In the Wake of Neoliberalism

Stanford Studies in Human Rights

In the Wake of Neoliberalism

Citizenship and Human Rights in Argentina

Karen Ann Faulk

Stanford University Press
Stanford, California

Stanford University Press
Stanford, California

Printed in the United States of America on acid-free, archival-quality paper

Library of Congress Cataloging-in-Publication Data

Faulk, Karen Ann, 1976- author.
 In the wake of neoliberalism : citizenship and human rights in Argentina / Karen Ann
Faulk.
    pages cm.--(Stanford studies in human rights)
   Includes bibliographical references and index.
  ISBN 978-0-8047-8225-8 (cloth : alk. paper)--ISBN 978-0-8047-8226-5 (pbk. : alk. paper)
  1. Human rights--Argentina. 2. Political rights--Argentina. 3. Neoliberalism--
Argentina. 4. Argentina--Politics and government--1983-2002. I. Title. II. Series:
Stanford studies in human rights.
  JC599.A7F38 2012
  323.0982--dc23   2012021909

Typeset by Bruce Lundquist in 10/14 Minion Pro

In memoriam Fernando Coronil (1944–2011)

Contents

Foreword

KAREN FAULK'S *In the Wake of Neoliberalism* is a compelling argument for how necessary critical ethnographies of human rights have become in broader debates over the relationship between international law and national politics, the changing nature of sovereignty after the end of the Cold War, and the limits of cosmopolitan ethics within grounded struggles over legacies of atrocity and its aftermath. Her book shows the value in responding to these key problems of our time from the inside out, in terms of the lives, reflections, and commitments of people who find themselves—willingly or not—on the normative frontlines in what has become a destabilizing moment of ambiguity and historical paradox. The triumph of human rights as a language of political change and moral protest over the last twenty-five years is grounded in a globalized ideology of human fulfillment and cultural evolution that has shaped the contours of resistance and provided a discursive toolkit that has proven to be remarkably versatile across a wide range of cultural, political, and legal vernaculars. But at the same time, underlying political economic vulnerabilities and multi-scalar structures of inequality have resisted the final coming of what Mary Ann Glendon called "a world made new"—a world remade under the sign of radical human equality protected in both form and spirit by laws.

Faulk's book is a carefully wrought study of these currents of ambiguity as they have swirled in and around Argentina over several decades. During this time, the experience and history of Argentina have become an iconic part of the story of human rights, from the images of the intrepid Mothers of the Plaza de Mayo holding vigil and demanding justice for the crimes committed by the military junta against their sons and daughters, to the more recent high-profile role played by a former Argentine lawyer as the first Chief Prosecutor of the International Criminal Court. Argentina has become one of the global touchstones for evaluating the promise and limitations of human rights—as a politico-legal mechanism for protection and redress, as a moral grammar with transcultural aspirations, and as a rallying cry for revolutionaries facing down the last authoritarian holdouts within what James Ferguson has called the "neo-liberal world order." Faulk parses these multiple dimensions of human rights and develops a theoretical framework that allows us to both appreciate and critically bracket the legacy of rights-claiming within contemporary Argentina.

Her book focuses on a key dynamic in this broader narrative of human rights in Argentina: the appearance of discursive and political fault lines when the logics of human rights were taken up beyond the political and social processes through which Argentine society struggled to come to terms with the Dirty War and its aftermath. Throughout the 1990s, as in other countries of Latin America, the Argentine political economy was restructured under the careful eye of the World Bank and the International Monetary Fund, which sought a hemispheric "consensus" on a specific economic and political model as a precondition for loan-making and the formation of new regional economies. As Faulk shows us, it was during this consolidation of neoliberalism in Argentina that human rights underwent a consequential shift in both meaning and application. She argues that the role of human rights was transformed when the strategy of right-claiming was broadened beyond the process of holding high-ranking officials to account for crimes against humanity. After civilian rule had been firmly established, Argentines thoroughly infused by a culture of human rights looked beyond torture and disappearance to other symbols of transgression.

They found them in violations not against physical integrity such as those that had accompanied the dictatorship-era political repression, but in those against the nature of the neoliberal subject itself. If the neoliberal subject was meant to be an autonomous agent, accountable for actions under law, and equal in access to opportunities, then "corruption" and "impunity" are markers of a failure by the state to create the conditions in which neoliberal subjectivity-as-citizenship can adequately flourish. Faulk uses an ethnography of two organizations—Memoria Activa and Cooperativa BAUEN—to demonstrate how the struggle to hold the state accountable for its failures led to new understandings of human rights themselves, as activists eventually reframed the implications of corruption and impunity *beyond* the neoliberal subject to encompass a collective account of well-being. The "dialogical analytics" that Faulk develops to understand this slippage toward an innovative human rights vernacular in Argentina reveals, as she puts it, the "mutually constitutive processes that link the language of rights, neoliberalist policies, and institutions of democracy, both in their philosophical premises and actual lived expression."

Mark Goodale
Series Editor
Stanford Studies in Human Rights

Acknowledgments

THINKING ABOUT all of those who have made this book possible is a monumental task. This project has been, in a multitude of ways, a collective effort. To mention those who have supported, accompanied, put up with, and challenged me in the long years of research and writing that went into this book is woefully insufficient in recognizing their role in the making of this project. Their efforts are woven into every page. Making explicit their names here is only a gesture toward recognition of their otherwise implicit but no less essential presence in the text.

My intellectual mentors, while of course not responsible for the failings of this work, are undeniably responsible for its strengths. Mark Goodale had the generosity to provide both insight and oversight in turning the book into a reality. I will be forever grateful for the brilliant care and support that Jennifer Robertson, Fernando Coronil, and Julie Skurski have offered me over the years. Many people have read, listened to, and commented on the chapters of this book or earlier versions. Noa Vaisman accompanied every step, and always understood what I meant, even better than I did. She and Leticia Barrera were always there to calm my doubts and refine my understanding. How many scholars can truly count themselves as lucky, able to send a rushed email with a question on the finer details of Argentine constitutional law and receive a detailed and accurate response from two such generous and capable experts (with relevant pdf's attached) in less than nine hours? Carlos Forment, Daniel Goldstein, and Sian Lazar were wonderfully incisive critical readers whose comments invariably pushed me to take it one step further. Kairos Marquardt heard me out, over and over again, lightening my mind and my heart with her generous ability to listen. Javier Auyero, José Blumenfeld, Sarah Muir, Michelle Cohen, Natasha Zaretsky, Mariano Perelman, Julia Paley, Carol Bardenstein, Michael Fisch, and the participants in the "Legal Subjectivity, Popular/Community Justice, and Human Rights in Latin America" conference at the Centre for Research in the Arts, Social Sciences and Humanities of the University of Cambridge all provided valuable feedback on portions of the text along the way. I am also obliged to the Departments of Anthropology at the University of Pittsburgh, the University of New Mexico, Marshall University, and CUNY–Staten Island for graciously inviting me to present portions of this research. I am very grateful to Kate Wahl, Joa Suorez, and Clementine Breslin at Stanford University Press for their careful and consistent efforts. Richard Gunde was a fantastically thorough and well-informed editor. My thanks go as well to my family, in the broadest of senses.

In many ways, this book is a tribute to all the people with whom I have shared time in Argentina. I hope I have been and will continue to be successful in contributing to their lives as deeply as they have to mine. Those who wished to have their words publicly attributed appear in the chapters that follow as they would prefer to be called. Others appear anonymously, and some names have been changed. Special thanks are due to José Blumenfeld, Sofía Guterman, Fabián Pierucci, Rolo Poire, Jorge Suárez, Federico Tonarelli, Luisina, Sarita, Marta, Noelia, Tita, Felisa, and los del Banchero, all of whom always found the time and patience to answer my questions and listen to my ideas.

Much of the research for this book was funded by a Fulbright-Hays Award from the US Department of Education, and by grants from the Rackham School of Graduate Studies, the International Institute, and the Department of Anthropology at the University of Michigan. The Departments of History and Global Studies and Modern Languages at Carnegie Mellon University also provided support.

Portions of this research appear, in a different form, in *Anthropological Quarterly* 81:1, Summer 2008, and in the volume *Economies of Recycling*, edited by Catherine Alexander and Josh Reno, published by Zed Books in 2012 (reprinted with permission). All translations throughout the book are mine unless otherwise noted.

My appreciation also goes to my colleagues at Carnegie Mellon University for providing an engaging and encouraging intellectual environment, and to my parents, for their unwavering support. Most of all, my love and appreciation go to Felipe, Ash, Céu, and Leticia, for being there forever and for always.

List of Abbreviations

AMIA Asociación Mutual Israelita Argentina (Argentine Jewish Mutual Aid Association)

ANTA Asociación Nacional de Trabajadores Autogestionados (National Association of Self-managed Workers)

APDH Asamblea Permanente para Derechos Humanos (Permanent Assembly for Human Rights)

APEMIA Agrupación para el Esclarecimiento de la Masacre Impune de la AMIA (Association for Shedding Light on the Unpunished AMIA Massacre)

BANADE Banco Nacional de Desarrollo (National Bank for Development)

BAUEN *Buenos Aires, Una Empresa Nacional* (Buenos Aires, a National Company)

CEJIL Center for Justice and International Law

CELS Centro de Estudios Legales y Sociales (Center for Legal and Social Studies)

CEPAL Comisión Económica para América Latina y el Caribe (see ECLA)

CGT Confederación General de Trabajo (General Confederation of Labor)

CONADEP Comisión Nacional sobre la Desaparición de Personas (National Commission on Disappeared People)

CTA Central de Trabajadores Argentinos (Argentine Workers' Central Union)

C.U.C. Cooperativa Unidos por el Calzado (United Shoemakers' Cooperative)

DAIA Delegación de Asociaciones Israelitas Argentinas (Delegation of Argentine Jewish Associations)

ECLA Economic Commission for Latin America

ESMA Escuela Mecánica de la Armada (Naval School of Mechanics)

FACTA   Federación Argentina de Cooperativas de Trabajadores Autogestionados (Argentine Federation of Self-managed Workers' Cooperatives)

HIJOS   Hijos por la Identidad y la Justicia contra el Olvido y el Silencio (Children for Identity and Justice against Forgetting and Silence)

IACHR   Inter-American Commission on Human Rights

ICCPR   International Covenant on Civil and Political Rights

ICESCR   International Covenant on Economic, Social, and Cultural Rights

IDELCOOP   Instituto de la Cooperación (Cooperation Institute)

ILO   International Labor Organization

IMF   International Monetary Fund

IMFC   Instituto Movilizador de Fondos Cooperativos (Mobilizing Institute for Cooperative Funds)

INADI   Instituto Nacional contra la Discriminación, la Xenofobia y el Racismo (National Institute against Discrimination, Xenophobia, and Racism)

INAES   Instituto Nacional de Asociativismo y Economía Social (National Institute of Associations and Social Economics)

MNER   Movimiento Nacional de Empresas Recuperadas (National Movement of Recuperated Businesses)

MNFR   Movimiento Nacional de Fábricas Recuperadas por sus trabajadores (National Movement of Worker Recuperated Factories)

MOSSAD   Israeli intelligence agency

NGO   Nongovernmental organization

OAS   Organization of American States

PJ   Partido Justicialista (Peronist Party)

SERPAJ   Servicio de Paz y Justicia (Peace and Justice Service)

SIDE   Secretaría de Inteligencia del Estado (Secretariat of State Intelligence)

UCR   Unión Cívica Radical (Radical Civic Union)

UDHR   Universal Declaration of Human Rights

UNASUR   Unión de Naciones Suramericanas (Union of South American Nations)

In the Wake of Neoliberalism

Defining Rights

I N DECEMBER 2001, Argentina was engulfed in the climax of a political and economic crisis. When President de la Rúa's administration tried to halt the tide of capital flight that was threatening to collapse the national banking system by freezing all deposits (the so-called *corralito*), the Argentine middle class joined with other sectors in expressing their frustration with all political representatives. This dissatisfaction with government was articulated as an ardent desire to throw out the lot of them (as summarized in the popular chant, *que se vayan todos*). Faced with widespread looting in the first weeks of this warm summer month (Auyero 2006, 2007; Cotarelo and Iñigo Carrera 2004), de la Rúa tried to stabilize the situation by declaring a state of emergency (*estado de sitio*). To a populace increasingly convinced of the government's ineffectiveness in addressing the nation's most serious economic crisis in two decades, this proved to be the final straw. Tens of thousands poured into the streets in defiance of his heavy-handed attempt at maintaining control. Indeed, not only was the injunction to stay home not obeyed, one of the most oft-repeated slogans of the day told the soon-to-be-ex-president what, precisely, he could do with such an order. Two days of massive street protests resulted in the deaths of some 37 protestors and ended with de la Rúa abandoning his post and being spirited off the top of the presidential offices (Casa Rosada) in a helicopter.

These protests are often seen as the culmination of an incremental process of economic disenchantment among the Argentine populace in reaction to the neoliberal structural adjustment policies implemented during the 1990s. While this is certainly the case, the events of December 19–20 were also part of broader discursive struggles over the meanings of elements of social life, including ideas of what constitutes rights of citizenship, human rights, legality, moral obligation, historical memory, and human dignity. These debates did not emerge out of a neoliberal vacuum, but were informed by and drew on a long history of contention over the role of the state in balancing the dual pillars of liberal notions of rights—the right to private property and the right to (meaningful) equality.

This book traces the language of rights in Argentina over the past few decades. The idea of rights became particularly salient in Argentine society following the brutal repression carried out by the state during the most recent military dictatorship, which lasted from 1976 to 1983. In the wake of this violence, "human rights" became the clarion call for activists, and the issue of human rights retains a central importance in public life and political discourse. In recent years, however, the focus on rights violations has shifted. Under the dictatorship, violations were most vividly exemplified and symbolically embodied in acts of torture and forced disappearance. This book shows how over the past two decades the concepts of impunity and corruption have become the primary lenses through which rights violations are conceptualized. That is, violations of human rights are seen as occurring primarily through endemic forms of impunity and corruption in the social, political, and economic spheres. As the 1990s unfolded and hopes for legal justice for the perpetrators of Dirty War violence receded, and as scandals highlighting corruption among members of the ruling political and economic elite dominated the media, the twinned phenomenon of impunity/corruption became so prominent that power itself became equated with impunity (Cernadas de Bulnes 2005:131 n30). These ideas have become the defining terms in the language of protest that seeks to describe and invent alternatives to the current reality.

The shift in the focus of rights violations was accompanied by and in many ways was the product of concurrent economic and political conditions. The linkage between impunity and corruption is one of the main legacies of the neoliberal era. This book identifies the unfolding and mutually formative effects of human rights and neoliberalism in Argentina, an issue that has received little attention. In doing so, it works to uncover the multiple meanings that rights hold and the relationship between these various and varying interpretations and the political and legal institutions that structure their governance. Fundamentally, through ethnographic attention to the use and circulation of notions of rights in and following the era of neoliberal reform, the chapters that follow show how activism around the issue of human rights in Argentina challenges and constitutes the limits of the neoliberal project.

Argentina and Global Human Rights

Understanding the meanings of rights in Argentina is an important task, given the place that the country has held in discussions of rights on a global scale. Argentina and Argentine scholars and activists have played a prominent role in the construction of transnational codes of human rights, both as an example of state terrorism and through the active participation of Argentine lawyers, politicians, and activists on drafting committees for international human rights declarations and courts. As an exporter of human rights tactics, ideas, and experts, Argentina has been a source of innovation and protagonism in the field of human rights (Sikkink 2008). Initiatives put forth by Argentine organizations and political representatives led to the creation of an Organization of American States (OAS) treaty against the practice of forced disappearances, as well as inspiring a new international forum, the United Nations Working Group on Forced Disappearance. The idea of the right to identity, the subject of a March 2007 Special Meeting of the Permanent Council of the OAS entitled "Children, Identity, and Citizenship in the Americas," has also come out, in part, of the issue of the children stolen from their abducted parents by the security forces under the last dictatorship. Argentina was also key agent in establishing the "right to truth" as part of the set of rights to justice as overseen by the United Nations Commission on Human Rights in April 2005.

These innovations were in part the product of a sharp focus on human rights in public discourse in Argentina, which intensified throughout the 1990s. Though the idea of human rights gained initial popularity through the particular issue of disappearances and torture during the dictatorship, it is now used broadly, in conjunction with a host of issues. It has become an essential feature of public discussion, and figures centrally in claims made by groups from across society about rights of citizenship and in legitimizing their struggles. The history of the discourse(s) of human rights that circulate and hold such power cannot be separated from the political and economic context that conditioned their emergence. This book traces the shifts that the idea of human rights has undergone within the context of the concurrent political and economic programs and policies. These factors, rather than being tangential, actively structured not only the conditions under which Argentines live but also the form and language that activism takes. Mark Goodale has argued that (neo)liberalist human rights discourse functions as a part of the empire of law used at once to structure the implementation of neoliberal changes to social, political, and legal organization and also to provide a source for resistance to these (Goodale

2007b, 2009). Excavating the liberal precepts of much human rights discourse, this book demonstrates how protest groups within Argentina use a modified version of this discourse to challenge the precepts of (neo)liberalism itself.

Commenting on the legitimacy, power, and potential that human rights discourses have come to posses internationally, Paul Rabinow has argued for the importance of learning more about the multiple forms and practices that human rights groups take on around the world, and the "preexisting moral landscapes" embedded in the choices these groups make in articulating their message of reform (Rabinow 2005:48). The more powerful normative transnational frameworks of rights become, the more important it is to investigate and understand how rights are conceptualized in different locations and at different times. As a critical ethnography of rights, this book explores the questions, How are rights being conceived by protest groups in Argentina? What issues are at the core of their demands? What violations do they perceive, and what are the (re)solutions they suggest? In addition, how do these demands relate to the political, economic, and social contexts within which they operate?

Critiques of normative visions of rights within international organizations or transnational NGOs largely center on the persistent domination within human rights discourse of certain basic liberal principles, to the exclusion of alternative perspectives. Liberalism is inherently embedded in the current normative framework of rights, most crucially in the primacy afford to the individual as the ideal liberal subject. From its inception, this univocal idea of rights has been criticized by those who favor either a more inclusive or more nuanced approach. The assumption that one view of rights, based on a particular Western philosophy, might be applicable universally begs the question:

> What if claims made in the name of universal rights are not the best way to protect people? In the 1840s, that is exactly what the radical Karl Marx was suggesting. In the 1940s, that is exactly what Hans Morgenthau, the conservative theoretician of political realism, and Melville Herskovits, the liberal cultural relativist, were arguing. All three were concerned about world peace, although each had a different way to get there: a violent lurch to the next stage of history, an ongoing balance of power, an increased respect for cultural difference. But, despite their very different sensibilities, all three were equally skeptical that some regime of liberal international law would do the trick. (Cmiel 2004:56)

In spite of the long history of such criticisms, the interpretations of human rights that predominate in international institutions and legal practice retain their liberal basis. As Sally Engle Merry has demonstrated, contemporary transnational human rights networks (like those detailed by Sikkink for Latin America) form part of a normative and fundamentally neoliberalist vision of modernity (Merry 2005). The legalist reasoning that structures the formalization, implementation, and (attempted) enforcement of transnational human rights regimes is itself also a historical product (Riles 2006). Argentina is an interesting case in this regard, as it has been both a producer and a receiver of the ideas and structures that govern human rights globally. Gaining a deeper understanding how ideas of rights circulate and resonate within a country like Argentina is critical if rights are to be used as a means of increasing well-being rather than as a new form of domination.

The attempt to remake governments or hold them accountable along the lines specified by normative transnational frameworks implies their imposition on systems that operate under their own unique cultural and political logics. The manifestation of a generalized discourse in any given context is necessarily conditioned by local particularities (Roniger 2003). These particularistic manifestations in turn stand in a dialogic relationship of mutual influence with the generalized discourses they partially absorb. In this book, I argue for a dialogic view of the construction of narratives of human rights violations and specifically of notions of justice and accountability as resolution to these violations. This view builds on work on the vernacularization of human rights discourses, which has shown how groups use international human rights to advance their claims while also imbuing them with local meanings (Merry 1997, 2006). By taking a dialogic view I emphasize the mutually constitutive nature of these transnational and local ideas of human rights and justice (Goodale 2007a).

As Ileana Rodríguez has noted, "To converse about human rights using th[e] contemporary vocabulary of liberal struggles simply acknowledges the standard idioms of the current ideological debate and tackles the questions within the same terrain" (Rodríguez 2009:8). This books shows how post-neoliberal protest groups in Argentina, while not fully departing from this "contemporary vocabulary of liberal struggles," do contest the ideas of individualism and universality embedded in transnational frameworks of human rights. Arising in the wake of neoliberal restructuring, they make a public case for the inclusion of a right to collective well-being or the collective good as a fundamental part of their demands, and do so in ways that draw on highly symbolic, historically charged notions of legitimacy. The forms of sociality they embody work to counteract the individualist focus of the normative discourse of human rights and its traditional elision of economic rights in favor of political and civil aspects. These groups insist that when primacy is given to the needs of the individual and the market, the rights of the collective are inevitably violated.[1] Once again, Argentina offers an essential contribution to discussion of human rights by illustrating how tensions between the individual and collective continue to permeate these discussions, and how different stakeholders from across the state and society have sought to resolve them.

Neoliberal Rights

In Argentina, the installation and popularization of the idea of human rights as such happened at the same time and in conjunction with the arrival and application of another transnational discourse, that of neoliberalism. The cotemporality of these discursive formulations within the Argentine context, far from being inconsequential, has meant they have had mutually formative effects. These effects go beyond the ways human rights and neoliberalism are intertwined in trans- and international institutions and legal precepts. Said another way, though it is the case that in Argentina the ideas of human rights have their roots in historical precedents and in the lived experience of many Argentines, all of the current variants have nonetheless been affected in one way or another by neoliberalism, even as they have influenced the form neoliberalism has taken, or at least the Argentine expression of it. This relationship has been largely overlooked, a lacuna this book seeks to address. In exploring the way "rights talk" is used and adapted locally by groups organized around a number of different issues, this book looks at the relationship between ideas of human rights, rights of citizenship, and the concrete and envisioned social relationships that form the basis for social activism in the wake of neoliberalism.

In using the term "neoliberalism," I refer to a particular set of economic and political policy proposals that had widespread adherence and enjoyed their heyday among economic elites and the major Washington-based international economic regulatory agencies, such as the International Monetary Fund (IMF) and the World Bank, from roughly the late 1970s through the late 1990s. These proposals include what has come to be known as the "Washington Consensus," and advocate a decreased role for states in controlling or regulating economic activity. They encourage free trade, privatization, reduced government spending, and deregulation of capital flows. Such policies, when applied to Argentina under the Menem administrations (1989–1999), included vast cuts to the size of state institutions, widespread privatizations of state-controlled resources, and severe reductions in social services like educa-tion, health care, and transportation networks.

Yet neoliberalism is more than a concrete set of economic and political practices. As a philosophy and a discourse, its policies and practices are accom-panied and reinforced by forms of governance and subject-making (Postero 2010:60 n1). Fundamentally, these forms of subject-making are based in the figure of the individual. In this sense, neoliberalism follows its roots in clas-sical liberalism, which gave primacy to individual choice and responsibility, primarily through the formalization and legalization of the liberal citizen and individual property rights. The right to own property, bestowed by liberalism on individual citizens, lies precisely at the heart of the liberal subject. Liberal-ism itself can be seen, as Aihwa Ong, following Foucault, describes it, as "a regime of normalizing whereby *homo economicus* is the standard against which all other citizens are measured and ranked" (Ong 1999:129). This locus of the individual as political subject through his (and eventually her) economic rights is fortified under neoliberalism, where opposition to collective entitlements such as labor rights takes on a force unequalled in prior instantiations.

This philosophical focus on the individual is both consequential and ironic. It is consequential in the long and lingering trail of effects that it has, particu-larly for conceptions of rights. It is ironic in that economic power under neo-liberalism at its height was only partially located in the individual. Macro-level policy was driven principally by transnational corporations and international economic decision-making bodies like the IMF, rather than within and by na-tional governments that could have been, in theory, beholden to and invested in power by individual voters.

The interaction of neoliberal philosophy and particular governments was not, however, devoid of consequences. Even in the Global North neoliberalism had a distinct flavor in its different expressions, whether through US Reagan-omics or British Thatcherism. Its manifestations in the Global South, where it was introduced through a coordination of international agencies and local elites, were inflected in even more locally specific ways in the different places in which it was applied. Neoliberalism carries with it an inherent ideological pre-disposition toward the construction of a certain notion of citizenship, through envisioning certain ideal forms of public participation in political life. These notions are likewise interpreted and applied in particular ways in local situa-tions (Comaroff and Comaroff 2004). As Carol Greenhouse has argued, "Neo-liberal reform . . . has restructured the most prominent public relationships that constitute *belonging*: politics, markets, work, and self-identity" (2010:2; emphasis in original). In Argentina and elsewhere in Latin America, neoliberalism as implemented advanced a new kind of relationship between the state and civil society. A minimalist conception of the state and democracy and the reduction of the political domain and its appropriate participants removed citizens from meaningful participation in political life. Rather, participation in the public sphere was (somewhat paradoxically) based on individual integration into the market, where citizens could voice their opinions and exercise their freedoms through the power of consumer choice. Furthermore, citizens were now expected to be self-responsible for social obligations, including the provision of basic and necessary services previously provided by the government (Escobar and Álvarez 1992).

Rights of Citizenship

Citizenship can be conceived of as the set of rights and responsibilities of members of a national community.[2] The Enlightenment ideal of liberal (European) citizenship conceived of an independent and free individual able to participate in the political life of the nation. However, the exclusions and limitations of citizenship, both de jure and de facto, make it a frequent site of contention. Furthermore, citizenship is not a fixed category, but subject to a multiplicity of interpretations and manifestations, both within a single national community and across different countries. As a form of ideological practice, ideas of citizenship are asserted, debated, modified, and resisted in accordance with the beliefs or agendas of those involved.

Maristella Svampa has delineated three models of citizenship that she argues were developed during the 1990s in Argentina in relation to its own version of neoliberalism (2005b: 280–285). The first of these is "patrimonial citizenship." This model has as its basis the idea of citizens as owners and controllers of their property and resources, with individual autonomy as an overriding principle. The commercialization of social services, such as education, health, and security, has led those financially able to provide for themselves to embrace the "improvements" to such services brought about by the increased reliance on options within the private sector. This model, which saw widespread expansion throughout the upper middle and ascendant classes during the 1990s, has its ultimate example in the rise of gated communities (known as *countries* in Argentina), which often function as complete, independent neighborhoods, with stores, health services, schools, and the like within their barriers.[3]

The second model is that of the citizen consumer. This idea is based on the inclusion of the individual in terms of his/her consumption and use of the goods and services provided by the market. As Néstor García Canclini has argued:

> The exercise of citizenship has always been associated with the capacity to appropriate goods and the ways of using them for oneself, but it was supposed that the differences [in one's ability to do so] were leveled out by the equality of the abstract rights that were made concrete through voting, in feeling represented by a political party or a union. Together with the decomposition of politics and the decline in its institutions, other modes of participation gain force. Men and women perceive that many of the inherent questions for citizens—where do I belong and what rights does that give me, how can I get information, who represents my interests—are answered more through the private consumption of goods and through mass media than as part of the abstract rules of democracy or through collective participation in public spaces. (2001:1)

The figure of the citizen consumer is based on a notion of individual advancement and an acceptance of the logic of the market. These ideas were promoted by the Menem administration as the new unifying values that could guide the nation toward stability and prosperity.

The third model of neoliberal citizenship is that of community assistance/participation. This model applies to the increasing number of those otherwise largely excluded from the other two models, and consists of a kind of low-intensity, restricted citizenship, to be operative under the watchful eye of the state and through the constant control of international lending and development agencies. This model advocates the development of community support networks to cover the survival needs of those left out of the formal economic system. In this way, "those paradigmatic expressions of Latin American social cooperation (like survival networks and the informal economy) that had for decades been seen as obstacles to modernization . . . were reinterpreted in terms of 'social capital,'" a term that Svampa says serves as "an ideological nucleus of the neoliberal model" (2005a:284).

These are the three models of citizenship that neoliberalism offered Argentines during the 1990s. However, it would be inaccurate to assume that the relationship of citizen to the market was an invention of the era. Inés Dussel's persuasive work on the making of citizens in early twentieth-century Argentina argues that viewing citizenship in terms of voting or the expressing of opinion in political matters is a particular historical articulation of the concept (and one that, I would add, is itself infused with a hegemonic exclusionary ideology). Rather, she asserts, citizenship "encompasses a variety of practices in which one relates to others as a public self; communitarian actions, collective groupings, even consumption" (2005:109–110). She also shows that regulating young bodies through uniforms at this formative moment in Argentine national history carried with it the intention of producing "enlightened consumers" who would be good citizens for their disciplined adherence to consuming products that conformed to the moral norms of modern hygiene and simplicity. These ideas of participation in shaping and directing public life through consumption that began to take hold during this era left a continuing legacy.

In contrast, the emergence of Peronism in the 1940s redefined the relationship of the populace to the state and incorporated masses of Argentines into the political machine in ways unseen previously. New articulations of the role of the state and what citizens could and should hold as their own rights and responsibilities as participants in the national community emerged, and political parties gained relevance in the daily lives of an increasingly large sector of the population. An important body of scholarship has explored the legacy of these changes and the persistence of certain patterns of clientalism and patronage through established political channels (e.g., Auyero 2001; Levitsky and Murillo 2005). However, in recent years much attention has been focused on the break away from these "traditional" forms of doing politics. Recent scholarship highlights what are often referred to as "new practices of resistance" (*nuevas prácticas de resistencia*), or new forms of political participation that arose surrounding the economic and political crisis that peaked in December 2001 (Colectivo Situaciones 2002; Dinerstein 2004; Mato 2004; Svampa 2002). While this body of work provides important information on the nature of contemporary forms of political practice and ideas of citizenship in Argentina, I contend that the tendency to view these as "new practices of resistance" overemphasizes the break with the past and fails to give sufficient attention to the ways the groups involved conform to and work within the structures of politics as practiced within Argentina. Rather, I find it productive to consider how assertions of rights respond specifically to the historical moment that led to their emergence in ways that both draw upon and diverge from previously established practices and ideas of citizenship, political practice, and state responsibility.

Such public articulations as to the nature of rights of citizenship provide insight into how citizenship can function as a site for the exertion of power.

Aihwa Ong highlights the role of the state in constructing and controlling ideas of citizenship and citizens. Drawing on Corrigan and Sayer's seminal work on the state as cultural formation, she argues for the way states undertake projects of moral regulation designed to condition and universalize citizens (Corrigan and Sayer 1985:4–5; Ong 1996:738). As such, citizens are created and homogenized in quotidian practice by the state through their ascription into definitive roles, such as students, workers, consumers, and patients.

These observations on the nature of state control over citizenship become even more acute in context of authoritarian rule, when the very notion of citizenship is undermined (though often, as in the case of Argentina, still appealed to by the ruling powers). The legacy of authoritarianism in Argentina has left an obdurate impression that citizenship is a condition ultimately controlled by the state, both in its unilateral ability to bestow the benefits and impose the obligations that accompany this status. The most recent military dictatorship retained the daily technologies of control practiced by democratic as well as authoritarian bureaucratic agencies to enforce the sensation that the state remains the ultimate arbiter of citizenship status and benefits, from architectural and spatial organization to the arbitrary and instrumental inefficiency of bureaucratic institutions designed to process the numerous forms of obligatory civilian registration. Beyond this, the military dictatorship also expressly used the status of citizenship as a political weapon, discursively and in some cases literally stripping dissidents of Argentine citizenship.

The impression that it is the state that maintains control over citizenship and defines its rights and responsibilities is one that is often carefully cultivated by those in power. Nonetheless, directing too much focus on the state as the ultimate controller of citizenship misses the way this concept is itself the site of a continuous process of contentious construction between multiple forces representing varying sets of interests. Rather, "citizenship [is] dialectically determined by the state and its subjects" (Ong 1996:738). One of the most profound and lasting impacts of the Argentine human rights movement under and following the dictatorship may lie in its having had the ability to create "a social base for democracy by encouraging participation, critical thinking, and other attributes of citizenship" (Brysk 1994:21), thus resisting and resignifying the definitions of citizenship projected by the dictatorship. Later activism for expanded rights is often credited to the example provided by the dictatorship-era human rights organizations. For example, the murder of María Soledad—a young, poor girl from the province of Catamarca—in 1990 provoked a scandal

when it became clear that local, entrenched elites had been involved, exposing the state as unable to fulfill its duties to protect or to bring rights to all
citizens, especially the poor, the dark-skinned, and females. Her death quickly
became a point for mass activism, and was a catalyst in the struggle to expand
rights to increasing swaths of the population. Though only one case, the girl's
murder came to symbolize "a type of violence and impunity that the Madres of
Plaza de Mayo had taught Argentinians to recognize" (Bergman and Szurmuk
2001:395). In the now more than twenty-five years since the return to democracy, the content of citizenship (and of human rights) has remained a site of
contention. The dialogic and always incomplete process of defining citizenship
can be best traced through attention to the multifaceted expressions of ideals
from official, media, and nongovernmental productions and practices. In doing
so, the research in this book highlights how ideas of citizenship and human
rights are being recrafted in contemporary Argentina.

Sociality, Collective Well-being, and the State

In the Introduction to the edited volume *Ethnographies of Neoliberalism*, Carol
Greenhouse writes that neoliberalism, with the many lines it draws in attempting to define the proper role of citizens/consumers, is resisted through the ways
people refuse these lines, "withdraw[ing] *into* another sphere, markedly *social*
and markedly *not* individualistic." As such, the social realms "recovered, re-
animated, or brought into being in the contexts created by neoliberal reform
. . . constitute the limits of neoliberalism" (Greenhouse 2010:8; emphasis in
original). With this book I argue that these social realms, strengthened or invented by those seeking to resist the conditions and identities into which they
are placed, form the basis of an imagined (and to some extent realized) alternative social reality for the actors involved. These imagined alternatives, I argue,
are based in submerged socialities that are revived, reinvented, and asserted as
the foundation for rebuilding the shattered nation.

In using "wake" in the title of the book, I draw on the multiple inflections
that the word can carry. In one sense, I invoke the idea that neoliberalism found
its limits in these forms of activism. As perhaps most vividly demonstrated in
the events of December 19–20, 2001, the economic and political policies of the
1990s could go only so far before resistance undid the stability that facilitated
their operation. The administrations that followed this dramatic collapse are
admittedly post-neoliberal only up to a certain point, as they have maintained
many of the foundations of the neoliberal economic program. And yet, in many

ways there has been a drastic change both in what Argentine governments since 2001 can say and do. In this way, we are in a post-neoliberal moment in Argentina, in the messy process of reconstruction in its aftermath, and holding vigil at its deathbed. While there are powerful sectors busily searching for signs of revival, this book focuses on those whose actions seek to construct alternative bases for organizing society and the role of the state.

In thinking about the state and groups that make demands upon it, I intend to reference not a concrete and knowable entity, but rather the abstract idea that informs the way protest groups direct their actions and formulate their demands. The state can be understood as a loose set of institutions, policies, symbols, and rituals (Abrams 1977), leaving its nature and purpose open to interpretation and debate by a variety of actors. How the state is envisioned and imagined, as it is and as it should be, is at the heart of social protest and social movement formation and practice (Fals Borda 1992). When these groups make demands of the state, they are constructing a particular imaginary of responsibilities and appropriate action. The book focuses on the ways the state is being imagined, invented, or proposed by these groups, as they work toward the construction of a state that upholds certain kinds of responsibilities. In doing so, they pressure for concrete measures for realizing this ideal, and derive their legitimacy by insisting on the state's inability or unwillingness to live up to the standards they demand. By showing how protest groups navigate different factions within the state, the book also demonstrates continual processes of negotiation, revealing how, far from being unitary, the state comprises a multitude of ever-shifting factions, actors, and interests (Striffler 2002). The always indeterminate nature of the state becomes the terrain upon which alternatives are imagined, as these groups strategically negotiate its physical and metaphorical spaces (Coronil 1997, 2005).

Two of the organizations that emerged during the 1990s and make demands for social change are Memoria Activa and the Cooperativa BAUEN. Throughout this book, the words and actions of these two protest groups will illustrate how, through the identification of corruption and impunity as violations of the social good, these key terms are defined and utilized in ways that challenge hegemonic conceptions of the role of the state and the sapping of the rights of citizens in the neoliberal era. In identifying corruption and impunity as ills that permeate and corrode the social environment, these groups draw on and deploy historical memory and the discourse of human rights in asserting their claims. Fundamentally, they embed a concern for and a responsibility toward collective well-being into their definitions of appropriate state action. In exploring the premises and meanings afforded to notions of rights in contemporary Argentina, this book demonstrates the mutually constitutive processes that link the language of rights, neoliberalist policies, and institutions of democracy, both in their philosophical premises and actual lived expression.

Memoria Activa

On March 17, 1992, a bomb tore through the Israeli embassy in Buenos Aires, leaving some 29 people dead and more than 200 injured. Two years later, on July 18, 1994, 85 people lost their lives in a flash of destruction that decimated the AMIA (Asociación Mutual Israelita Argentina, or Argentine Jewish Mutual Aid Association) building. Along with the DAIA (Delegación de Asociaciones Israelitas Argentinas, or Delegation of Argentine Jewish Associations), also housed in the same building, the AMIA forms the principal organizational pillar of the Argentine Jewish community. It has provided a host of social services to the community in the over a hundred years since its foundation. Alongside many offices and social programs, including the coordination of the city's Jewish cemeteries and schools, the AMIA building also housed the largest Judaica library in South America. The destruction of the AMIA/DAIA building was a devastating moment, a direct assault on Argentine Jewish secular and religious life.

Shortly after the AMIA building exploded, those most deeply affected by the blast met and agreed to gather publicly in the Plaza Lavalle the following Monday morning in a silent memorial/protest (*acto*) that appealed for justice in the attack. By holding a public gathering, the victims' relatives intended to bring immediate pressure on the government to conduct a serious and thorough investigation into what had happened. The investigation into the embassy attack two years earlier was by that time seen as highly problematic. The continuing lack of credible information and dismay at what was felt as a lack of protection offered by the Argentine government garnered widespread condemnation. Many felt that had the Argentine government been more efficient or diligent in uncovering responsibility for the previous attack, the AMIA tragedy would never had occurred. In addition, the attitude of President Menem in the aftermath of the AMIA bombing was cited as an immediate cause for concern and seen as an indication of a continued lack of political responsibility. His reaction to news of the attack had been to call the Israeli prime minister to offer his condolences, even though the building in question, unlike the embassy, was an Argentine Jewish institution located on Argentine soil. Through manifesting a visible "symbolic representation of the destruction" (Gurevich 2005b:15–16), the *actos* called for by relatives of the victims were designed to provide a voice for the suffering of the families and a call for justice.

As the months and years passed, the group gained a more organized format, eventually taking on the legal status of a not-for-profit civil association (*asociación civil*), maintaining their focus on the victims by mandating that the rotating board of directors consist of direct family members of those killed and wounded in the attacks. They took the name *Memoria Activa* (Active Memory), in recognition of their stated desire that the memory of their loved ones serve as an active force in the pursuit of justice. Over time they would become the public face for criticism of both the investigation into the attack and the AMIA/DAIA leadership itself.

The chapters that follow explore how Memoria Activa draws on the rhetoric and practices of other Argentine human rights organizations in asserting justice as a fundamental right, in contradistinction to the impunity and corruption they see as characterizing the handling of the investigation. It also shows how Memoria Activa's actions and demands insist on the role of Argentine Jews as full citizens within the nation, embodying the right to difference in contrast to historical pressures for cultural assimilation and in direct reaction to an accompanying spate of limited inclusionary politics, or the Argentine manifestation of neoliberal multiculturalism. Finally, the case of Memoria Activa demonstrates an embedded concern for collective well-being over individual resolution and for the construction of a governing body based in institutional democratic practices founded upon and respectful of these principles.

Cooperativa BAUEN

The other group discussed throughout this book is the Cooperativa BAUEN, a workers' cooperative formed by former employees following the closure of a major hotel during the dramatic economic crisis of 2001. Part of a phenomenon known as the recuperated businesses movement, the cooperative took control of the installation and reopened it under the workers' own direction, following a principle of worker self-management. Located at the intersection of Callao and Corrientes in the *microcentro* of Buenos Aires, the Hotel Bauen was originally built using state loans as part of the preparations for Argentina's hosting of the 1978 World Cup. Later, it was a favored meeting spot for the political elite. However, years of self-interested management practices and the diversion of profits into other investments left the 4-star hotel with accumulated debts that ran into the millions of dollars/pesos.[4] At the end of December of 2001, in the midst of the economic and political crisis that saw a rotation of five presidents in a span of two weeks, the management of the Bauen closed its doors, leaving its few remaining employees out of work. The hotel remained closed for over a year. By early 2003, some former workers had begun to meet with representatives of other recuperated businesses and the umbrella movement the Movimiento Nacional de Empresas Recuperadas (National Movement of Recuperated Business, or MNER). The MNER advised them to gather as many former employees as they could and occupy the installation. Finally, on March 20, 2003, a small group of workers entered the hotel. Shortly after, they registered as a workers' cooperative. In the years since, it has become one of the most emblematic examples of the recuperated businesses movement.

The members of the Cooperativa BAUEN (*Buenos Aires, Una Empresa Nacional*) have found it necessary to take to the streets on numerous occasions in defense of that which they propose to be their fundamental right—the right to work. This right, they insist, has been repeatedly violated by the corruption and impunity that have characterized the neoliberal Argentine state, and by the continual attempts to take away the material conditions for the source of labor that they themselves created. In reasserting work as a right, the cooperative draws on a long history of activism around workers' rights in Argentina in articulating and legitimating its demands. However, it also draws on a different history, by appealing to the notion of cooperativism, which has become a central feature of the recuperated businesses (*recuperadas*). The use of the word "cooperativism" (*cooperativismo*) by the members of recuperated businesses refers to the idea of labor being organized collectively and oriented toward the benefit of all. It also includes a moral sense of cooperation, both between the members of a cooperative and of these to the larger society. This idea of *compañerismo* or working together is seen as an inherent aspect of *trabajo sin patrón* (working without a boss), the kind of worker self-management practiced by the BAUEN and other recuperadas. These groups contrast worker self-management to the alienation experienced when selling their labor to a boss. As such, in demanding that work be given priority as a fundamental right, they are also constructing a vision of the state as a protector of a certain kind of work, one that gives primacy to a revitalized and reinvented figure of the worker.

While Memoria Activa was formed in response to a violent, intrusive act, the BAUEN Cooperative was a direct response to the violence of poverty, inequality, and neoliberal structural adjustments. In both cases, however, it is the centrality (and ambiguity) of impunity and corruption that gave shape to the claims and actions of each group. The construction of an alternative form of sociality, based on collective well-being over individual interest, is facilitated by and facilitates the language of expression these groups use in articulating their demands.

While this book undertakes a focused and a historically grounded ethnography of these two microcosms of Argentine social life and practices of resistance, the insights these groups provide have implications far beyond their direct sphere of engagement. The lessons they show, and their poignant articulations of the effects of actually lived neoliberal reforms on their lives and life opportunities, speak to broader patterns that are relevant across many parts of Latin America and beyond. Their voices reach out from within the trail of destruction, dismay, hope, and recomposition that neoliberalism has left behind. Neoliberalism "has profoundly altered, if unevenly in space and time, the phenomenology of being in the world" (Comaroff and Comaroff 2001:14–15). This book shows some of the ways this change has been felt, experienced, interpreted, and *shaped* by the members of Memoria Activa and the BAUEN Cooperative.

Corruption

The notion of corruption functions as a fundamental part of the confrontational language and assertions of legitimacy on which these protest groups base their ethical challenges to the state. In changing the focus of human rights violations, these groups take corruption as a defining feature of the problems they face. "Corruption" becomes a catch phase to designate immoral behavior and social ills. This aligns with transnational concerns during this era. However, even while accepting the transnational interpretation of corruption as a major cause of social malady in contemporary Argentine society, they adopt this interpretation without subscribing to its particular definitions or attributed causes. Rather, they use it to challenge precepts of neoliberal discourse.

In considering corruption, I build on the recent interventions of anthropologists in disputing its treatment as an objective phenomenon, as is often assumed or proposed in academic or prescriptive literature. The idea that corruption is a universal category of a distinct set of social actions, or is a readily definable and understandable social phenomenon concerned primarily with embezzlement, bribery, or nepotism, particularly characterizes its treatment within the sphere of development agencies (e.g., Eigen 2002; Goldsmith 1999;

on Latin America, Blake and Morris 2009; Tulchin and Espach 2000). This position is epitomized by the global monitoring and advisory agency Transparency International. This organization was founded by lawyer and World Bank development worker Peter Eigen in 1993, and has been fundamental in promoting the vision of corruption as the key obstacle to achieving economic and political stability in "developing" countries by eroding civic trust, decreasing governmental legitimacy, and inflating the cost of business transactions (Muir 2011). According to Arthur Goldsmith, the idea behind Transparency International is "to spotlight corruption the way Amnesty International has publicized human rights violations" (1999:865).

In contrast, recent ethnographic work from around the world suggests that what is perceived as corruption needs to be itself an object of study, and that such perceptions rely heavily on cultural influences (Haller and Shore 2005; Hasty 2005; Lazar 2005; de Sardan 1999, Smith 2008). What constitutes corruption depends on culturally recognized registers of appropriate behaviors. That which may be considered a corrupt dealing by an outside observer could be locally interpreted as appropriate behavior on the part of those committing the act (Gupta 1995). Another contribution from this literature is recognition of the entanglement of equally ethnocentric ideas of modernity and democracy with corruption. The ways international development agencies and their promoters use the word "corruption," or, more exactly, the kinds of actions they define as corrupt, become a signal for the inability of local institutions to properly behave according to international standards of modern bureaucratic governance. This concern has extended to international organizations, as seen for example in the 1996 signing of the Inter-American Convention against Corruption. The formation of an Ethics Committee by the second Menem administration (1995–1999) showed its sensitivity to the new restrictions international lending agencies placed on developing countries "where fraudulent activities have significant macroeconomic implications" (Goldsmith 1999:865).

The circulation of the term "corruption" in Argentina during and in describing this era undoubtedly owes much to the international discourses that were becoming increasingly influential at the time. The idea that corruption was a serious problem that must be remedied was replacing the "functional theory of corruption"—that is, that corruption in developing countries has macro-level economic and political benefits (Merton 1968)—which had previously held sway among the intellectuals whose thinking influenced the policy decisions coming out of Washington and its economic institutions. This "narrative of corruption," to use a phrase coined by Gupta, had in fact become a primary basis of the neoliberal agenda:

> Striped to its basics, the neoliberal thesis holds that since corruption is primarily a pathology of the public sector, the solution lies in reducing public spending and rolling back the frontiers of the state. Shrinking the public sector, so the argument goes, reduces the scope for public officials to engage in malfeasance. It also subjects public officials to the regulatory disciplines of the market, to cost-consciousness, and to entrepreneurial business ethics. (Haller and Shore 2005:18)

However, Sarah Muir argues that "the Argentine case, at least, disallows a too-hasty distinction between bureaucratic and cultural ethics, demanding instead an analysis that can grasp corruption as a folk category of moral critique" (2011:199). In Argentina, "corruption," or rather, its antithesis, has become a lens through which the proper role and ethical basis for governance is envisioned. Yet this sense of corruption defies a simple interpretation. Used nearly ubiquitously to describe the era of neoliberalist politics, the idea of corruption as permeating Argentine society has gained a powerful interpretive force as a shorthand way of describing the local "source" of the nation's difficulties. The marked increase in "watchdog journalism" in Argentina and elsewhere in Latin America greatly contributed to the public perception of the scale of corruption (Waisbord 2000). Not only are the politicians who held power during the 1990s widely seen as having engaged in multifarious "corrupt" practices, but community leaders, state workers, union bureaucrats, judges, businesspeople (*empresarios*), and many others are all considered to have been complicit in this "era of corruption."

The protest groups discussed in this book operate within the context of the widespread circulation of the specific idea of corruption set forth by international lending institutions and widely propagated through local mainstream media. While they certainly do accept the idea that corruption is a major problem in contemporary Argentine society, Argentine protest organizations and the alternative media have their own, different definition of the term. Some scholars have noted how the discourse of corruption emanating from the Global North rests on an inherent public/private dichotomy, clearly delineated in the definition of corruption by the World Bank as "the abuse of public office for private gain" (Haller and Shore 2005:2–5). However, these protest groups, I argue, emphasize not a public/private dichotomy, but a difference between individual and collective benefit. In this context, a "corrupt" act is quite specifically one that places personal interests above the public good. Noteworthy perhaps is that, despite listing 14 different definitions for the term, neither the Oxford English Dictionary nor the Real Academia Española mentions corruption as having to do with putting individual interest above collective good. This limited and specific usage is what allows its application across such a broad sector of society, indicting all those who hold positions of power and are expected to act for collective benefit. In the case of invested officials, whether of the state or in the private sector, it is those who have been entrusted with the care of the collective who are seen as violating this trust. Memoria Activa condemns both state and Jewish community officials as "corrupt" for their failure to protect the interests of those they are supposed to represent, and asserts the rights of citizens and members to protection under their leaders. The BAUEN Cooperative accuses business owners of corruption for having failed in their moral obligation to work for the benefit of the business they run. They contrast the logic of capitalism and the primacy given to an ethics of (individual) financial gain to what they see as the owners' ethical obligation to act for the benefit of the business as a productive unit, one that includes the workers. For both Memoria Activa and the BAUEN Cooperative, corruption, in this sense, represents a predominant form of rights violations in the neoliberal era.

Impunity

Impunity for those who infringe upon the public good, either through criminal acts or the breach of responsibilities, is the other predominant issue that these groups identify as a violation of human rights and a major source of societal ills. The term "impunity" first saw widespread use in the struggles to bring legal action against perpetrators of the brutal repression under the last military dictatorship. The idea of impunity gained particular force in reference to the unpunished designers and perpetrators of state violence during the Dirty War. The perception of widespread political corruption in both chambers of the National Congress and throughout all levels of the judiciary were directly tied to impunity in the form of diminishing hopes that those responsible for the Dirty War violence could ever be tried in Argentina. The negation of justice, understood as legal prosecution by an impartial judiciary, became symbolic of the endemic institutional failures of the Argentine state. However, this notion of impunity has taken on a broader significance in Argentine society, and is widely used as an interpretive trope for understanding the cause of social ills, the self-interested behavior of government officials, and the inefficiency of both state and non-state public institutions. It has been broadened to include a failure to prosecute post-dictatorship police brutality, repression of public protest, politically motivated murders, and the widespread violation of contract and labor laws.

In a semiotic as well as a practical sense, corruption and impunity are intertwined. Widespread impunity meant that the business elite and state actors could commit corrupt acts and get away with it. In this sense, impunity shielded corruption, with those in power confident that their actions would remain free of negative legal consequences. Furthermore, the idea of impunity is linked to that of corruption in that it is widely believed that acts defined as criminal, such as the AMIA bombing or violations of labor and business laws for the BAUEN, remain unpunished due to the webs of relationships and interests that define the workings of politics. That is, the corrupt relationships that operate as the basis of politics inhibit the resolution of these (illegal) acts, thus creating a self-perpetuating climate of impunity. For years, the AMIA investigation was directed toward Buenos Aires police officers as major accomplices in the attack, only to have it later revealed that this accusation was based primarily on political interests seeking to discredit this institution and its recognized leader Eduardo Duhalde, who was embroiled in a battle for control of the Peronist party. In the case of the BAUEN, workers' rights were systematically violated during the 1990s, and attempts to halt the tide of these violations were subordinated to the delicate balancing of interests between traditional unions, business owners, and newly organized workers' groups.

Impunity can serve as an impediment to healing damage to the social fabric caused by periods of intense or prolonged violence (Jelin 1995; Roht-Arriaza 1995). Upon the return to democracy in 1983 and in the decades since, human rights groups in Argentina have focused attention on the issue of impunity. They argue that justice for those responsible for the violence is essential for overcoming the legacies of fear and ruptures in societal participation. They view impunity for those responsible as only compounding damage to individuals who lost friends and loved ones and to society as whole in the aftermath of the terror. Many in the human rights movement in Argentina have sought to counteract this damage and to bring both personal healing and social reconstruction or "the healing of the body politic" through activism against impunity (Sikkink 2008:22).

Impunity can also be a form of domination. When power holders are immune to accountability for their actions, those they rule are incapable of protecting their interests against the actions of their rulers. Likewise, when the economic elite is able to personally profit from irregular financial transactions or from the bonanza of privatization of state-held industries, the public pays the price of reduced services and increased costs, with little recourse to prevent or remedy their new and untenable situation. Lesley Gill notes:

> Impunity is an aspect of power that reinforces a highly unequal social order. Although it generally refers to the lack of accountability enjoyed by militaries, police forces, and paramilitary organizations, impunity can be usefully conceptualized in a more dynamic fashion as an aspect of power that is embedded in the process of social differentiation . . . and that extends from the military and powerful civilian elites to the oppressive economic policies of international financial organizations. When experienced from above, impunity allows perpetrators to harm others without suffering consequences themselves, and when endured from below, it restricts the ability of people to limit violence—political, economic, and cultural—and hold perpetrators accountable. (2004:20)

If impunity is the problem, then what is the solution? The word "impunity" can mean exemption from punishment. However, among Argentine protest groups, the word has come to denote fundamentally the lack of legal justice. In this way, it is quintessentially tied to the notions of democracy and the rule of law institutionalized in an effective and independent branch of government. As an ideal means for redressing violations, the right to justice becomes "the right to all other rights" (Caldeira and Holston 1999:723). When these groups signal impunity as an endemic problem, it is fundamentally this lack of access to justice through the legal system that they are lamenting. This contrasts, for example, to the use of the term in contemporary Spain, where *impunidad* refers to the state's failure to dismantle the legal structures and sentences of the War Councils and special tribunals put in place during the reign of Franco, i.e., to a lack of rectification of juridical forms and decisions perceived as illegitimate.

Even as this understanding of justice as fundamentally dependent upon legal prosecution and condemnation over and above other forms of justice-making gained force over the course of the 1990s and first years of the 2000s, perceptions of the justice system in Argentina became increasingly negative.[5] While the Supreme Court provided perhaps the most extreme example of executive intervention and control, the system as a whole was widely considered inefficient, nepotistic, and subservient to political interests (Barrera 2010; Huneeus 2010; Smulovitz 2010). Though many reforms undertaken by the administration of Néstor Kirchner (2003–2007), such as the renovation of the Supreme Court, were successful in improving the independence, functioning, and image of the system, others, such as the widely criticized reform of the Judicial Council (Consejo de la Magistratura), continued to locate the judiciary as among the most problematic of the nation's institutions in public perception.[6] Critics cite the control the executive branch retains over the administrative aspects of the justice system. These include influence over the naming of judges, requisites for their appointment, and fiscal control over not only the amount of money the system receives but also the way it can be distributed (Chávez 2007). The sense of justice as something that remains always out of reach is enhanced by the way it is commonly referenced. The term "la Justicia" is used in news media and common speech to refer to the entire justice system, in many cases with no further specifications. For example, when a major television news channel covered the opening of a new subway line in Buenos Aires in 2007, it noted that "*la Justicia* define si da lugar a una denuncia por falta de seguridad" (*the justice [system] is in the process of defining whether to accept an accusation for lack of security*) (From Noticias TN, Oct. 18, 2007; emphasis mine). Such usage further alienates most people from the workings of the institutions of justice that are available to them and/or to which they are subject, by failing to provide basic information on which facet of this huge and labyrinthine branch of government is involved. With the manner of its functioning obscured, the justice system becomes even more impenetrable.

In spite of these complications and the fact that normative perceptions of the law and evaluations of the performance of the judiciary have worsened, the use of legal procedures and the process of judicialization have intensified in the past two decades (Smulovitz 2005:238). Their bond to a notion of legal justice has conditioned both the ethical demands asserted by these groups and their choices and possibilities for action within the legal sphere. While demands for an effective, transparent, and politically neutral judiciary are at the core of these groups' rhetorical demands, in practice they have had to learn to navigate the judicial system in its current manifestation, even while maintaining pressure on the executive branch to provide solutions that could circumvent it. Actors increasingly opt "to use institutionalized procedures to 'solve' not only legal disputes over established positive rights but also as a strategic tool to advance political and social goals. . . . They situate judges and tribunals as legitimate parties in a given conflict and introduce legal precedents and pre-established rules as mechanisms to address political disputes" (Smulovitz 2010:235).

The realities of the structure and operations of the legal system have led to protest groups working within the system, by serving as plaintiffs (in the AMIA case) or filing judicial petitions (for the BAUEN), while simultaneously pressuring for its reform. They see the use of the system and working to increase its efficacy through exposing the damages wrought by pervasive impunity and corruption as essential to improving the quality of Argentine democracy and society. In doing so, these groups explicitly seek a collective, rather than an individual gain, by bringing about solutions designed to benefit society as a whole. For the BAUEN, this is based on a fundamental reformulation of economic principles, placing solidarity over profit. For Memoria Activa, the focus is on what it perceives as a dire need for improved governmental institutions, in ways that can better respond and attend to the needs of all members of society, regardless of religious or economic status. For both groups, justice, impunity, and corruption come together in the definition of the social ills left behind by the destructive storm of the neoliberal era.

Methodology

This book is based on ethnographic field research I conducted during a number of research sessions in Buenos Aires between 2000 and 2009. However, my initial contact with Argentina on an personal level came in 1992, when I spent six months in the small town of Reconquista, nestled on the banks of the Paraná River and surrounded by the *pampas santafesinos* (grasslands of the province of Santa Fe) in the country's geographic center. In addition to providing me with trial-by-fire experience, this formative time also provided a lasting emotional connection to a place to which I find myself linked in a cycle of continuous return. I returned to Argentina in 2000, and then 2001, for two eight-week fieldwork sessions in which I explored the public performance of memory and practices of monumentalization, including the way monuments functioned and affected the experience of public spaces (cf. James 2000, esp. ch. 1). This research led me into contact with the group Memoria Activa, and during my 2001 field session, I attended several of their public events and organizational meetings, and conducted interviews with members of the directive board (*mesa directiva*).

These initial research sessions in Buenos Aires laid the foundation for my extended period of field investigation, from October 2004 to March 2006, with a return visit in September–October 2009. I also maintained an active research agenda in between these sessions and afterward, through continued personal communication via letters, email, and phone conversations, and through careful attention to local developments through newspaper and other media. In doing this detailed ethnographic research, I was interested in accessing the mutually constitutive processes that link ideas of rights, justice, and the institutions of democracy at this critical juncture and time of rapid change, as expressed in the lived experience of the members of the group. As such I was interested in hearing what people had to say, both in answer to my questions but even more centrally in their conversations with those around them (myself included). I also listened carefully to their public proclamations, spontaneous and prepared (through speeches at protest events, testifying in court, or making media appearances). My work included participation at public and private events, semi-structured and open interviews with participants, hundreds of informal conversations with individuals and groups of individuals in coffee houses, restaurants, plazas, theaters, and private houses, and a careful (and, in my field informants' eyes, perhaps leaning toward obsessive) collection of published and printed documentation of the group's activities and the many facets of the AMIA case. I also interviewed a number of people closely connected to the investigations, including high-level government and community officials, as well as participants in varying aspects of the legal cases.

In addition to my work with Memoria Activa, I was also interested in working with organizations making demands upon the state concerning economic rights. In late 2005, a participant in Memoria Activa provided me with an introduction to leading members of the BAUEN Cooperative, shortly after it reopened of large portions of the hotel. After conducting several initial formal interviews, I began to participate in the daily activities of the hotel, in a variety of forms including as a teacher of English. My research with the cooperative over the next few years consisted of in-depth participant observation in the most literal sense of the term, encompassing, among other things, attendance and participation in cooperative organizational meetings, observation of daily life within the hotel, and participation in numerous protest marches. As time went on, I also began working with BAUEN's internal press committee, on the distribution and translation of its press releases. I also conducted semi-structured and open interviews with individuals and small groups of cooperative members, state officials, and activists, as well as conducting archival research on the hotel. In addition, I studied the extensive legal documentation surrounding different aspects and legal entanglements of the hotel's construction, ownership, and operation, as well as following the various court cases that arose concerning the cooperative's possession and habilitation of the establishment, and its interactions with state officials concerning these cases.

In taking a historically grounded view of the events unfolding in the moment, I attend to the economic, political, and cultural forces that have shaped the nation and the people within it. However, this also entails taking into consideration the construction of histor(ies) (official, semi-official, or otherwise), and paying attention to the ways these are built upon, challenged, or renovated through the daily actions of the people with whom I worked. One outcome of this perspective was that the formative interactions and interstices between local and transnational visions of human rights became clear. It was possible to observe how powerful ideas of human rights were in granting an organizing framework for understanding and a deep legitimacy to the struggles of the protest organizations. Yet, also evident were the precise ways they were consistently adapted to the on-the-ground and in-the-moment needs and experiences of those choosing to invoke them. By doing so publicly (regardless of whether the audience was one, five, or five thousand others), these constant reworkings also fed into the reconceptualization of the dominant understandings.

Structure of the Book

In this Introduction I have outlined some of the theoretical considerations that underlie the issues discussed in this book, laying a foundation for understanding the fluidity of the discursive categories operative in twenty-first-century Argentina, and their relevance for citizenship and human rights globally. In Chapter 1, I trace a history of ideas of rights within Argentina. From the early days of state formation through the present, the question of rights—what kinds of rights, for whom, and the role of the state in promoting, protecting, and enforcing these rights—has been based on culturally salient notions derived from the particular local context. Concepts of rights in Argentina have historically been constructed through the interplay of local and global ideas. The language of rights exists within a system of claim-making that is at once specific to Argentina and in dialogue with transnationally validated visions. By paying attention to this history, this chapter sets the stage for exploring how the language of rights has changed in recent years and the conditions for its emergence.

Chapter 2 traces the shift from disappearance and torture to impunity and corruption in the local language of human rights under neoliberalism. This shift, and the intimate relationship between the era of neoliberal reform and perceived endemic corruption and impunity, are illustrated through the cases of Memoria Activa and the BAUEN Cooperative. In the years since the AMIA bombing, the members of Memoria Activa have come to define and articulate the centrality of impunity and corruption to their understanding of the nature of the problems they faced and the obstacles to their resolution. They condemn the investigations into the attack as riddled with deliberate inefficiency. They seek an end to impunity through judicial punishment for those responsible for the event and for the subsequent attempts to misdirect the investigation. Similarly, members of the workers' cooperative BAUEN protest what they see as the illegal and immoral actions of profit-driven, socially irresponsible business owners and their allies. They assert that this corruption in the economic sphere and the impunity that guarantees it are part and parcel of the neoliberal state. In exploring these cases, this chapter also takes up the broader issue of the relationship between neoliberalism and human rights.

Chapters 3 and 4 trace specific features of the demands of these groups, exploring how these groups conceptualize and use the idea of rights in confronting the issues that directly affect their lives. Chapter 3 shows how, for Memoria Activa, the right to equal protection and justice is violated by the state through its failure to properly respond to the attacks and for the deliberately flawed investigations that followed them. For the BAUEN, it is the right to work that is being violated, both through the initial closure of the business and by subsequent attempts to deprive the workers of the material conditions of the source of labor they created in response. In crafting their claims and demands, each group is also advancing a particular vision of the proper role of the democratic state. Chapter 4 focuses on the right to collective well-being embedded in the demands of Memoria Activa and the BAUEN Cooperative. It traces the shift in the national discourse on human rights under the Kirchner administrations, and shows how ideas of sociality underlie the demands of many Argentine protest groups and animate their vision of what a better society would look like. Finally, Chapter 5 serves as a reflection on the prospects for the realization of these visions.

Chapter 1

Land of Equality and Assassins

Rights in the National Imaginary

The Idea of Rights

How have rights been imagined in Argentina throughout its history? This chapter focuses on the tension between individual and collective rights that has permeated the social field, exploring how the dominant political philosophy has tended to vacillate between one formulation and the other. This tension is crucial to contemporary debates, yet it is not a new phenomenon. Rather, individual and collective rights and the different meanings attributed to these terms have historically been essential features in the way the nation has been imagined and experienced by its members, and this history influences and is drawn upon by those who engage in these debates.

The idea of a national imaginary as fundamental to the formation and development of the modern nation-state was proposed by Benedict Anderson in his book *Imagined Communities*. In it he traces how the modern nation came to be understood as an "imagined political community . . . both inherently limited and sovereign" through the use of new mechanized technologies by institutions of power, including printing, counting (of populations), and mapping (1991:6). A number of scholars have criticized Anderson's treatment of the formation of the nation as too centered on the literary (i.e., elite, male) class, and for ignoring that these ideas existed within a field of power relations that extended beyond these privileged enclaves (see Guha 1985; Skurski 1996). In addition, and fundamentally, the pattern of development of the (European) nation-state is not a formula that can necessarily be applied in very different contexts across the world. Even if the form of the nation-state has been influential globally, the trajectory of its development in each place must be understood within the context of specific local conditions. While not contending that a national imaginary was necessarily compelling for all groups across Argentine society, nor that its development precisely coincided with Continental patterns, I draw on Anderson's insights in considering the foundations of the philosophy of rights that took root in Argentina. Specific formulations of a national imaginary in Argentina have operated in conjunction with competing political philosophies in influencing public policy in practice, notably in relationship to ideas of rights. The formation of a creole identity as part and parcel of colonial subjectivity encouraged incipient understandings of the nation and, importantly, of the rights of its citizens.

Ideas of rights in Argentina have been inextricably bound to the political and ideological currents that have affected the formation and historical development of the nation from its inception. The idea of rights that took hold among liberals in the River Plate following independence closely mimicked that circulating throughout Western Europe. This was a particular idea of responsibilities and obligations developed in relation and reaction to monarchical society, growing out of and forming an integral part of Enlightenment ideals. Lynn Hunt has shown how changing conceptions of the self and the body toward the end of the eighteenth century led to the sense of these rights as being "self-evident," and to their codification in formative political treatises and documents at that time (2007). The United States Declaration of Independence in 1776 and the French Declaration of the Rights of Man and Citizen in 1789 clearly and explicitly delineated an idea of rights that was to mark an irreversible shift in the formalization of rights and the responsibilities and limits of the state. Essential to this conception of rights was their location in the figure of the individual. The individualist nature of rights marked a revolutionary difference from the monarchical social system that preceded it, where the sovereign held rights over the people as a whole.

European liberalist ideas greatly influenced the perspective of Argentine founding fathers like Bernadino Rivadavia, whose fascination with non-Iberian European culture was to profoundly inform his social, economic, and cultural policies in ways that continue to have repercussions today. Rivadavia's "doctrinaire democratic idealism" sought to remake Argentina in the model of Enlightenment-era Europe, free from the influence of local oligarchs and ecclesiastic authority. While encumbered by virulent elitism, the Rivadavians nonetheless sought to encourage a brand of equality among men through peace, prosperity, and (European) high culture, with this final element to be achieved through the creation of numerous cultural institutions. The liberal fascination also served to further entrench the country in its colonial position as an export-based economy. The signing of the Anglo-Argentine Treaty of Friendship, Commerce, and Navigation under Rivadavia essentially gave Great Britain unrestricted access to the nation's markets, "devastat[ing] local manufacturing . . . and limit[ing] the country's economic future to one of provider of agricultural goods and raw materials to an industrial power" (Shumway 1991:99).

Liberalist economic policies affected the emerging nation in other ways as well. Property rights were in many respects the foundation of the post-monarchical society. The original meaning of being endowed with rights in the River Plate was, to a certain degree, founded on shifting the notion of property from being a privilege to a right. The inherent individual nature of private property embedded in liberal conceptions of rights was born out of rebellion against the monarch's abusive authority over its control and regulation. However, the protection of private property and its contractual basis required a stable and legitimized state capable of preserving legal order. This need illustrates the tension within liberalism between public representation and private property, where the government must serve as a legitimate representative of the interests of the people while upholding and enforcing private contractual property law. Thus, in Argentina as in other American countries, the formation and formalization of the nation was inextricably bound to creating and maintaining a balance between the prerogatives of political institutionalization and the right to private property (Adelman 1999).

Part of the formalization of this kind of state came with nation's first constitution, enacted on May 1, 1853. A version of liberal idealism is embodied particularly in the first of the two major sections of this constitution, consisting of a set of rights and guarantees (*derechos y garantías*) laid out explicitly in its 31 articles. These include protections for equality before the law, rights to property, free circulation, and freedom of expression. This portion of the constitution was largely borrowed directly from that of the United States of America. However, it also contains certain important provisions that distinguish it from its Northern counterpart. Significantly, it has specific articles concerning the abolition of slavery and the establishment of free primary education, the latter moving beyond the so-called first-generation civil and political rights.

The 1853 constitution also expresses one of the foremost concerns of the Argentine liberalist philosophy. This is most famously contained in Alberdi's phrase *gobernar es poblar* (to govern is to populate). One of the most concrete and lasting effects of the liberals' vision was the change they effected in the composition of the Argentine populace. Immigration began to be encouraged as a means of modernizing the nation, and economic incentives were implemented specifically for European immigration. Accordingly, the preamble to the constitution declares that it is to apply to "todos los hombres del mundo que quieran habitar en el suelo argentino" (all those in the world who want to inhabit Argentine soil). Article 20 declares equal rights for citizens and foreigners, and Article 25 mandates state support for European immigration.

Behind these incentives and protections lay Domingo Sarmiento's characterization of Argentina as the battleground for the forces of civilization against the powers of barbarism. This ideology of purportedly ethical domination influenced many of the political elites of his time, and promoted the idea that the nation would be built through the influx of (preferably Northern) Europeans, who would come to outnumber and override the "racial backwardness" of the gaucho and Native American populations. The devastating losses among indigenous populations through directed genocide under the Desert Conquest in the second half of the 1800s was a concrete and tragic result of this ideology. Disparaging the country's Spanish heritage, which they saw as full of "stultifying piety," Catholic superstitions, and "bereft of industrial capacity" (Alberdi 1852, cited in Shumway 1991:138), thinkers within this strain believed that an influx of Northern European immigrants would prove the key to the development of the nation as an agricultural and industrial power. The attempted erasure of the indigenous populations of the arable pampas was reasoned within the law that instigated it as justified since "the presence of the Indian impedes access to the immigrant who wishes to work."[1] The brutal "desert campaigns" at once brought about the large-scale land expropriations that fueled the emergence of agrarian capitalism and left the *indio* as an absent presence in the national imaginary, to be reviled and feared (Gordillo and Hirsch 2003).

Concerns over the shaping of the nation's body public were also embedded in Article 22 of the constitution, which was maintained even through the reforms of 1994. This article prohibits all forms of direct democracy, and reflects the drafters' discomfort with the participation of the masses in public life. The equality of rights they proposed and enshrined in the document was not intended to be equally applicable to all, but rather to an entitled, educated, and elite subset of the citizenry. As Adelman notes, "the republic would only realize a robust notion of citizenship at the end of a very long process of social change—one the citizens were not necessarily invited to define or elect" (1999:215). The realization of equality of rights remains a work in progress.

Becoming Liberal Citizens

With the passage of the constitution and the absorption of previously occupied lands, the government opened the door for immigration to Argentina. These measures, alongside concurrent civil and economic unrest within Europe itself, led to a vast number of immigrants making their way to Argentina in the ensuing decades. However, in practice, the majority of those who chose to make the journey did not depart from Northern Europe. Overall, Argentina saw an influx of 2.5 million immigrants in the period from 1888 to 1913.[2] Over half came from the Italian peninsula, another 20 percent from Spain, and the rest from France, Germany, Great Britain, and other Latin American nations.[3] This influx would fundamentally change the national imaginary of who "the Argentine people" were. Surviving indigenous populations and the significant urban Afro-Argentine community (Andrews 1980) would be relegated into near oblivion in the new demographic.

The vision of nation-building that held sway during the last decades of the nineteenth century and early twentieth century assumed the ideal of assimilation as a means to achieving equality. Assimilation, while envisioned as the means through which immigrants could obtain full membership in the nation, carried the attendant implication of homogenization and minimization of difference (Grimson 2006; Halperín 2008). Proponents of assimilation endorsed a new national identity based on a melting pot model of culture (*crisol de razas*). Ultimately only certain immigrant cultures were recognized as formative of this new cultural mix, with influential sectors of society often dismissing "undesirable" groups like Jews as foreign and inassimilable.

Assimilation was encouraged and enforced through various means. An example is the approved lists of names which could be given to children born in Argentina, as a means of facilitating easy pronunciation and understanding. The laws providing for state education of all residents also formed part of the broad set of policies that were the codification of this ideal. Throughout the first half of the twentieth century, public schools played an active role in instilling patriotism in the children of immigrants. This included the creation and promotion of national rituals and the standardization of the teaching of national history (Plotkin 2003). Policies such as school dress codes functioned to implement Enlightenment principles of egalitarianism while disciplining and defining the emerging citizenry. Inés Dussel argues that these policies spoke "of a particular construction of the nation, a construction that equated homogeneity with democracy, and equality of people with equal, identical appearances" (2005:101–

102). New masses of people, many of them recent immigrants, were coming to understand and view themselves as citizens of the Argentine nation. Concern over the habits and political participation of these newcomers engulfed not only the conservative opposition but also those who supported egalitarianism. "The principle of equality," Dussel argues, "had to navigate turbulent waters, and a safe port could only be reached if self-discipline and enlightenment were generalized and the enlightened citizens participated in public government" (2005: 109). As Donna Guy has also shown, the body became a focus for attempts to mold this new citizenry (Guy 1991, 2000a). The use of basic white smocks (*guardapolvos*) in schools was designed to at once provide a release from the markers of difference and to educate citizens as modern "enlightened consumers," able to pick democratic, healthy, and affordable clothing, monitoring bodies in ways that readied them to act as producers in the emerging form of capitalism (Dussel 2005).

As immigrants built new lives, their labor transformed the nation they adopted as their own. Early in the twentieth century, Argentina was enjoying a degree of economic stability and prosperity that rivaled that of its Northern European interlocutors (Romero 2002). It was this prosperity and the ruling elite's interest in cultivating architectural and artistic fame that endowed Buenos Aires with the nickname the Paris of Latin America. Yet, unlike the early economy of North American immigrant-dependent nations with their many small landowners, the Argentine economy was largely dependant on the exportation of grain and cattle produced on large latifundias controlled by the local oligarchy and worked by the influx of immigrants. As refrigeration and canning technologies improved, the profits from the cattle industry grew even larger. Due largely to foreign investment, industry, controlled by a small number of elites, began to develop, and Argentina continued to cultivate a privileged relationship with Great Britain in both infrastructure development and trade.

The waves of new immigrants, however, were for the most part not easily incorporated into the existing structures of oligarchic domination. The new mass of urban workers, furthermore, could not fall back on subsistence agriculture to weather fluctuations in the global market for exports. Rapid industrialization brought on in part by new technological innovations and the expanding urban populations led to ever louder demands for stronger protections for rural and urban laborers. Increasingly, these demands came to focus on the inclusion of immigrants and other non-landowning residents into the ranks of full citizens. The passage of the Sáenz-Peña laws in 1912 fulfilled this demand, making voting obligatory, secret, and universal for all males (though not yet for females).[4]

The attempts to expand first-generation rights to ever greater swaths of the populace were accompanied by movements that sought to place economic and social rights in the center as well. The idea that these rights must be attended to if a true equality was to be achieved gained increasing support in many places throughout the world during the late nineteenth and early twentieth centuries. In Argentina, ideas of social entitlements and group rights were joined to notions of popular sovereignty and found a ready constituency in this mass of urban immigrants, presenting a challenge to existing patterns of representation and governing institutions (Adelman 1999:290–291). These currents found their strongest expression in the growing numbers of activists in socialist and anarchist political (or anti-political) organizations.

The most visible face of this activism in Argentina is in the figure of Simón Radowitzky. In the Buenos Aires of the early 1900s, Chief of Police Coronel Ramón Falcón was infamous for his brutal repression of workers and activists. Enraged by his actions in response to the May Day demonstrations of 1909, which left at least five people dead and dozens more wounded or imprisoned, 19-year-old Russian immigrant Simón Radowitzky shot and killed Falcón in reprisal. The assassination turned both men into legendary figures, to be remembered and memorialized by different factions of Argentine society. It is worth noting how such events hold contemporary relevance. Meaning remains contested and inescapable for the inhabitants of Buenos Aires, embodied in the materiality of the urban landscape, the street signs, cars, and buildings of their everyday travels. The current police school for the Federal Police (Policía Federal), took on Falcón's name in 1928, as proudly displayed on its website and television recruitment commercials.[5] As of 2009, a monument to Ramón Falcón, in the porteño (Buenos Aires) neighborhood of Recoleta, bears graffiti that reads "Simón lives" above the anarchist symbol.

In part as a result of the growing unrest, by 1919 the "liberal consensus" had begun to crack.[6] A reactive nationalist sentiment had developed against the growing tides of immigrants and the policies of Radical president Hipólito Yrigoyen (1916–1922 and 1928–1930) that benefited the urban working and middle classes.[7] In particular, the conservative oligarchy feared the spread of communist and anarchist ideologies, and led media campaigns focusing on the supposedly destabilizing influence of Jewish (Russian), Bolshevik, and Catalonian immigrant activists. This culminated with the *Semana Trágica* or Tragic Week of January

1919, when President Yrigoyen backed away from his earlier support of labor's demands and sent police and military forces to break an ironworkers' strike. This sparked a wave of anti-immigrant and anti-Semitic sentiment, and murderous bands incited by the ultra-nationalist Liga Patriótica Argentina (Argentine Patriotic League) rampaged through Jewish and Russian shops and neighborhoods, leaving some 850–1,000 people dead and thousands wounded.[8]

In 1930 a military coup—the first in a long series of coups in Argentina history—brought a premature end to Yrigoyen's second term as president. This so-called Conservative Restoration of the 1930s also saw a withdrawal from international markets in reaction to the increase in protectionism in European and North America, as the world economy was drastically altered by the effects of the Great Depression. The conservative government's harsher policies toward union and labor activism increased popular unrest and arguably set the stage for the emergence of the Peronist movement in the 1940s.

The Right to Collective Well-being

Juan Domingo Perón won the elections of February 1946 to become President of the Nation, shortly after the massive demonstrations of his popular support on October 17, 1945 (James 1988a; Plotkin 1995). Perón's first two governments (1946–1955) adopted many contradictory policies, but overall expanded first-generation political and civil rights to include women and indigenous groups (Gordillo and Hirsch 2003). The Peronist vision of social justice, based in large part on the assurance and protection of collective rights, is perhaps nowhere better expressed than in the 1949 reforms to the constitution. These contained a long set of explicit rights for workers, the family, children, and the elderly (Article 37). The inclusion of these rights into the constitution itself placed economic and social well-being at the center of government's role and responsibility toward the populace. Furthermore, Chapter 4 of this constitution, consisting of Articles 38–40, is dedicated to "The social function of property, capital, and economic activity." These articles insist that the function of these economic cornerstones be oriented toward the collective good of the people ("el bienestar del pueblo").

The rights embedded in the 1949 constitution thus included recognition of what have come to be known as second-generation rights, or rights concerned with realizing social and economic equality. The Peronist reforms were part of a broader movement toward social constitutionalism, or the enshrinement of these rights into formal governing documents. The constitution produced in 1917 by the Mexican Revolution served as an early example for the inclusion of this class of rights. Internationally, the formation of the International Labor Organization (ILO) in 1919, initially as an agency affiliated with the League of Nations and transformed into a specialized agency of the United Nations in 1946, demonstrated the growing strength of concern for the establishment and protection of the rights of workers. The ILO was founded "in the wake of a destructive war, to pursue a vision based on the premise that universal, lasting peace can be established only if it is based upon decent treatment of working people."[9]

The United Nations Universal Declaration of Human Rights (UDHR), adopted on December 10, 1948, also accords second-generation rights a fundamental importance. The atrocities of the Second World War gave impulse to further codifying a comprehensive, internationally agreed-upon set of rights for all people. In distinction to earlier declarations like the Rights of Man, the UDHR covers both first-generation and second-generation rights. Argentina joined with other Latin American states in championing the passage of the Declaration.

In spite of international recognition of such collective rights, the 1949 reforms to the Argentine constitution came at a time of increasing instability for the Peronist government. The first Perón administration enjoyed the high prices of meat and grains that followed the destabilization that World War II brought on European food production and populations. However, by 1949, prices were returning to normal and an increasingly industrialized Argentine economy had become dependent on imports for fuel, machinery, and intermediate goods. The ensuing crisis in foreign trade was aggravated by drought, and the early 1950s marked a change in state policy. The government began to encourage foreign investment, in a fundamental departure from Perón's earlier emphasis on economic independence, and in contradiction to the sentiments expressed in Article 40 on the non-transferability of national resources and state control of public services. However, the attempts to redirect the economy did not lead to stability, and another military coup in 1955 sent Perón into exile.

The 1949 constitution was revoked in 1956 following the coup that deposed Perón. De facto president Pedro Eugenio Aramburu mandated a return to the 1853 constitution.[10] In 1957 the government called for a commission to reform the constitution again. Political tensions within the convention, from which Peronists were excluded, prevented it from enacting any revisions, with the exception of Article 14bis on the rights of workers. While Article 14bis did retain some of the rights and protections of the previous reforms, no Argentine constitution to date would provide the same level of protections and entitlements for economic and social rights as the 1949 reforms did during that constitution's brief life.

Escalating Violence and the Violation of Rights

Fluctuations in the world economy continued to have dramatic effects on Argentina throughout the politically volatile years that followed Perón's exile. The next two decades saw a great increase in foreign investment and an even greater increase in the influence of foreign capital. The rise to prominence of dependency theory during this era provided a tool for describing the constraints that policy makers in countries like Argentina faced. In spite of the traction this theory gained locally, especially though the work of Argentine economist Raúl Prebisch, Argentina's dependence on foreign capital grew and the economy stagnated under the weight of a growing foreign debt. The possibilities for a state-directed policy that could address these problems were reduced by the climate of competition and shifting alliances between the ruling economic interests that dominated the era. The passion play of rival interests included factions within the military, unions, non-unionized workers engaged in new forms of social protest, industrialists, landowners, and representatives of foreign capital. Constraints on governability reached a point where

> it was a game without logical or predictable rules; no sector could impose rules on the rest. Although the state's actions were of paramount influence, the state did not design policies autonomously but was at the mercy of those who could capture the state for the moment and use it to take as much advantage as possible. (Romero 2002:157)

Tensions between radical labor unions, student activists, and militant revolutionary groups on the one hand, and the military and right-wing death squads on the other, led to spiraling political violence and increasing state repression (Robben 2005). Events like the Cordobazo and Rosariazos in 1969 and the Viborazo in 1971 left many businesses, national and multinational, keen to secure their interests in the country and reassert their dominance over the workers' unions inside the plants (Robben 2005; Brennan 1994; James 1988b). All sides competed in the escalating scales of violence, with emergent guerilla groups undertaking ever bolder and more violent actions, and the state directing and tolerating increasingly intense repression.

Perón's eventual return to the presidency in 1973 came after several punctuated military regimes were forced to yield to public demands for the relegalization of Peronism. While heralded by both the right and left of his party, his return only exacerbated the fighting, increasing the divisions between the Peronist factions and radicalizing the militant left.[11] Perhaps inevitably given the circumstances, the return of the leader at that time failed to bring about fundamental changes in the structure of the economy. Perón's death in 1974, with the assumption of power by his third wife, María Estela Martínez de Perón (Isabelita), allowed the right-wing factions led by José López Rega to implement even harsher measures against the militant left and society in general, while ineffectually managing an already volatile economy.

On March 24, 1976, a military coup put an end to the chaotic presidency of Isabelita de Perón. If Perón's first presidencies signaled the expansion of rights to include economic and social rights, the end of his second presidential era brought the violation of civil and political rights to a new extreme. Within days, Congress was dissolved and all high level courts, including the Supreme Court, were adjourned. Major political party activities were shut down, with communist and socialist parties banned entirely. The military intervened in the major unions and the right to strike was suspended. The state of siege, in effect regularly since the late 1960s, was maintained, and the military leaders threatened to impose severe penalties, including the death penalty, on any who attacked members of the security forces, military installations, or public services.

The dictatorship rapidly began implementing what it called the Process of National Reorganization (*El Proceso de reorganización nacional*, or simply *El Proceso*), calculated to redesign Argentine society and cure it of the social ills that it argued were brought about by the revolutionary Marxist groups and left-wing Peronist ideology. This was to be achieved by the complete destruction of the opposition. Evidence from survivors and extant documentation demonstrate how individuals were abducted and taken away to clandestine detention centers, held often for years without recourse to legal procedures or any official acknowledgment of their detention. These "disappeared" were extensively and brutally tortured, and although some were eventually released, many were killed and buried in anonymous graves or thrown, drugged but still alive, from military aircraft into the Río de la Plata (Verbitsky 1995).

Marguerite Feitlowitz has described how the terror imposed by the dictatorship permeated and appropriated even everyday language, leaving deep scars in society even after the return to democracy. She studied the way the

Argentine language was warped by the actions of the dictatorship, asking people, "What words can you no longer tolerate? What words do you no longer say?" (1998:xi). The deformation of language delved deep into Argentine social life, taking over and resignifiying cultural aspects in an almost playful appropriation that decisively locked horrific scenes of torture into the negotiation of quotidian life. For example, the *submarino*, a common form of hot chocolate, became the name for one of the methods of torture imported from the French in Algeria; the *parilla*, or grill, a ubiquitous feature in Argentine *asados* or cookouts, was the metal bed prisoners were strapped to during torture sessions with electric prods. Perhaps the most pervasive and lasting example of this distortion of the everyday was precisely the transformation of the word "disappear" into a transitive verb. Someone could now be "disappeared" by someone else.

An estimated thirty thousand people were disappeared by state forces, mostly from 1975 to 1978.[12] The armed revolutionary groups were largely in disarray by 1976, having suffered greatly at the hands of the ultra-right-wing death squads and the faltering of their base of public support following the return of Perón. After the coup, the main victims of this repression were not armed combatants. Nearly anyone concerned with social justice was a potential target, from high school students asking for state subsidies for student transportation to soup kitchen volunteers and priests and nuns influenced by liberation theology.

The military viewed the struggle as primarily a cultural war over the future and direction of the Argentine nation, one that necessitated at the same time the merciless cleansing of the national body and the reestablishment of cultural and historical order among the populace at large. De facto president General Videla insisted that the coup that brought the military to power in 1976 was "a fight that we neither sought nor desired, a fight that was forced upon us, but which we accepted because nothing more and nothing less than the national being was at stake."[13] The rhetoric of nationhood embraced by the dictatorship was based firmly on a vision of divine hierarchy and moral right (Graziano 1992). This worldview contrasted sharply with the view of an ideal society expressing the fundamental equality of all people, which the military denounced as a threat to Christian values and the Western cultural heritage. "Theirs was not just a contest about power but a contest about the space of culture, about the cultural confines and social conditions within which the Argentine people were supposed to lead their lives" (Robben 2005:172).

The idea of the nation as a beleaguered body in need of saving was used to defend the military's seizure of power and as a guide for social reform. In waging a cultural war, the dictatorship and its supporters manipulated the media to propagate a prolific and authoritative discourse that divided the world into black and white, us and them, the morally right and the "subversives." This discursively established a subclass as less than human, and not a part of the Argentine self. The military appealed to "citizens" to help in the battle against subversion.[14] In doing so, it discursively expelled those who opposed the regime and others considered less Argentine, such as indigenous groups, from the national body, rhetorically (and in some cases actually) stripping them of their citizenship. "The repression is directed against a minority we do not consider Argentine. . . . A terrorist is not only someone who plants bombs, but a person whose ideas are contrary to our Western, Christian civilization."[15] The dictatorship used the designation of "subversives" as "internal externals" to justify repression and the struggle against the "cancer" that threatened society.

This dichotomization of society into two uniform wholes, and the demonization of the created Other, is in no way particular to Argentina, nor was it devoid of historical resonance within the country. The category of the "subversive" was as much a transformation of Sarmiento's "barbarians" or the characterization of anarchists at the turn of the century as it was a reaction by the Right to the perceived danger of the Cuban revolution and radical trade unionism. Though powerful economic and political sectors of society feared revolutionary change, they borrowed and adapted well-known discursive tropes that, for their familiarity, resonated and made sense in intuitive ways.

The political bloodshed in Argentina reached a scale that few seem to have been prepared for or expected. While there was some vocal opposition to the use of violence in the spiraling waves of attacks in the years leading up to the 1976 military coup, it was only with the onslaught of organized state terror that groups began to come together in a concerted attempt to, first and foremost, stop the violence and discover the fate of the disappeared. These groups rapidly adopted the language of human rights in defining and attempting to counter the repression.

The Search for Justice

The establishment of military regimes in this era coincided with and in many ways provoked the adoption of human rights as the primary language of dissent and response across Latin America. A strong institutional and legal foundation for human rights had been established with the passage of the UDHR and the American Convention on Human Rights, and by the 1970s both states and social movements had begun to increasingly frame their actions and demands in these terms. The military regime in Argentina implemented state terrorism through the indiscriminate use of torture, hiding information, creating a climate of fear, marginalizing the judiciary (and with it, all possibility of legal reckoning of wrongs), and spreading deliberate confusion and uncertainty among family members of victims and throughout society (Jelin 1995).[16] The local organizations that arose in response adopted the name "human rights organizations" very early in their formation. Internationally, these Argentine organizations became an important force in what became the Latin American human rights network. This loosely connected set of organizations was fundamental in raising awareness and pressing for the enforcement of human rights in Latin America. Characterized by informal, non-hierarchical links and flows of information among its constituents, it consisted of local human rights organizations, international NGOs, global and regional interstate organizations, and private foundations, many of which were established or strengthened during this time (Sikkink 1996).

Such was the force of this emerging discourse of human rights that the Argentine dictatorship felt compelled to respond to its critics in like terms, in an early example of what would become an international trend in the appropriation of the language of human rights by those accused of violating them. The first military junta defensively proclaimed themselves to be *derechos y humanos*, especially as international pressure against them mounted around the 1978 World Cup soccer games, held in Argentina. In doing so, they played with the multiple meanings *derecho* has in Spanish (as in English), and in using the words for "human rights" (*derechos humanos*) they were claiming that they were "just," in the sense of fair or righteous.

The 1970s was not the first time human rights had become a focus of attention in Latin America, and human rights movements drew on the structures already in place. The decades of experience of the Liga Argentina por los Derechos del Hombre—organized in 1937 by leftists (Bickford 2000:173; Villalba 1984)—in cultivating international ties were a useful resource in garnering support outside of Argentina in the 1970s. What was newer was the emerging use of human rights as a mobilizing concept and directive for action, both internationally and locally.

Within Argentina, organizations that responded to the repression fell into two main categories (with considerable overlap between them): those organized by the directly affected, such as ex-detainees or family members, and groups concerned more broadly with rights violations.[17] One of the major issues these organizations faced concerned defining their field of struggle. The initial tactics of the human rights organizations had focused on concrete legal actions such as writs of habeas corpus and the search for and compilation of information on cases of disappearance. The more family members and activists made their actions known internationally, the harder it became for the dictatorship to ignore their demands. International attention to the dictatorship's tactics, including the 1979 fact-finding mission by the Inter-American Commission on Human Rights (IACHR) and the awarding of the Nobel Peace Prize to activist Adolfo Pérez Esquival in 1980, gave strength to increasingly open public debate within Argentina. The international community became part of an "insider-outsider coalition," where activists focused on domestic change but were able to draw strength from supportive international structures (Sikkink 2008; Grugel and Peruzzotti 2010).

Indeed, the events in Argentina in the lead-up to and during the last military dictatorship, publicly symbolized through the figures of torture and disappearance, were major elements in the perceived need to create and strengthen international institutions capable of stopping and preventing such violations. Human rights organizations during this era played a major role in drawing global attention to what was occurring inside the country. The regional human rights treaty, the American Convention on Human Rights, entered into force in 1978, but as still more a potentiality than an actuality. As Kathryn Sikkink notes, "Activists from countries like Argentina and Chile, with the support of state and NGO allies, mainly from Europe and the United States, were crucial in using the potential in these institutions and thus transforming them from potential into actual mechanisms of human rights change" (2008:3).

However, as activists' demands garnered support, they were also canalized and prioritized according to the interests and politics of the era. The dictatorship-era human rights organizations had to operate within the polarized Cold War climate of the time. This context of their emergence influenced both the form and possibilities for action. While during the early decades of the twentieth century moves to expand political and civil rights to more members of society were accompanied by an equal concern for economic rights, the Cold War saw a conceptual separation in the formalization of different classes of rights. The emblematic and formative case of this separation is the division of rights in the International Covenant on Civil and Political Rights (ICCPR) and the International Covenant on Economic, Social, and Cultural Rights (ICESCR), both of which were adopted by the United Nations in 1966 and entered into force in 1976. The division of rights into these two classes marked a distinction that would be reflected in the transnational human rights organizations that were emerging, as well as in some, like the Liga Argentina, that had been operating for some time. International human rights institutions have tended to concerned themselves more with punctual (though at times widespread) violations of individual liberties by a defined and identifiable institution (usually the state), and pay less attention to the generalized violation of social and economic rights by actors more difficult to localize and identify (those responsible for economic inequalities and structural violence) (Farmer and Gastineau 2009). For example, Amnesty International, founded in 1961, originally limited its sphere of action to violations of civil and political rights, specifically the deprivation of political rights and the violation of physical integrity. These included the deprivation of liberty through imprisonment, torture, and political assassination, but not, importantly, physical deprivation through the lack of resources for adequate nutrition, or access to medical care, unless as a result of imprisonment, for example. In recent years, Amnesty International has broadened its sphere of action to include some cases of violations of economic rights. Many other international institutions including the United Nations, the Organization of American States (OAS), and the Inter-American Institute for Human Rights (founded in 1980), also focused primarily on civil and political rights. The violations they most frequently covered included bodily violence against the person, such as torture, assassination, or the deprivation of liberty through incarceration for political motives.

However, the focus on torture and disappearance within Argentina, to the exclusion of all other issues, was contentious within the local human rights community. Many felt the need to include as a fundamental part of the definition issues that went deeper than the return of the disappeared and prevention of future violence. This deeper need had a number of elements, including demands for truth, justice, accountability, memory, and meaningful social and economic equality, all of which have contributed to the form human rights activism in Argentina has taken in the ensuing decades. The first of these to be widely articulated were the demands for truth and justice. What many within the human rights movements sought became encapsulated in the phrase "Aparición con vida" (give them back alive). This phrase expressed a unifying potential that included an implicit demand for truth and an incipient focus on accountability (which would become much stronger over the years). The emphasis was still on the recuperation of the disappeared. However, by demanding that the disappeared be not only located but also returned alive, human rights organizations discursively placed responsibility for their well-being on the state (Jelin 1995:116). In doing so, human rights organizations were laying the foundation for the struggle for justice that was to ensue.

Justice in Transition

After seven years in power, the military government in Argentina called for general elections in 1983. Part of the reason involved the increasing pressure from local human rights groups, demanding an end to the ruthless repression and, increasingly, accountability for what had occurred. The military was also faced with general public unrest under declining economic conditions. The junta that seized power in 1976 had immediately concerned itself with economic reform as a necessary part of political stabilization. The architect of the dictatorship's economic program was José Alfredo Martínez de Hoz, who served as economics minister under Videla. A member of a powerful landowning family that included founders and leaders of the Sociedad Rural Argentina (Argentine Rural Society), his assessment was that state intervention in the economy and the establishment of the welfare state had been the principal cause of Argentina's problems since the 1930s. Influential currents within Argentina, working mainly under the auspices of the UN Economic Commission for Latin America (ECLA, CEPAL in Spanish), had been advocating a vision of development throughout the 1950s and 1960s that emphasized state-directed regional integration and equity in trade relationships. However, the dictatorship chose to lessen trade protections and embrace free market reforms as the path to growth and stability. The market was proposed as "the instrument capable of equally disciplining all the social actors, rewarding efficiency, and discouraging unhealthy interest-group behavior" (Romero 2002:221). Ultimately, the reforms they implemented concentrated economic power within the country into even fewer hands.

The methods of implementing this plan were concordant with the era, and provide a telling example of the interweaving of political violence and economic policy. Martínez de Hoz, or Joe as he is known in Argentina, was convicted in 2010 of participating in the kidnapping and extortion of two local businessmen with the intention of forcing their business to renegotiate a contract with Hong Kong from which the dictatorship hoped to benefit.

Such tactics failed to secure fiscal solvency, and, by the end of the dictatorship in 1983, a severe banking crisis had sparked massive capital flight and the foreign debt had risen to an unmanageable US$45 billion. The breaking point came, however, with the military's disastrous defeat in the War for the Malvinas. Needing to bolster its public support, in 1982 the military government tried to retake possession of the Malvinas Islands, which have been occupied by the British since 1833. Banking on the hope of encountering little resistance, on April 2 then de facto president Leopoldo Galtieri began a concerted offensive with the deployment of Argentine warships to the island.[18] The move was extremely popular at first, and garnered the military some of the support it sought under the banner of nationalist sentiment. But the British responded with unexpected vigor and, in spite of the military's repeated assertions that the war was going well, it soon became clear that Argentina was in for a disastrous defeat (Escudero 1997). The war, which ended in July 1982, cost the lives of almost seven hundred Argentines, many of whom were young conscripts fulfilling their year of military service. The military government was left even more discredited, and the Thatcher government received the boost it needed to win reelection while diverting attention from its own implementation of unpopular neoliberal structural adjustment policies.

Shortly afterward, on December 10, 1983, the Argentine military government handed over power to the newly elected civilian president, UCR (Unión Cívica Radical) leader Raúl Alfonsín. Coincidentally, but symbolically resonant nonetheless, December 10 is also the day in 1948 when the UDHR was adopted by the General Assembly of the United Nations, and has become International Human Rights Day.

With the election of Alfonsín, the demand for justice took center stage as an inextricable part of the call for human rights. This demand, which had formed part of the debate within the human rights organizations from their inception, became a defining feature of the meaning of democracy itself. However, what justice meant and what it would look like were far from easy questions to resolve. From a political standpoint, the return to nominal democracy was dominated by an uneasy balance of power. Pressure from foreign creditors and international lending institutions limited the options of newly elected Radical president Alfonsín. Locally, the major economic powers located in the GEN (Grupos Económicos Nacionales), the military, and the unions all exerted pressure on the new government in attempts to secure concessions. Even so, under the new government the notion of human rights as a subject of state policy would begin to take hold.

Upon coming to power, Alfonsín took the landmark steps of calling for the creation of an independent commission to investigate human rights abuses and ordering the trial of the military junta leaders.[19] CONADEP (Comisión Nacional sobre la Desaparición de Personas, or National Commission on Disappeared People), gathered evidence on the disappearance of almost 9,000 persons and the existence of 365 clandestine detention centers.[20] The commission's report, *Nunca Más* (Never Again), was a national bestseller immediately upon its release in 1984, and the information it revealed was used in the subsequent trials of the military leaders, known as the *Juicio a las Juntas*. The trials led to numerous convictions of high-ranking officials.

The trials opened up renewed debate among the human rights organizations over how to pursue justice. Since as early as 1979, the question of justice had been a source of controversy within the movement. While some groups emphasized the need for peace, a return to democracy, and the release of information about what had occurred, others insisted that peace needed to include both truth and justice. Once the dictatorship had ended, the demand for "juicio y castigo a todos los culpables" (trial and punishment for all those guilty) gained strength. However, how to assign and limit responsibility? Should unelected officials responsible for the economic plan, which led to the impoverishment of the nation and unemployment and hunger for many, be held criminally responsible? What of the military commanders who led hundreds to their death in the Malvinas? Different groups held varied opinions and goals, but the position that came to be most representative was that which demanded criminal legal proceedings against those directly responsible for physical acts of torture and disappearance, either through directing the repression or carrying it out. This position held that history will judge those who have a presumed capacity to influence the decisions of those in power: politicians, union leaders, priests, and journalists, with judicial prosecution reserved for those who kidnapped, tortured, killed, and those who ordered them to do so. "The circle of responsibility is drawn around those who were in touch with the body of the disappeared" (Jelin 1995:134).

Even as the Alfonsín administration was able to take steps toward democratic consolidation and political inclusion, the possibilities for action were severely limited by pressure from the military to counteract the legal prosecutions against its members for the Dirty War (see Tedesco 1999; Melamud 2000). These pressures from the military included the 1987 rebellion by a small faction within the armed forces referred to as the *carapintadas*, or "painted faces," for the camouflage paint they used. In April of that year, a group of military officers took control of the Campo de Mayo military installations, refusing to turn themselves or their fellow military personnel into the justice system as ordered in investigations into Dirty War abuses. The Alfonsín administration eventually called for a public demonstration in opposition to the rebellion. Massive numbers of people filled the Plaza de Mayo in defense of the fledgling democracy, using their bodies and their presence to express their vision for the nation. Alfonsín dealt a crushing disappointment to many of those assembled and to those involved in the struggle for human rights through the "Felices Pascuas" speech, in which he granted the military the immunity they were demanding, which led to the passage of the laws of Full Stop (*Punto Final*) (1986) and Due Obedience (*Obedencia Debida*) (1987). These laws, usually referred to as "immunity laws" in the English-language media, are commonly called the "impunity laws" (*leyes de impunidad*) in Argentina, and ended prosecutions of further military personnel for crimes committed during the repression. These events made it seem increasingly clear that achieving legal prosecution and accountability for all but the most high-ranking perpetrators of state violence locally would be a difficult if not impossible task.

After Alfonsín

Although Alfonsín launched a new currency plan, known as the Austral, his years as president were characterized by a rampant permanent inflation that drastically limited the state's ability to govern. Ultimately, his presidency would be overshadowed by the economic instability he inherited. Spiraling inflation reaching over a thousand percent led to the transfer of power to president-elect Carlos Menem in late 1989, six months ahead of schedule. By this time, governments across the region were increasingly including the language and certain ideas from human rights discourse into official policy. Human rights had become an issue that could not be avoided, and governments and institutions from across the region found ways to incorporate a particular rhetoric and practice of human rights into their stated and, in some cases, implemented objectives. In many instances, this included institutional reforms and/or modification or addition of laws on the state's obligation to protect human rights. In adopting human rights policies or making human rights a campaign or governing platform issue, democratic regimes across the region espoused a version of human rights influenced by (and influential upon) the concurrent discourse of neoliberalism and government reform along neoliberal lines. However, human rights violations of many kinds continued to a certain extent under democratic regimes, even as the arenas for the practice of these violations and often the major actors shifted.

This posed a new challenge for human rights networks locally and internationally. Violations received less attention when the state was nominally democratic, and international institutions like the OAS continued to grapple with issues concerning state sovereignty. While the Inter-American Commission on Human Rights openly condemned violations of human rights by dictatorial governments, there was an initial reluctance to investigate or denounce violations occurring under democratically elected regimes (Sikkink 1996:69). During this period, institutions and foreign governments were disinclined to pressure democratic regimes on the issue of human rights, and thus human rights networks had difficulty raising support for many continuing cases of repression (especially cases of restrictions on and violent repression of free speech, electoral fraud, and police brutality).

Apart from the issue of a changing climate for addressing the continuing violation of civil, political, and physical rights, organizations concerned with human rights in Argentina also operated during this period under a profoundly different political climate. Whereas the Alfonsín government sought initially to encourage legal prosecution, the Menem administrations (1989–1999) made it clear early on that such prosecutions, already largely impossible under the concessionary laws of 1986 and 1987, would not be tolerated. Furthermore, military officials who had been convicted in the *Juicio a las Juntas* in 1985 were pardoned by Menem through one of his many presidential decrees.[21]

Frustration over the lack of avenues for achieving judicial accountability led local human rights organizations to look abroad for other ways to achieve this idea of justice. With the precedent of seeking international condemnation of the military's violation of human rights during the dictatorship, local human rights organizations began to file criminal complaints and support criminal trials against dictatorship officials in foreign courts. The first of these were brought in 1983 (in Italy) and 1985 (in France) by plaintiffs with dual citizenship. These precedents opened the door to further trials. However, these cases were generally limited to the prosecution of Argentine military officials for the abduction and murder of foreign nationals in Argentina. As the Argentine judicial system would not accept the extradition of the accused, the cases frequently concluded with the condemnation of the accused in absentia.

Justice and Democracy

Why have the various local human rights movements chosen to specifically agitate for legal accountability of members of the military governments and security forces under the fragile conditions of gradually reemerging democracies? What was at stake in maintaining this focus on judicial prosecution and justice and why are these demands so central for those who suffered from the political violence of the 1970s and '80s? This was not the primary solution adopted or attempted in all situations of massive and/or state-sponsored political violence. For example, the Truth and Reconciliation Commissions in South Africa (established 1995) and Guatemala (1994) did not have legal prosecution at their core. At the same time that many within the Argentine human rights community applauded the search for justice abroad, some also worried that the pursuit of justice in foreign courts was insufficient and diluted the attempt to build stronger institutions domestically. Many have argued that as long as the Argentine state and institutional structure remained incapable of prosecuting people accused of human rights violations, the nation as a whole suffered (Jelin 1994; Roht-Arriaza 1999). In this point of view, legal prosecution is intricately linked to notions of the proper role and nature of the state. Justice through legal prosecution is a concrete enactment of the rule of law.

The focus on institutionality is underscored by the concomitant demand that many human rights organizations also made upon the return to democracy. In addition to justice through the legal system, they pushed for a bicameral commission to investigate what happened and in this way achieve condemnation from all branches of government. The horrific violence that led up to and permeated the 1976–1983 military dictatorship created fundamental changes in a country where authoritarian modes of governance had a long history. The discourse of democracy took on a desperate vitality following the return of free elections in 1983. Alfonsín's defeat of the Peronist candidate, the first ever such defeat the Peronist party had faced when allowed to participate, was due in no small measure to a carefully worded campaign platform centered on the importance of democratic institutions and human rights and on Alfonsín's track record in working toward these goals. In Argentina, the demand for legal prosecution for violent repression is also a rejection of authoritarian tactics. The focus on these goals, initially but also throughout the last few decades and even as other sorts of solutions were implemented in other places, is part of a broader (international) discourse of democracy. In return, this focus has helped to install and maintain the idea of legal prosecution within the international sphere as a key component of the discourse of human rights.

By the 1990s, members of the political apparatus in Argentina were nearly unanimous in embracing the belief that any appeal to legitimacy, to be effective locally as well as internationally, must hold at its discursive center the ideal of modern democracy. This belief found an able partner and formative expression in the philosophy of neoliberalism that was gaining force at this time. The key pillars of modernity through institutional reform, democracy, and free markets were presented as the way to lead Argentina back to the greatness it was seen to have once held within the international community. This, coupled with short-term economic success for those able to take advantage of the cash boom, garnered an initial acceptance of neoliberal policies by many in Argentina. Even among those who opposed neoliberalism from the beginning, the idea of enacting institutional reform was important. In this vein, to achieve legal prosecutions was not only about punishing the perpetrators, but also about asserting a particular vision of the state.

The ability to effectively prosecute and punish through legal channels those accused of committing or ordering the violent acts of state terrorism gained increasing (though by no means uniform) public acceptance as an essential part of a functioning democracy. However, for many within the human rights organizations, achieving the desired legal prosecution locally could not alone resolve the question: What are the rights that a democratic political system should be expected and obligated to protect? If the focus on the judicialization of protest tactics was part of a broader strategy to construct and strengthen democratic institutions capable of protecting human rights, what is the content of these rights that should be guaranteed? Fundamentally, are rights individual or collective? As early as 1985, the Madres of Plaza de Mayo were asserting that they were the mothers not of individual disappeared, but of *el pueblo*, and they were accompanying "the people" in their struggle for a better world where work, housing, and food are not a privilege of the few, but the right of all (cited in Jelin 1995:122). Questions concerning governmental responsibility to ensure and protect third-generation rights to peace, development, and a clean environment and fourth-generation rights of the people as a global and collective entity, also became part of the discussion within the transnational network of human rights activists and institutions. After more than a decade of neoliberalism, the debates within Argentina over what rights the government must protect took on an ever-increasing urgency as the twenty-first century dawned in crisis.

There was, in addition, another significant reason why legal prosecution was so important for those seeking justice. Struggles over the memory of the era began to emerge immediately following the return to democracy. For the human rights organizations, legal prosecution and condemnation became a way of receiving official legitimation of their version of historical memory. Achieving legal prosecution locally would be a highly significant conduit for the state itself to agree to this vision, publically and officially condemning the accused perpetrators of authoritarian violence.

Constructing Memory

The theme of memory began to underlie discussions of the dictatorship era from the very inception of the return to democracy. This is another of the fundamental elements embedded in the concerns of many Argentine human rights organizations. Those fighting to know the truth about the fate of the disappeared soon begin to include the idea of memory as equally a right to be respected and protected (Jelin 1995). Just how memory was to be used or defined itself became a site of debate and construction, among factions of the human rights, within the government, and across diverse sectors of society. This is not surprising. Memory is not an objective univocal rendering of past events. Rather, it is subject to canalization through social discourses that give shape and form to the kinds and ways of remembering (Halbswach 1992; Lambek and Antze 1996). Across Argentina, the idea of memory as a right and the debates over how the past is to be remembered and defined became an integral part of the discussion of rights.

As the transition to democracy was underway, the military government was immediately concerned with establishing its own version of how its time in power would be remembered. There are reports of the widespread destruction of records documenting the detainment and captivity of the disappeared. This destruction of evidence, like the destruction of bodies, both protected the armed forces against future prosecutions and intensified the degree of "disappearance," making future knowledge of the fate of the missing even more inaccessible. Immediately before leaving power, the military also issued statements vindicating its actions. The dictatorship's attention to constructing a social discourse that legitimated its actions was at least in part due to anxieties over the threat of legal prosecution or other retribution (such as those that were later initially realized under Alfonsín). It was also related to the continued interest of the armed forces in maintaining their position as a political force. The carapintada military rebellions had had symbolic importance as moments that expressed the military's desire for vindication as an institution, in addition to the practical effect of eliminating criminal prosecution for all members of the armed forces at that time. These mutineers, who named their actions *Operación Dignidad* (Operation Dignity), insisted on the recognition of the political violence as part of a war between the military and a dangerous opposition (Brysk 1994).[22] This desire on the part of the military to continue to assert its role in society constrained and in some ways determined how the dictatorship era and its legacy were dealt with politically over the subsequent two decades.

The *Juicio a las Juntas* marked the Alfonsín administration's distancing of the democratic government from the military's attempts to legitimize its actions as justifiable and necessary. Nonetheless, pressure from the military and the fragility of the democratic institutions, particularly under the unstable economic conditions in which the Alfonsín regime operated, led to a different official stance toward the memory of the dictatorship era, one that was to be continued throughout the rest of the twentieth century. The initial inability and unwillingness of subsequent political leadership to meaningfully incorporate the position of the human rights organizations into the discussion over memory prolonged and intensified the salience of these debates within Argentine society.

In order to calm military opposition and to serve their political agendas, both the Alfonsín and Menem administrations adopted a "politics of forgetting," designed to silence all discussion of what had happened and thereby "heal" the deep divisions that still rent Argentine society (Vezzetti 2002). This politics of forgetting was brought into effect on many fronts, including such tangible acts of erasure as the destruction of former clandestine detention centers or their conversion into renovated shopping malls. However, both Alfonsín and Menem were aware that they could not vindicate the military's actions. Rather, they needed to invoke a discourse of democracy in order to maintain their own legitimacy, at once condemning the military's actions and attending to its demand for recognition of its vision. The attempt to perform just such a delicate and convoluted balancing act led to the creation and propagation of the "Theory of the Two Demons," a version of history that interpreted the violence as the struggle between two groups of misguided fanatics, the military and the armed leftist opposition. While condemning the military's "excesses," this version of history left space for the military's claim that its use of force was justified. Taking this stance was an attempt by Argentina's fragile democratic regimes to quell opposition from both sides, through a policy of enforced forgetting. However, for the human rights groups that argued against this vision, legal prosecution of the perpetrators of the violence was another way of asserting a vision of the Argentine state as a modern democracy. Each side in the debate appealed to notions of memory, justice, and democracy.

As Jonathan Boyarin argues, memory and forgetting are not opposites, but rather are intricately connected to one another (1992). He denies the positivist assertion that memory implies presence and forgetting absence. For, absence, he says, lies outside of all possible history; it does not exist. Forgetting, on the other hand, is both social and historical, a necessity of domination. It is constructed, as memory is. Certainly, he argues, Benjamin's angel of history stares back at forgetting, and not at absence (Boyarin 1992:2). The attempts by nearly two decades of civilian government in Argentina to instill a forced forgetting did not lead to a quelling of discussion about what happened during the dictatorship or how it should be remembered. Rather, the efforts of the government to maintain a measure of stability by foreclosing public debate instead strengthened the desire of large sectors of Argentine society to pressure for the incorporation of their need for information and closure as to the events of what was becoming an increasingly distant past.

Indeed, from their inception human rights organizations have played an important role in providing a space where people affected by the repression could find an echo of their experiences in others, and together construct an alternative- or counter-memory. Natalie Zemon-Davis and Randolph Starn use the idea of counter-memory to stress that memory is subject to the pressure of challenges and alternatives (Zemon-Davis and Starn 1989). They draw on Foucault in seeing counter-memory as "designat[ing] the residual or resistant strains that withstand official versions of historical continuity" (2). During the more than two decades that the government officially upheld a policy of forgetting, the efforts of organizations like the Mothers of Plaza de Mayo, SERPAJ, CELS, and APDH helped locate the individual memories of those most affected by the repression within an increasingly influential collective counter-memory narrative, one that highlights impunity as itself a violation of rights. The success of these organizations in gaining and maintaining the high level of respect they have come to possess was due in great measure to their providing a space within which to counter the official silencing.

Ultimately, the politics of forgetting may have had the paradoxical effect of multiplying memory by denying those affected the possibility of officially recognized public remembrance, keeping the debate over the past relevant to the present (Jelin 1998:28). As Robben argues, the continued exploration of historical memory "led to a polyphonic reconstruction of the past which pushed conflicting memories of violence and trauma to the forefront of each group's political concern" (Robben 2005:350). The politics of forgetting gave a particular structure and language to the historical memories as they took shape in a continuous process of construction. Specifically, the politics of forgetting led to the idea of impunity being adopted as a central and orienting feature in public discourse and in the understanding and interpreting not only of past events but also contemporary circumstances. In the 1990s, corruption was added to impunity as both took center stage as targets in the struggles for citizen and human rights.

Chapter 2

Spaces of Corruption
and the Edifice of Impunity

T HE 1990s saw both the height of neoliberalism and the consolidation and popularization of human rights in Argentina. Human rights became and remain the inescapable referent for ethical conduct, political responsibility, and social action. At this same time, the language of human rights shifted, expanding beyond its previous focus on disappearance and torture. Instead, the dual pillars of impunity and corruption came to serve as the central sites for identifying societal ills and for organizing resistance and repudiation. For the members of Memoria Activa, the violations of their rights as citizens and their human rights comes in the form of the lack of effective legal prosecution and the complicity of the government in obstructing investigation into the 1992 and 1994 bomb attacks in Buenos Aires. For the workers in the BAUEN Cooperative, the rampant corruption and impunity among business owners violates their rights to social and economic justice. This chapter traces this shift from physical and psychological violence and toward the violence of impunity and corruption in the language of human rights.

Impunity and Disappearance

The violations of individuals through widespread torture and disappearance have had lasting social effects. Impunity as an interpretive trope grew out of and depended upon the discourse of the trauma of disappearance as a personal and social reality. I argue that the notion of impunity and the need for legal justice took on such force within human rights organizations and, eventually, throughout large sectors of Argentine society, through an emotional identification between the effects of disappearance and those of impunity. Here, impunity mimics disappearance by denying social reckoning after a traumatic event. Much as the military denied having kidnapped the disappeared, impunity for acts of violence is seen as denying relatives, friends, and ultimately society the right to official recognition of their suffering. The political attempt to move past the dictatorship era by institutionalizing impunity for the perpetrators only intensified these feelings by denying the voices of those affected and negating the existence of their narrative of history based on experience, thereby foreclosing the possibility of a true social reckoning of events. In highlighting impunity as a major issue, human rights organizations in Argentina popularized a new interpretive trope for identifying and contesting social ills and added a new language to the discourse of human rights. This new language became so important that human right organizations (*organizaciones de derechos humanos*) are at times referred to as counterimpunity organizations (*organizaciones contra la impunidad*).

In proposing that impunity holds an ineludible relationship to disappearance, I argue that the idea of impunity as used in Argentina depends and draws on the earlier frame of disappearance as producing a particular kind of damage to the social fabric. The figure of the disappeared person or, more precisely, the concept of the act of disappearance and the notion of impunity have been stitched together into a unified way of understanding and interpreting the recent past, thus impacting the current construction of a notion of human rights in need of protection. I think of disappearance as forming a kind of counterpoint to the idea of impunity. The idea of a counterpoint as I use it here is in the sense of the necessary underside or counterpart, something apart and different from the first but at once inextricably intertwined within a contained whole. The entangling of the traumatic past (disappearance) with the injustice of the present (impunity) affects how current events are interpreted and encoded within the language of human rights that has gained widespread popular and political support in recent years.[1] This application beyond the sphere of the Dirty War reveals the overarching significance and emotional and moral resonance that the idea of impunity has taken on as an interpretive frame. In order to better situate, then, the idea of impunity as an episteme for interpreting contemporary society and, especially, as a violation of human rights, I first trace the contours of "disappearance."

Disappearance as a Public Secret

Disappearance in Argentina exhibits many aspects of the idea of the "public secret." Michael Taussig in his book *Defacement* discusses the "public secret" as that which everyone knows but no one can say, and perhaps not even think: "that which is generally known, but cannot be articulated," the core of social knowledge that consists in "knowing what not to know" (1999:5, 2). In Argentina, disappearance was created as a kind of public secret that allowed the dictatorship to conduct widespread repression while simultaneously denying its involvement in what were even then extrajudicial acts of violence, as part of a rhetoric aimed at establishing its legitimacy as a governing body. At the same time, and perhaps more importantly, the inability to articulate the reality of the denied yet undeniable missing spawned debilitating social patterns, including fear of engagement and atomization. The human rights organizations were perhaps primarily effective in that they were able to overcome and counteract these effects to some degree through their public presence and open defiance.

The public secret that they worked against can function in a number of ways. Though the practice of forced disappearance has historical resonance with the Nazi *Nacht und Nebel*, in which prisoners would "vanish in the night and fog,"[2] it was not systematically practiced in Argentina before the 1970s. Political violence was nothing new in Argentina, and indeed, the spirals of political violence and social traumatization in the 1950s, 1960s, and early 1970s set the stage for the dictatorship's *Proceso* (Robben 2005). Yet the act of disappearance converted the known threats from history into an uncertain and unknown danger threatening in the present.

By officially denying its involvement in the disappearances, the military could publicly proclaim a position of moral right, and thus avoid jeopardizing its legitimacy within Argentina and abroad.[3] Its worries over international retributions were particularly acute ahead of the 1978 World Cup. This event, hosted by Argentina and culminating in the country's first world championship title, put the country and the military government in the international spotlight. The dictatorship used major publicity campaigns in seeking to legitimize its rule to an attentive global audience (Gilbert and Vitagliano 1998; Llonto 2005; Mason 1995). In doing so, it frequently reversed the blame of the disappearances back onto the victims, claiming that the missing were either killed in open combat against the (officially) armed forces or had chosen to run off and were living happily in a self-imposed exile. Furthermore, by couching this Cold War–era repression in terms of counterterrorism measures waged against communist insurgents, it enjoyed tacit and active support, particularly from the United States.[4]

However, the flip side of a public secret is that what is being denied must also be known. The dictatorship's strategy was dependant on instilling in the populace a sense of uncertainty and fear about the possible consequences of dissent. Thus, while openly disavowing responsibility for the disappeared, the dictatorship also relied on public knowledge of the dangers of opposing the regime. The military explicitly talked about its "war against subversives," broadly referencing or staging armed confrontations and utilizing measures that allowed a certain degree of visibility, such as having many abductions conducted in broad daylight on busy streets. In an oft-quoted statement from May 1976, Gen. Ibérico Saint Jean, then governor of the province of Buenos Aires, said, "First we will kill all the subversives, then we will kill their collaborators, then . . . their sympathizers, then . . . those who remain indifferent, and finally, we will kill the timid."[5]

The deliberate spreading of uncertainty concerning the disappeareds' fate, even beside the explicit denial of their existence, acted as another form of psychological torture for the loved ones of the missing. That some disappeared were occasionally allowed to make phone calls to relatives, and that rumors persisted through the end of dictatorship that the disappeared were still alive and being kept in forced labor camps in the interior, are often cited by the family members as only feeding the uncertainty they suffered.[6] Many relate having retained hope of the disappeareds' return even up to the restoration of democracy.

It was this "organized destruction of meaning" (Sveaass 1994b), through a combination of widespread knowledge with public denial of responsibility and the construction of systematic roadblocks to the search for information about the disappeared, that made the public secret of disappearance and torture a daily reality in dictatorship-era Argentina. The dread and uncertainty these tactics produced contributed to the climate of fear that permeated Argentine society during this era (Corradi et al. 1992). The fear of public space and outside engagement form part of a vivid memoryscape. "You couldn't gather even three people on a street corner, stop to chat, anything. The street wasn't safe."[7] This culture of fear "was conducive to an extreme individualization and privatization of human beings" (Perelli 1994:43) and contributed to the atomization of society during this era (Sarlo 1988; Jelin 1994). The erosion of confidence in the public sphere had concrete political and social implications at the time, and many see this atomization as laying the foundation for the emphasis on individualism that accompanied the neoliberal experiment that followed.

Disappearing Memory

Disappearance as a method of repression has effects that go even beyond this resignification of sociality and public spaces. Antonius Robben has argued that the treatment of dead bodies in particular affected culturally relevant ideas and practices of remembrance. After assassination, many of the disappeared were buried in unmarked graves. Some of the remains were later dug up and dissolved with acid, ahead of a 1978 fact-finding commission of the OAS sent to investigate the allegations of military brutality. Other disappeared were drugged and thrown, still alive, out of airplanes into the sea.[8] This treatment of the bodies shows how "state terror . . . was as much inflicted on the dead as on the living" (Robben 2000:93).

Disappearance and the subsequent vanishing of the corpse functioned to 1) prevent revenge on the direct perpetrators from the deceased's friends and family; 2) prevent the mobilization of international opinion; and 3) avoid future judicial and historical condemnation through the erasure of evidence. However, there were deeper cultural reasons and effects behind this extension of terror into the afterworld, including the desire to invalidate the social and political struggles of the victims (Robben 2000:108–109). The erasure of the dead body accompanied the denial of the disappeareds' continued existence as a person and converted a recognized social entity into a void. This figure of the missing thus has come to represent a hole in the fabric of society. With no records and no trace of their passing available to the relatives, the disappeared were denied their social existence, effectively ceasing to exist outside of their loved ones' memories. The act of disappearance created the social death of persons without the concomitant physical death, denying this culturally valued piece to the processes of grieving and remembering. By entering into houses or snatching victims from public spaces, the security forces left families in a liminal state. The parental ability to protect their children was violated, as it was with the appropriation of the victims' children, and no certainty of death or destiny was left behind. In this way, the disappeared were to be gone forever, permanently desocialized and removed from the Argentine social fabric. This worked as an attempt to prevent their reincorporation into society as deceased persons, whose deaths could be mourned and commemorated and whose struggles could be vindicated.

It is this desocialization and the appropriation of the right to commemoration that is forcefully repudiated in the actions of the human rights or counter-impunity organizations. From the anonymous silhouettes plastered across city walls and the bars of detention centers, to the blocks' long strips of photos carried during the "resistance marches" (*marchas de la resistencia*), the presence of the missing is a powerful and recurrent trope taken up by these organizations in rebuttal of the denial of their memory.

The discursive power that forced disappearance has gained within the human rights sectors of Argentine society as a symbol of trauma is evidenced in the hierarchization of victims and their relatives and friends. One active and constant participant in Memoria Activa's weekly actos lamented that the leaders of that group had refused to let her serve even once as one of the weekly speakers. This, she insisted, was because they did not recognize her as holding the same importance as the Madres of Plaza de Mayo. Though her support for their struggle was unwavering, she herself chose not to don the iconic *pañuelo blanco* or white headscarf that identified the Mothers. Her explanation for her difference from the group rested on the fact that "A mí también me mataron un hijo. Pero a mí me entregaron el cuerpo" (They also killed one of my sons. But they returned his body to me). That she could bury her son at the time when he died led to a minimization of her suffering on a cultural scale of trauma that, in response to the dictatorship's denials and justifications, gave primacy to the anguish of disappearance.

As it became clear that the return to democracy would not result in extensive judicial prosecution or in legal punishment for most of those involved in carrying out the repression, nor in the kind of careful reckoning and production and validation of knowledge through its presentation as legal evidence, the human rights organizations that had formed previously began to increasingly use the idea of impunity to describe the social and political ills against which they were struggling. Human rights groups in Argentina argue that during the 1980s and 1990s the official politics of forgetting included an institutionalization of impunity. In addition to questions of governmental responsibility and the construction of democracy discussed in the preceding chapter, the search for justice through the judicial system is in part also an attempt to have the knowledge about what happened discovered, unearthed, revealed, and presented to those involved and to society in general. In looking to reveal information and receiving judicial condemnation of what was done, many relatives of the victims seek to establish a kind of officially recognized legitimate truth that affirms the unacceptability of what they and the disappeared have suffered. They consider this kind of moral truth essential for the closure of the events and a beginning of the grieving process. In essence, they seek reappearance through the establishment of a legal truth.

More broadly, impunity itself is interpreted as a kind of disappearance through its denial of wrongs committed. Locally, the language of impunity speaks clearly of the damage impunity wreaks on society as a whole.[9] Impunity has become an orienting principle for understanding current social problems and is framed as a direct violation of the right to justice.

Impunity is discursively linked to corruption, either as the facilitating mechanism that allows impunity to prevail or the original wrong for which justice is denied. In part, the shrinkage of the state under neoliberalism meant that government agencies no longer had the capacity to monitor their own officials, nor did they provide them with sufficient funds to fulfill the tasks with which they were charged. The judicial system also saw a weakening of its ability to investigate and prosecute political and business leaders, even as a rise in watchdog journalism (Waisbord 2000) focused public attention on widespread fraud, favor-mongering, and politically motivated assassinations. The exposure of scandals became the dominant way of practicing politics under neoliberalism. Media can reflect and are used to reflect specific understandings of the state, and in this way, coupled with quotidian interactions with local state representatives, work to shape public understandings. The role of scandals in cementing corruption as a figure to protest against placed the media, with all their limitations, in the role of the guardian of the common good. The government and public officials, on the other hand, came to represent the way private interests had colonized public life. In Argentina the depoliticization of democracy and mediatization of politics and the attendant discursive shift to impunity/corruption were all constitutive of neoliberalism, shaping the way the state was popularly interpreted.[10] With the unresolved bombings of the Israeli embassy in 1992 and the AMIA in 1994, family members of the victims quickly adopted this emerging local idiom and denounced the scandal-ridden investigations as part of the impunity and corruption that they allege permeated and structured the government's response.

Impunity and Corruption in the Aftermath of the Embassy and AMIA Bombings

To try to explain what happened in the 1992 and 1994 bombings in Buenos Aires is, ultimately, impossible. By this I mean not only the simple admission that senseless violence makes no sense. When over a hundred people die and hundreds more are wounded in deliberate flashes of blind destruction, responding to some distant logic the victims had nothing to do with, any attempt at explanation in the sense of revealing meaning is necessarily doomed at the outset. As Michael Taussig writes in relation to his work in Colombia, his job as an anthropologist is to make sense out of situations like these, but what if they have no sense (Taussig 2003)?

Of course, it's worth asking, How *could* we ever know what happened in such moments of anonymous, orchestrated violence? What do we need in order to feel we have a certain "knowledge"? Who is responsible for providing that "knowledge"?

But there is also a more perverse element at play here, undermining my capacity to relate what happened. Not only are certain aspects highlighted and others disregarded in the usual process of the construction of sense, but for both of these attacks even the most basic facts remain uncertain and disputed. Official reports, where they exist, have been inconsistent, and a myriad of provocative statements made by high-ranking politicians, security officials, and individuals close to the investigations have either been later retracted or remain unsubstantiated. To describe either attack, then, requires deliberate selection from among contradictory pieces of information.

My attempt here to relate a brief and partial history of the events and the subsequent investigations carries within it the inconsistencies left behind by conflicting interpretations of evidence and their selective dissemination. But this is intrinsic rather than contrary to an understanding of the nature of these attacks and their aftermath. What has developed is a haze of (mis)information that only grows denser the further back in history the attacks fall. This is not accidental, and speaks to how the attacks and their understanding derive from and respond to their use in different and ambiguous ways by an uncountable number of personal and political interests. To the extent possible, the information I have chosen to present here is that which is agreed upon by most journalistic, investigative, and judicial sources. Additional information is presented in the context within which it is claimed. But in doing so, I try to attend to the indeterminateness that is an essential part of what those who seek a sort of truth have faced.

The Embassy Bombing

Shortly before 3 pm on March 17, 1992, the Israeli embassy, on the corner of Suipacha and Arroyo Streets in central Buenos Aires exploded, leaving perhaps 29 people dead (the number of fatalities is still debated) and more than 200 injured. The attack was investigated by teams from at least six countries, principally the local intelligence service (Secretaría de Inteligencia del Estado, or SIDE), Israeli intelligence (MOSSAD), and the US Department of Alcohol, Tobacco, and Firearms Control. These agencies report that the blast was produced when a truck loaded with explosives pulled up in front of the embassy building and detonated. However, this international assortment of intelligence teams presented different conclusions about the type of explosives used and whether they were manufactured in Argentina or brought in from the exterior, along with other aspects. A communiqué purportedly issued by Islamic Jihad claimed responsibility for the attack shortly after it happened, saying it was in retribution for Israel's assassination of Hezbollah leader Sheikh Abbas al-Musaw on February 16, 1992. However, this claim was quickly retracted, and Hezbollah has denied any involvement.[11]

Pressure fell on the Argentine government to actively participate in uncovering the details of the planning and execution of the bombing. This was especially urgent given the mounting suspicion that Argentine nationals and officials may have been complicit in the attack. Reasons for this suspicion included the rumor that three of the four federal police officers assigned to be on guard at the embassy were missing from their posts at the time of the explosion. One of the three claims to have been accompanying the Ambassador Yitzhak Shefi, but the ambassador has refuted this. The other two officers are reported to have walked off the scene five minutes before the explosion.

Due to jurisdictional considerations, justices from the Argentine Supreme Court (rather than the federal circuit) headed the judicial inquiry into the bombing. This inquiry, which failed to lead to any prosecutions or arrests, also failed to arrive at conclusions as to the origin or type of explosives used, the provenance of the truck-bomb, or whether the truck had been detonated by a suicide bomber or remotely. Nor did it shed any light on possible local knowledge of or involvement in the attack. After seven years without results, in 1999 the court abruptly pronounced the unsubstantiated claim that Imad Mughniyah and Islamic Jihad had been responsible for the bombing. Mughniyah, an elusive Lebanese national, is cited on the FBI's most wanted terrorists list as the head of the security apparatus for Hezbollah and was "indicted [by the United States] for his role in planning and participating in the June 14, 1985, hijacking of a commercial airliner," TWA Flight 847. He is also alleged to have participated in numerous bombings and kidnappings throughout the 1980s and 1990s.[12] The assigning of responsibility to such a well-known foreign suspect without a corresponding body of evidence, led many to dismiss the court's findings as too convenient and perhaps as a way to avoid responsibility for further action.[13]

The Argentine Supreme Court already had a reputation for being particularly subject to political manipulation. The body has held limited independence from the executive branch since at least the 1940s. Throughout the twentieth century, Argentine politics consisted of unstable periods of democratic rule punctuated by military coups. In this context, it became common practice for military leaders to appoint Supreme Court justices who would legitimize their seizure of power. The return to democracy would then bring a renewed opportunity to remove and appoint justices to the court, often resulting in near complete renovations.[14]

Public disapproval of the Supreme Court only increased in the 1990s, as confidence in the legal system, and particularly the Supreme Court, reached a low point. When Carlos Menem assumed power at the end of 1989 he enlarged the Supreme Court from five to nine justices, allowing him to stack the court with his political allies and thus form what quickly became known as the "automatic majority."[15] Accordingly, public polls from throughout the 1990s consistently rated the Supreme Court and the judiciary in general as among the least respected Argentine governmental and social institutions (Miller 2000: 372–373). For example, a poll taken by a leading domestic polling firm in November 1991 found 70 percent of the public expressing little or no confidence in the judiciary.[16] By March 1997, the same polling firm found that 93 percent of lawyers and law students considered the Supreme Court to be completely or largely dependent on the executive branch.

It was this court of the infamous automatic majority that was called upon to investigate the attack on the Israeli embassy. This has deeply undermined the sense that a full investigation following every probable lead was ever carried out, compounded by the widespread suspicion that this attack and the AMIA bombing were at least in part the result of failed political machinations by Menem and his government. For example, many still voice doubts concerning the "Syrian connections," a body of evidence that seems to indicate the involvement of some of Menem's close relatives and allies in the cover-up following the attacks as well as their suspected implementation by Syrian nationals. Some argue that evidence that seemed to point in this direction was deliberately left aside and not investigated. Others allege that the bombings were the result of unfulfilled preelection promises that Menem had made in exchange for financial support for his campaign or of the involvement of Argentina in the 1991 war against Iraq.[17]

These concerns are clearly reflected in the demonstrations held each year in commemoration of the bombing. The demonstration in 2005 revealed frustration with the lack of government efforts to fully investigate the bombing. I approached the site, held outside the Plaza Seca that replaced what had once been the facade of building, accompanied by Juan, a member of Memoria Activa. Then in his early 70s, he never ceased to reiterate during our conversations his contentment that all of his children had successfully established lives for themselves and their families outside of Argentina. For this retired engineer, the endemic problem with Argentina was its lack of effective institutions. The government's unwillingness and inability to adequately resolve the embassy bombing was just one more effect of the lack of a strong and trustworthy political and legal system.

This particular late summer day was hot, with a relentless sun beating down on the thousands who had assembled. Security was tight, both approaching the site and once inside the police cordon. This was undoubtedly partly because of the general security measures taken at any "Jewish" event (the monthly commemorations held in front of the AMIA had sharpshooters placed at intervals in neighboring windows), and partly because of the presence of high-level government and international officials, including then-senator and first lady Cristina Fernández de Kirchner and Israeli ambassador Rafael Eldad. Several local Jewish youth groups were also present, wearing identifying T-shirts and carrying signs that accused the Kirchner government of continuing the impunity consolidated under Menem and continued by successive administrations. Though the crowd in the Plaza Seca overall listened quietly and respectfully to the line of official speakers, it was clear from their signs and conversations that few believed the renewed promises to uncover the truth and secure justice would be realized.

The AMIA Attack

The sense that official Argentine investigations were under pressure to deliver suspects to society, even without an accompanying body of credible evidence, was to overhang the investigation of the second attack as well. On July 18, 1994, two years after the attack on the embassy, another building exploded in Buenos Aires. This time the building belonged to the AMIA and housed the central offices of both the AMIA and DAIA, constituting the core of Jewish organizations and services in Buenos Aires. Eighty-five people were killed and over three hundred injured in the blast, which destroyed the entire front of the building and knocked out windows throughout several city blocks. Coming early on a Monday morning, the attack claimed a wide range of victims engaged in their routine weekday activities.

The legal investigation fell to the young federal judge Juan José Galeano, whose turn in the case rotation it happened to be at the moment of the attack. Galeano had no experience with cases of this kind or magnitude. He had only recently acquired his post, some claim through an aunt's political connections, others emphasizing his close ties at the SIDE, whose head, Hugo Anzorreguy, was known to pull strings in the federal judiciary during the Menemist decade. Almost from the beginning, Galeano's investigation was plagued by inconsistencies and accusations of malfeasance. To follow here each bit of information that has been produced would be a vast and consuming undertaking, and numerous books, reports, articles, and pamphlets have been written on aspects of the investigation and the various persons involved in producing or covering up information.[18]

The official investigation into the AMIA bombing illuminates the slippery realm of political intrigue and the real workings of politics throughout the three main branches of government over a decade of Argentine history. I have selected two examples as illustrations, which, though they fall short of encompassing the dozens of serious irregularities noted by family members of victims and judicial tribunals, give a sense of how the investigation proceeded, some of the problems it presented to both those conducting it and those following it, and the difficulties and frustrations it posed and poses for those most profoundly affected by the attack. They show how clandestine relationships and competing political and personal interests conditioned the handling of the AMIA investigation from its inception through to its only judicial prosecution to date.[19]

Counting the Dead   For years, the number of dead was said to be 86. However, in 2000, one of those listed as killed in the AMIA was discovered to be alive, even though compensation had been paid on his behalf. According to reports from the Argentine judiciary, the remains of this individual were recovered from the rubble. The passage reads "Patricio Irala. Paraguayan. According to the statement made by his life partner he had begun to work in the AMIA as a driver that same day. *Only remains were found*" (emphasis added).[20] This particular error may have been due to sloppiness rather than being intentional, and Galeano himself was partially responsible for uncovering the fraud perpetrated by the woman who received the compensation. Nonetheless, members of family organizations often hold it up as indicative of the carelessness with which the investigation, including the technical examinations, was carried out and the desire of the investigators to arrive at definitive "facts" about what had happened, even when lacking actual supporting evidence.[21] Diana Malamud, whose husband Andrés was killed in the attack, expressed the pain and frustration that this kind of disregard for something as significant to family members as bodily remains caused: "So, did they find remains or not, whose were they, who ran the tests [on the remains] that should have been run, maybe the prosecutors made a mistake, or maybe they were trying to cover [something] up, or maybe just nobody cared. All of this is just one more sign of the atrocities committed during this investigation that those of us in Memoria Activa have been denouncing."[22]

The 400,000 Pesos   Perhaps the most widely known irregularity in the investigation is the 400,000 pesos that Judge Galeano agreed to pay or was ordered to have paid to the principal accused in the first and only case to be brought to trial over either of the attacks. This trial began on September 24, 2001, and involved twenty defendants accused of having handled or participated in the preparation of the vehicle used in the AMIA attack. The longest in Argentine history, the trial finally concluded nearly three years later with a resounding verdict that absolved the defendants of all charges related the AMIA bombing. The three presiding judges in their extensive final sentence signaled that the investigation had been oriented toward "constructing an incriminatory hypothesis, with the intention of responding to society's demands, while satisfying the shady interests of unscrupulous governing officials."[23] This verdict also called for the investigation of several top-ranking government officials, including the head of the SIDE, for their suspected role in orchestrating the cover-up.

A cornerstone of the verdict was an accusation of Judge Galeano for his conduct, including most importantly the payment of these 400,000 pesos for (false) testimony on the part of the man last known to have had in his possession the van that the court ruled had carried the bomb. This was perhaps not the most serious of the accusations—other charges against Galeano involved kidnapping and torturing witnesses—but it was the most widely reported and credibly confirmed.

The prosecution's case, based on Galeano's investigation, evolved around the provenance of a van, a Renault Trafic, that the trial verified was used in the attack.[24] This van was traced back to Carlos Telleldín, who was well-known to the local police for illegally altering and selling totaled and stolen cars. Arrested soon after the bombing, Telleldín admitted to having bought the Trafic from a local dealer following an accident after it was declared a loss by an insurance company. Telleldín claims to have rebuilt the van, placing it inside a different frame whose serial number had been erased, and then put an ad in the paper to sell the reconstructed vehicle. Telleldín admitted that as of July 10, eight days before the bombing, the Trafic was still in his possession.

But what happened after that is unclear. For over a year after his arrest Telleldín apparently said little about who took the Trafic from there. According to a video tape made by Galeano and later stolen from his office and leaked to the press, in 1996 Galeano met with Telleldín and offered to pay him if he would testify that he had turned the Trafic over to officers from the Buenos Aires Provincial Police Force. One theory holds that, as the second anniversary of the attack was approaching, Galeano was under pressure to produce results. This group of officers, under Commissioner Juan José Ribelli, had reportedly extorted money and goods from Telleldín before, thus allowing him to continue his lucrative illegal operations while themselves maintaining their status as the highest yielding corruption ring in Buenos Aires.[25] In paving the way for this particular accusation, Galeano may have become trapped within the intrigues of the political forces that governed at the time. The Buenos Aires Provincial Police Force was under the control of Provincial Governor Eduardo Duhalde, President Carlos Menem's chief political opponent within the Peronist party. Implicating the *bonaerense*, as the police force is known, in the AMIA attack would have been in the political interests of Menem and his vice president Carlos Ruckauf, and would deflect any investigation away from the previously mentioned "Syrian connection," the line of investigation surrounding the attack that uncovered uncomfortable information and implicated Menemist allies in a number of scandals.

It seems that Telleldín may have obliged, as his female companion was paid his 400,000 peso asking price in two installments. The money came from the SIDE, and though Galeano later insisted that it fell under the rubric of the reward for information that the government was offering, the judicial commission that eventually removed Galeano from his post concluded that the payment had been made illegally and outside of the proper channels for reward payments. In addition, the leaked videotape seemed to show Galeano instructing Telleldín on what to say, not offering payment for information the accused provided. Based on his testimony, Ribelli and several other officers stood trial along with Telleldín. On average, they each spent eight years in prison awaiting resolution of the case. In the end, the trial judges decided that there was no proof that could link them with the AMIA attack and that way the case had been conducted necessitated their absolution. Furthermore, they found that

Galeano had "engaged in behavior contrary to the law, behavior in which he had the collaboration, by action or by omission, of several organs in the three branches of government that gave him political support and cover for his irregular and unlawful acts."[26]

The family members of the AMIA victims have played an important role in constructing and publicizing the debates over the government's conduct in the investigation. Built around one group of the family members of victims killed in the AMIA, Memoria Activa formed immediately after the bombing to demand that the perpetrators be brought to justice. As soon became clear, they would dedicate much of their energies to disentangling the misinformation and obstruction surrounding the investigation. The mounting evidence that Galeano's investigation responded more to political interests than concrete evidence led many of the family members of victims to feel they were being deceived and to become increasingly discontented with the government's handling of the issue. For more than a decade Memoria Activa held weekly public protests demanding a full and impartial investigation into the AMIA and Israeli embassy bombings. The organization, which also acted as a plaintiff in the criminal trial, was instrumental in drawing and maintaining attention to the irregularities in the official investigation and ultimately pushing forward the removal of Judge Galeano from the case and his eventual disrobing.

The Accuser Accused   The day had been long in coming. Memoria Activa had for years been accusing Judge Juan José Galeano of grave irregularities in the investigation of the AMIA bombing. In September 2004, when the verdict in the trial against Telleldín and Ribelli and co. backed up these allegations and called for an investigation into Galeano's conduct,[27] the Consejo de la Magistratura (Judicial Council) began to act. This body, formed as part of the changes mandated under the 1994 constitutional reforms, is charged with selecting judges and overseeing their conduct. Following formal procedures, Galeano's performance in the AMIA investigation had been the subject of a hearing in November 2004 held by the Accusatory Commission (Comisión de Acusación) of the council. In February 2005 the commission would finally vote on whether to recommend to the council as a whole that Galeano be subjected to a political trial, which could end in his destitution as a judge. To be sure, it was a small step in a long line of bureaucratic proceedings, each of which contained endless opportunities for dilatory tactics and political machinations designed to derail the process. Perhaps that was why of the 1,200 complaints the council had received in the seven years of its operation (its formation not having been realized until November 1998), only one or two a year had ended in sanctions against the accused judge.[28] Though the commission had heard Galeano's case in November, the lack of a quorum at several sessions and the insistence by one of its members to suspend the vote until after the summer recess forced another long wait for those anxious to hear the outcome, while buying more time for the exertion of political pressure upon the voting members. Meanwhile, Galeano remained an active judge.

Now with the moment of the vote finally approaching, tensions were high among the family members of victims in the AMIA who were following the proceedings. It was not certain that enough members would recommend that Galeano be tried, and a vote against moving the case forward would end it on the spot. Even more dangerous than votes in Galeano's favor was the possibility that too few members would show up.

I headed out early that warm February morning, stopping along the way for a quick *cortado* and a glance at the morning paper. My eyes, having been wearily conditioned to pick out certain key words from among endless fields of newsprint (AMIA, Galeano, BAUEN, etc.), honed in on a short article buried in the middle of the paper, which mentioned that the audience I was headed for had been moved across the street from the Palacio de Justicia (Palace of Justice, commonly known simply as Tribunales) into a smaller building on the Calle Libertad. It seems that the move had been decided (or at least announced) in the middle of the night. Manipulation of information being an old tactic and integral part of politics, and this trial being more political than legal, even seemingly routine matters like fixing the time and place for holding sessions became contentious sites for the exertion of power. Rumors later abounded that the move was made because the president of the Supreme Court had ordered the removal of the table that had been in the room slated for that morning's hearing.[29] The Judicial Council was embroiled in its own political battle with the nation's highest legal authority (mainly over members' salaries, which the council at that time had the power to regulate). But many family members told me it had been an attempt to diminish their presence at the hearing.

Regardless of the reasons for the move, it provided an illuminating look at how information flowed among people who followed judicial proceedings. I asked those who made it that morning and, later those who didn't, how they found out about the change of venue. Most made it there in spite of the change, though a few had gone to Tribunales, only to be sent uselessly from floor to floor by emblematic agents of bureaucratic operations who, in impeccable fashion, unwaveringly offered incorrect information. It seems that those most directly invested in the case, the members of Memoria Activa involved in bringing the accusation to this point, had received a call from their allies on the Accusatory Commission. These then notified some others, and a limited chain reaction of phone calls ensued to ensure the presence of at least a few relatives.

Equally interesting were the reactions of the people who had not planned to go at all. I spoke with several who, though they faithfully participated in the acto held every Monday in front of Tribunales in the Plaza Lavalle, expressed hesitation in responding to Memoria Activa's call to attend the hearings. The Monday morning following another of the meetings I had attended, I was immediately questioned on what it was like to get in. Although the hearings were open to the public, my companions anxiously asked me, "Do they ask for your *documento* [national identity card]? Do they register your name? Were you searched?" In fact, none of these things happened, neither to me nor to anyone else. These individuals tirelessly placed their bodies in front of the imposing facade of the Palace of Justice in a stance of defiant insistence, yet they were clearly intimidated at the prospect of crossing that external line and entering into its neoclassical halls. I admit also feeling a sense of timid foreboding the first time I passed over its threshold. The architecture intended to endow an air of grandeur on the institutions of the state effectively fulfilled its related purpose of evoking the citizen's sense of vulnerability.

Galeano did lose the vote that February morning, and the commission recommended 6–0 that he be subjected to a political trial. A week later a full session of the Judicial Council approved this recommendation, and with this move Galeano was provisionally suspended from his position. The trial that would decide his future as a federal judge began four months later, in June 2005.

The jury for that trial comprised nine (white male) members, headed by the vice president of the Supreme Court, Augusto Belluscio. The other members included two senators, a legislator, and three lawyers. House Representative Marcela Rodríguez and lawyer Beinez Szmukler, both members of the Judicial Council who had been responsible for writing the accusation, acted as the prosecution. The trial took place in its entirety within Tribunales, in the grandiose auditorium that had, some two decades earlier, been the site of the *Juicio a las Juntas*, the trials of the military leaders of the 1976–1983 dictatorship. This opulent chamber still held the sense of weighty importance its designers had clearly attended, with intricate stained glass windows, ornately carved wooden benches, and elegant fixtures. The thick coatings of dust that enveloped even the crucifix above the judges' heads attested to the layers of judicial history that the room had conditioned and contained.

The division among the members of the Jewish collectivity showed acutely at this trial.[30] Memoria Activa was only one of three organized groups of family members of AMIA victims by this time. In 1997, differences between Memoria Activa and the leadership of AMIA/DAIA had become acute as Memoria Activa grew frustrated with the community leadership's accommodations to avoid criticizing the government. During an event held on the third anniversary of the attack, a member of Memoria Activa read a speech that directly accused then-President Menem and Interior Minister Carlos Corach of obstructing the investigation. Immediately after, the president of the DAIA, Rubén Beraja, went over ("cruzó la vereda") to the House of Government and personally apologized to President Menem for her statements, thus in their eyes privileging his relationship with those in power over the interest of the Jewish community in the success of the investigation. Allegations that Beraja and the DAIA's legal counsel, Marta Nercellas, had been aware of the payment made to Telleldín and complicit in the attempt to close the investigation exacerbated these tensions.[31] In 2001, a former member of Memoria Activa founded her own group, APEMIA (Agrupación para el Esclarecimiento de la Masacre Impune de la AMIA), which was even more critical of the government's attempts at handling of the investigation.[32]

While the members and supporters of Memoria Activa and APEMIA were roundly critical of Galeano at his trial, much of the official representation of the DAIA was actively supportive of the soon-to-be-ex-judge. Two members of Memoria Activa testified against him, criticizing him so harshly that one had her testimony thrown out after openly declaring that her interest in the case was to make sure that Galeano was found guilty. Key members of the DAIA, on the other hand, testified on his behalf. Galeano's defense consisted largely in his assurances that he had acted in good faith, with the sole objective of uncovering the truth about the attacks. He admitted that the investigation had problems, explaining the failings with the insistence that the country was not prepared for such an attack and that no Argentine federal judge could possibly have been prepared to undertake such an investigation. Amid the murmurs of disapproval at Galeano's answers, which adroitly managed to go on and on but offered little to no information, a staunch supporter of Memoria Activa leaned over and whispered to me, "Of course, they'd kill him if he said what he knows." He didn't say who exactly could be so direly implicated if Galeano disclosed his purported knowledge of what the other tribunal had called "shady interests of unscrupulous governing officials," but he was quick to assert that Galeano himself was not immune to the politics behind the (mis)handling of the investigation.

In itself, Galeano's argument that Argentina was not prepared for such an attack was not disputed by the family members of the victims. It was, in fact, the privatization of public security and policing combined with the effects of spending cuts to many other government agencies under neoliberal reform that they considered the core of the problem. In their eyes, the implementation of neoliberal reforms under President Menem undermined the government's own ability to provide citizens with the type of physical security and legal protection that states owe their citizens. Neoliberalism became a necessary accomplice to the security failures that permitted the attack to occur, the disorganization that characterized the immediate aftermath—when no coordinated emergency response was in place to attend to the dead and wounded or preserve evidence at the site—and the botched investigations. The elimination, reduction, or privatization of state agencies thus created the conditions under which the state was unable to fulfill its public duties. For Memoria Activa, these limitations were compounded by the corruption among politicians, security officials, and members of the Jewish community leadership more concerned with protecting their own narrow interests than with achieving truth and justice for the bombings. Impunity for the perpetrators of the attacks and for the corruption that surrounded them adds another wound to a community already shaken by the violence.

The verdict in Galeano's trial came on August 3, 2005. Security was high on this tension-filled day, and this time it was required to exchange a picture ID for an entrance pass, though as far as I could tell no one was denied entry. A colleague and I were mildly reprimanded by a nervous young police officer for audio recording the proceeding, but he did not take our devices or the recordings we had already made. Galeano was convicted on three of the most serious counts against him and formally removed from his post as a federal judge. As a consequence, he would not be entitled to the pension that accompanied his post. He had tried to retain this privilege by offering his resignation at the end of 2004. This move, which would also have spared him the political trial, had been rejected by President Kirchner. Criminal proceedings against Galeano remain pending at the time of this writing.

In spite of Galeano's removal from his position, the family members of the AMIA victims and many others interpreted the lack of effective criminal proceedings against him and the very need for a trial as a sign of the endemic impunity that gripped the nation. Drawing on the language of the human rights organizations concerned with bringing justice to the perpetrators of Dirty War violence, the family members of the AMIA and embassy victims join with groups from across society in locating impunity and corruption as the key contemporary violations of human rights. In doing so, Memoria Activa and the other organized groups of family members of victims have played a central role in locating impunity and scandalous corruption as major impediments to the personal and communal process of healing after the embassy and AMIA attacks.

Entrepreneurial Corruption and the "Habitus of Impunity"

The AMIA case shows how impunity can be the source of widespread ills throughout the social body. But the language of impunity has not been limited to cases where a lack of legal justice follows acts of brutal violence. The notion of impunity has been equally applied to the widespread violation or irregular alteration of business, labor, and property laws.

Groups like the Cooperativa BAUEN view these violations, the corruption that accompanies their enactment, and impunity for the actors involved as an infringement of their economic rights. Alternative globalization organizations and some governments, especially in Latin America, have begun to exert pressure for additional attention to economic rights within international institutions. The idea of economic rights as human rights is enshrined in the UDHR and the Covenant on Economic, Social, and Cultural Rights. Under the neoliberal program implemented in Argentina, citizens indeed held economic rights, but as consumer or beneficiaries of (civil or religious) charity services. Though vestiges of the welfare state persisted even in the most extreme forms of neoliberalism as implemented, these were often reduced as far as politically viable or even more so. Pressure from Latin America for the meaningful inclusion of these rights into the transnational human rights regime (Goodale 2007b) has come largely in the trail of increased unemployment and reduced job security and social benefits left behind by neoliberal programs.

Neoliberal Economic Rights

It was during the 1990s that neoliberalist principles became openly and wholeheartedly embraced and promoted by the Argentine national government as the way to stabilize the nation's economy and lead the country out of the hyperinflationary spirals that had plagued the Alfonsín administration.[33] Yet many of these ideas have roots prior to the 1990s and coincide with other fundamental shifts in social organization. The social disruption brought on by the state repression of the 1970s, including the weakening of unions, social atomization, and the undermining of national industry through increased reliance on foreign capital and international loans, set the stage for the neoliberal reforms that followed. Fundamentally, the application of neoliberal policies coincided with (and worked to enact) changes in conceptions of citizenship and the meaning of participation in civil and political life. As García Canclini emphasizes, the consumerism that has become central to contemporary formulations of citizenship was not only promoted by the capitalist state (and the business and media interests that lay at its core), but was also accepted and inculcated by the people as filling a void not otherwise being satisfied (2001). That is, the disruptions to social life that industrialization and urbanism occasioned, and later the dismantling of and public disenchantment with traditional structures for political participation, left a space that could be readily filled by emerging ideals of consumerism. Consumerism as the most important, most visible, and most viable form of social capital became increasingly acceptable and desirable (Sarlo 1994).

The installation of the notion of the citizen-consumer in Argentina is illustrated in the history of changes to the Argentine constitution, especially the 1994 reforms. The reforms, finally approved through negotiations between Menem and Alfonsín in the so-called *Pacto de Olivos*, or Olivos Agreement, included new "rights and guarantees" (*derechos y garantías*). These included protections against the overthrow of democratic governments (Article 36), and rights such as habeas corpus (Article 43), a major concern during the dictatorship era, when family requests of information about their missing loved ones using this legal notion were often denied or ignored. They also included clauses for environmental protection, including the right of all inhabitants to a healthy environment (Article 41), and mandate the establishment of proactive norms to assure "the true equality in opportunities for men and women in their access to elected government and party offices" (Article 37). Importantly, the 1994 reforms also gave constitutional rank to international human rights conventions to which Argentina is a ratifying party (Article 75, section 22).[34]

At the same time, the 1994 rewriting of the constitution incorporated changes that reflected neoliberal versions of citizenship. Article 42, also within the section on *nuevos derechos y garatías*, establishes the rights of the consumer as social actor and the obligations of the state toward consumers. While providing significant protections for the quality and equality of access to goods and services, the extensive and explicit attention paid to the rights of consumers (*comsumidores y usuarios de bienes y servicios*) demonstrates the extent to which citizens' rights had come to rest on and include their integration into the market.

This aspect of the constitution demonstrates one of the ways citizenship and human rights are intertwined with neoliberal economic and political philosophy. The division of rights into two general categories, enshrined in the separate covenants of 1966 (the ICCPR and the ICESCR), set the stage for further conceptual division of these kinds of rights into distinct categories. The constitution of 1994, still in effect, upholds a vision of economic rights distinct from that proposed in the ICESCR, perpetuating the division between these rights and the civil and political rights that, conversely, receive considerable reinforcement. The "economic rights" incorporated into this constitution are a reflection of the values and definitions integrated into neoliberalist philosophy. The focus on certain rights (civil and political, defined as separate and separable from other rights) at the expense of economic rights (except for the kind in the 1994 constitution) was permitted and encouraged, coupled to the new economic model.

In this way, the 1994 Argentine constitution exemplifies what the Comaroffs have called the "rash of new constitutions" across the world. Linking citizenship to human rights, they argue that "if law underpins the langue of neoliberalism, constitutionalism has become the parole of universal human rights, a global argot that individualizes the citizens and, by making cultural identity a private asset rather than a collective claim, transmutes difference into likeness" (2001:39–40). The Argentine constitution, like the others they reference, does not "actually spea[k] of an entitlement to the means of survival. [These instruments] do not guarantee the right to earn or produce, only to possess, to signify, to consume, to choose" (2001:40).

One of the most cogent challenges to the neoliberal model of economic rights has been the recuperated businesses movement. The rise of this movement in Argentina came in response to the more than five thousand factory closings during the latter half of the 1990s. These closures, combined with the erosion of worker protections through "flexibilization" and the drastic decline in regular and salaried positions from these and other structural adjustment policies, led to a sharp increase in unemployment. Given this economic context, workers affected by the closure of a business or factory faced difficult odds in the search for reinsertion into the regular workforce. Toward the end of the

1990s, some workers began to resist, opting to take over the closing businesses and put them into operation themselves rather than allow these sources of labor to disappear.[35] Most of these recuperadas are organized as workers' cooperatives. The movement promotes a vision of economic production based on cooperativism and worker self-management. In doing so, it uses the language of impunity and corruption to challenge the consumerist notion of rights. The Hotel Bauen, one of the most emblematic of these recuperadas, is both site and example of the alternative proposals advanced by this movement.

Buenos Aires, Una Empresa Nacional (BAUEN)

Cooperative member Gerardo has astutely described the Hotel Bauen as "a twenty-story summary of Argentine history from the past thirty years" (see Figure 1). The building, located at Callao 360 between Corrientes Avenue and Juan D. Perón Street in the heart of Buenos Aires, was initially built under the direction of Marcelo Iurcovich in collaboration with two navy officers who facilitated his securing of a government loan. Construction of the 4-star installation was thus made possible through credit from the Banco Nacional de Desarrollo (BANADE, or National Bank for Development), as part of the dictatorship's efforts to prepare the country for the 1978 soccer World Cup tournament. Argentina's role as host came on the heels of the most severe period of Dirty War violence, and the dictatorship faced increasingly intense international criticism as information on its heavy-handed methods at crushing opposition and the plight of the disappeared were slowly coming to light. The military government tried to use the World Cup to divert local and international attention away from the violence and to capitalize on the nationalist sentiments that the tournament provoked. Nascent human rights groups like the Mothers of the Plaza de Mayo, SERPAJ, and the APDH had some success using the increased media coverage to draw attention to their struggles, but the successful transpiring of the events and Argentina's culminating victory as first-time World Champions undoubtedly worked, at least temporarily, in the dictatorship's favor. Now, however, the memory of the 1978 World Cup is for many shrouded in a haze of embarrassment for the popular exuberance it provoked, and the Bauen's association with the event inevitably evokes its emblematic status as a repository of the material traces of political machinations.

Throughout the 1980s and '90s the Bauen continued to serve as a political stage, becoming renowned as a favorite venue for entertainment and business by the political and economic elite. President Menem frequently held personal

Figure 1 The Hotel Bauen. Photo by the author.

and political events within its walls, including using it as a campaign headquarters. Not reserved for any one party, but catering across the spectrum of elite actors, it has been cited as also having been home to the many secret meetings between the Duhalde faction of the Partido Justicialista (Menem's political rivals within his party) and members of the opposition Alianza Party. In the era of "pizza and champagne" during Menem's first presidency, so named for the consolidation of established fortunes and the rise of a nouveau riche able to capitalize on the easy profits arising from decreased regulation, the Bauen was the iconic space for the closed-door negotiations and public posturing that characterized political practice.

The credit that Iurcovich and his associates received from BANADE in 1976 totaled $US37 million, and was intended to finance 80 percent of the construction costs. By 1982, the terms of the loan were being challenged in court. Iurcovich and his associates claimed that the credit had only served to finance 40 percent. BANADE was later absorbed into the Banco Nación, and the legal dispute was not closed until 1994, when the Banco Nación accepted only US$6 million in exchange for considering the loan cancelled (i.e., paid). By 1997, Iurcovich, having failed to invest in the Hotel Bauen (preferring instead to use profits to build other luxury hotels, including the nearby Bauen Suites), passed its management to a Chilean company, Solari, S.A. The hotel was by this time deeply in debt, largely for nonpayment of taxes and services. By 2000, this group had entered into bankruptcy protection (*concurso de acreedores*) and claimed to be operating under accumulated debts of over US$8 million. Under commercial law in Argentina, a business that cannot fulfill its financial obligations enters into this preventive status. The intent is to bring together the owners with the creditors to ensure payment of the debts. However, the law also stipulates that, to protect jobs, an attempt must be made to save and reactivate the business. To this end, the commercial judiciary intervenes and appoints a *síndico*, typically an accountant who takes control of the business's finances.

In this way the hotel remained opened and operated under a *síndico* until it was finally closed on December 28, 2001. At that time, only days after the tumultuous events of December 19–20 that had led to President de la Rúa's (literal) flight from office, another judicial order instructed that the doors to the hotel be closed and the few remaining personnel were abruptly dismissed.[36] The workers often reflect on the irony of having showed up on that particular day, only to find the business shut down. December 28 in Argentina is the *Día de los Inocentes*, something akin to April Fools' Day in the United States. Many of the workers recount how losing their jobs on that day, with scant possibilities of finding work in the height of an economic crisis, made a mockery of their dire situation.

The Bauen remained closed for over a year. By early 2003, some former workers had begun to meet with representatives of other recuperated businesses and the umbrella movement the Movimiento Nacional de Empresas Recuperadas (MNER). The MNER advised them to gather as many former employees as they could and occupy the hotel. Finally, on March 20, 2003, a small group of workers decided to enter the building. Shortly after, they formed their cooperative.

Once inside, they were faced with the utter desolation that abandonment and pillage had left. In the year that had intervened, the former owner had stripped the hotel of everything of value, in violation of remaining labor laws (which would have demanded the sale of the goods and proper allocation of proceeds to creditors, including the former workers). Before the workers could reopen for business they needed to rebuild the hotel. The workers manually reconstructed the installation (sewing the bedspreads, laying phone lines, rebuilding floors, etc). Over time, the cooperative was able to not only repair but also to expand the usable portions of the hotel. It invested much of its profits in renovations, and in 2004 was able to open to the public a full café/bar not previously there. By 2005, 80 percent of the hotel was in operation, and the ground floor hosted a bookstore, hair salon, gift shop, and point of sale for a new line of originally designed and manufactured shoes by the recuperated factory C.U.C. (Cooperativa Unidos por el Calzado, ex-Gatic).

The workers of the BAUEN Cooperative have struggled from the beginning with the pressure of the legal uncertainty that surrounds their occupation and operation of the hotel. Their situation was made more complex by the legal haze that surrounds the circumstances of the hotel's closure. As mentioned above, in 1997 the owners of the Hotel Bauen turned the management of the hotel over to the Chilean group Solari, which was to buy the business for 12 million pesos (at that time equivalent to US$12 million). When the hotel closed in December 2001, Hugo Iurcovich, son of former owner Marcelo Iurcovich, presented a complaint in court requesting that the hotel be returned to them, on the basis that the Solari group had made only one payment of 4 million pesos toward the purchase of the hotel. They won the case, which legally removed the hotel from bankruptcy, but the decision contained the provision that the Iurcovich family return the 4 million pesos they had received. As they have not done so, the ownership of the hotel remains encased in legal ambiguity.

While each case presents its own idiosyncrasies, in general within the recuperated businesses phenomenon in Argentina there are four actual or desired resolutions to the situation that arises once the workers take over a factory or business (Fajn et al. 2003:102–109). In some cases the state, through either law or decree, has validated (usually temporarily) the workers' expropriation of a factory or business. In other cases, the workers have agreed to contracts, either through direct negotiations with the former owners or through judicial decisions that allow them the right to rent the installations. In still other cases, where a business is in bankruptcy and the creditors have the strongest legal claim on the business, the workers have made arrangements with the major creditors and stockholders. Finally, in cases such as FaSinPat (Zanón) and Bruckman, the workers have chosen to demand the nationalization of the business, having it operate under worker control and for the benefit of the entire nation.[37]

Since the Hotel Bauen was technically removed from bankruptcy through a legal decision, the workers were limited in their possibilities for a resolution. As one cooperative member, Fabio Resino, relates, "When we entered here at first we wanted, as a solution, to sign a rental agreement with the owner, since as the hotel wasn't bankrupt, it was difficult to expropriate: everyone in the Legislature told us, since the hotel isn't bankrupt, nobody's going to expropriate it. But for that same reason we couldn't rent it either."[38] In September 2003, six months after occupying the hotel, the workers were able to achieve a preagreement that allowed them the right to operate a part of the hotel. This agreement was decided between the cooperative, the former owners, the government of the City of Buenos Aires, the MNER, and the lawyers for the former creditors. Under this agreement, which was overseen by the Commercial Judicial Circuit No. 9 under Judge Paula Hualde, the cooperative was able to put into operation the first three floors of the hotel. These included the large meeting rooms and halls, which the workers were able to renovate and rent out. However, as the hotel became profitable, the pressure from both the former owners and political forces whose interests lay in the protection of property rights increased. Each of these has mounted persistent legal attacks against the cooperative's right to occupy and operate the hotel.

Following counsel by the MNER, the BAUEN Cooperative has responded to the legal uncertainty surrounding its status by demanding that the state expropriate the hotel and turn it over to the cooperative. As was the case with the organized groups of family members from the AMIA bombing, the workers identify particularly conceived notions of corruption and impunity as the principal obstacles to the movement's objectives. "Corruption" here acts particularly as a frame through which their practice, that of occupying and operating businesses, is legitimated. In appealing to a notion of corruption, the workers contrast the logic of capitalism and the primacy of an ethics of (individual) profit to what they see as the owners' ethical obligation to have acted for the benefit of the business as a productive unit, one that includes the workers.

This perception of widespread corruption was intimately connected to the issue of privatization. Neoliberal policies demanded the deregulation and privatization of the industries and services that had remained under state control. Control of these operations was typically decided through bidding, with foreign and local companies competing to make the most attractive offer. Many of the concessions for operating everything from railroads to water and sewage services went to the companies or conglomerates that promised the most efficient service at the lowest price to users. However, in many cases the bidding has been questioned for its transparency and the ability of government officials to take advantage of the process for personal gain. In addition, in many cases the companies that won the concessions have frequently failed to fulfill even the minimum obligations to invest in expanding infrastructure or to keep costs to users (now redefined as consumers) low, provoking crises in many cases.[39] These concessions, most often to foreign bidders, have been severely criticized for operating under a logic of profit for the principal players and unrelated to concerns for the public good. Deregulation and poorly supervised privatization generated highly visible examples of private interests trumping public welfare, and the exposure of these acts and the lack of accountability for those involved contributed to the focus on corruption and impunity within political language. From this point of view, the corrupt practices of the former owners and the impunity afforded to the business class under the era of Menemist politics came together to form the principal cause of the severe unemployment and debilitation of the primary and service industries in Argentina around the turn of the twenty-first century.

The example of privatizations extends to private businesses as well, as members of the movement argue that many of the factory and business closures that plagued the second half of the 1990s were fraudulent. The workers highlight that even under the capital-friendly laws passed or decreed during the era of neoliberal reform, many of the actions of business owners remained illegal, and that this illegality was in fact an integral part of the system. The weight given to profitability in the 1990s often led to business owners having little regard for the continuity of the business and overemphasizing the transportability of capital, manifested both in widespread capital flight and preferential investment in other, often foreign-based businesses.

That business owners did not follow the law, even though it overwhelmingly favored them over workers, is clearly exemplified in the much-contested Law of Insolvency and Bankruptcy (Ley de Concursos y Quiebras). The rewriting of the bankruptcy law, one of Menem's neoliberal reforms, facilitated owners' ability to evade paying their debts, particularly to workers. The former workers of a bankrupt business are themselves its creditors, with both back pay and benefits due to them. Although this is often recognized in bankruptcy cases in Argentina, former workers are rarely able to collect on any of what is owed them since bankruptcy law, both as written and in practice, gives the lowest priority to this group. The 1995 rewriting also invented the notion of the "cram-down" that allowed interested parties a favorable position from which to buy businesses under protection and renegotiate their debts. This led to many cases of "phantom associations" controlled surreptitiously by the former owners, and allowed business owners the possibility of authoring fraudulent bankruptcies as a method of debt evasion, a route many took (Fajn et al. 2003; lavaca 2004; Rebón 2006).

The ethics of profit maximization, even over and above business and labor laws, was so pervasive as to lead some to speak of a "habitus of impunity."

> Within the business sector was installed the idea of legal and moral deregulation, forming a kind of "habitus of impunity," in which many businesspeople placed little value in the most elemental aspects of following the law. Only by taking into consideration this supposed social climate of *immunity* in which they were inserted and a profound anomie, can we understand the set of fraudulent practices that many developed. (Fajn et al. 2003:35; emphasis in original)

Within the BAUEN, these kinds of business practices are singled out as the primary facets of the illegitimacy of the owners' claims to the property. Though considered to be part of a widespread phenomenon, members of the BAUEN Cooperative detail with adept precision the specifics of their case. They disseminate their claims through a variety of means, including press releases, an email list, public speeches during protests, interviews with members of the alternative media and researchers, and, more recently, through social media such as Facebook.

In explaining the details of their case, they stake their claim to legitimately operate the hotel in terms of the owners' illegal and illegitimate practices. Major features of their allegations include accusations that:

- The former owners deliberately failed to properly maintain and invest in the hotel to keep it viable. Rather, the cooperative argues, they amassed millions of dollars of debt by failing to pay the hotel's service providers, and used the profits they thus gained to construct other luxury hotels in Argentina and Brazil.

- The former owners and management violated labor laws regarding the maintenance and closure of a business. For example, by the time the doors formally closed, the number of workers employed at the hotel had already been drastically reduced by the management under varying reorganization schemes and the slow reduction of the hotel's offer of services. Workers who had maintained their jobs report having suffered months of underpay and nonpayment of mandatory benefits.

- For years the former owners engaged in predatory management. As evidence of this, workers cite how they changed social service providers five times, with each change forcing the entire workforce to resign and be rehired. The cooperative claims this move allowed the owners to avoid paying their debts and to deny workers the rights they accumulate for continuous tenure.

- The former owners are guilty of *vaciamiento*, or the emptying of the premises of all saleable goods after bankruptcy had been declared, thus preventing their liquidation toward repayment of the amassed debts.

- The former owners orchestrated a post-bankruptcy "sale" of the business to a phantom corporation that is in fact controlled clandestinely by the former owners, in a move designed to allow them to evade responsibility for having led the business to bankruptcy.

This appraisal of the former owners' actions influenced the way workers chose to confront the hotel's closure. Anger over their mistreatment, the denial of their legal rights as workers, and the fraudulent practices of the owners are all reasons frequently cited to justify the occupation of the business. That these factors are important in a number of situations is supported by the low incidence of businesses being recuperated when the proper indemnity was paid to the workers upon their dismissal (Rebón 2004:43). In referring to these fraudulent bankruptcies, Rebón notes:

> This behavior by businesspeople is perceived as "intolerable," making space for acts of resistance. In this perspective, it is important to point out that in the literature [on recuperated businesses] and the consciousness of the workers moral explanations of the "inappropriate behavior by the owners" as determining the business crisis abound. These hypotheses don't take into account that the very nature of capital is the maximization of gain and its reinvestment. If the conditions for the realization of the cycle of accumulation don't exist, withdrawal at the lowest cost is the morally capitalist alternative to follow. (2004:65)

However, for the Bauen workers, it was the perception of corruption across the business sector in ways that directly affected them and their families that galvanized many into action. Many workers also view the fact that the former owners first allowed the hotel to fall into disrepair and then to strip it of its useful parts as criminal, wasteful, and disrespectful of the place of work. This was often expressed as one of the most painful features for many members of the cooperative, who had invested many years of their lives in the care of the hotel. In the account of one member, her accumulated anger and sense of indignation were central to her decision to join the cooperative:

> When the Bauen closed, I kept working for Iurcovich in Bauen Suites; later I had to choose between continuing to work there or recuperate the hotel. It was a difficult decision because I had four children to care for and who was going to provide for my household? . . . [I decided to come because] my compañeros were there. But beyond that, while I was in the Bauen Suites, which is connected to the Bauen Hotel across the back, I saw that the Iurcovich family was taking things from here [the Bauen Hotel] to use there [Suites]. I'm a maid, and when I cleaned the rooms I recognized the stolen furniture. They had left us without work and now they were stealing even the night tables. That, which is what made me feel more powerless, was what made me decide to change.[40]

The perception of the actions of the former owners as corrupt and immoral motivated the workers to act. They further strengthen their denouncements of the owners by highlighting the connections of these with the dictatorship. For workers in the BAUEN Cooperative,

> the defense of our jobs is not just a labor issue, but also a struggle against the darkest elements in our country, personified today in an economic group that

was capable of conducting the shadiest financial maneuvers, connected within a network of relationships that they began in the 1970s, with the closest ties being those that linked them to the bloodiest military dictatorship in the history of our nation.[41]

Identifying corruption and impunity as violating Argentine workers' fundamental right to survival and as the principal causes of the nation's troubles, they were galvanized into seeking alternative resolutions.

Conclusion

The structural reforms that characterize neoliberalism did not begin in the 1990s under President Menem. Rather, privatization of state-run industries, the erosion of workers' rights and protections, and the general lessening of government regulation of the economy were all aspects of the economic program implemented by the dictatorship. The lasting wound of disappearance finds its companion in the erasure of suffering under a neoliberal political economy. "Human bodies apparently disappear under the neoliberal logic, just as the last military dictatorship in Argentina disappeared the real, material bodies of many people who opposed precisely that kind of socioeconomic organization" (Sutton 2010:29). The politics of forgetting and the invisibility of the human effects of structural adjustment are both forms of denial and are intricately linked. And yet, these erasures are precisely what came under fire in the moment of crisis in December 2001.

> In a country that has a history of denying the disappearances, torture, and horror inflicted by the last military dictatorship, the reality of pervasive poverty in the making could perhaps for a while still be covered up by politicians and economic elites or overlooked by members of the middle class holding on to illusions of economic prosperity. However, with the crisis that erupted in the new millennium, this kind of denial was no longer possible. The new disappeared, the "economic disappeared" as they have been called in social movement circles, showed their existence with their physical presence when they claimed, through individual demands and collective protests, their rights to partake in citizenship and the goods that democracy was supposed to deliver. (Sutton 2010:43)[42]

In Argentina, the struggle for human rights has shifted. The disappearance and torture of the 1970s have receded and the dual pillars of impunity and corruption have become the interpretive tropes for defining social ills. A narrative of corruption became a way of making ethical claims about the obligation of the state to protect human rights and serves as a point of resistance and a way of legitimizing alternative actions. The rise and spread of a global discourse of rights throughout the 1970s and 1980s meant that neoliberalism came to be expressed and justified within these terms. Furthermore, as the next chapter shows, the emergence of a neoliberal human rights discourse lent further legitimacy to the increasing traction of the idea of human rights in Argentine society. However, it also led to significant differences in interpretation and contradictions in expression. People who mobilized to protect or secure their rights have resisted neoliberal formulations of what those rights are. Groups like Memoria Activa and the BAUEN contest the neoliberal injunction to embrace (neoliberal) citizenship and human rights by focusing on the implications of the neoliberal project itself.

Chapter 3

Streets, Plazas, and Palaces

Asserting Justice and Work as Rights

Soy madre de una víctima del atentado a la AMIA, soy una mujer que llora la pérdida irreparable de su única hija, soy una más de los que luchan sin descanso para esclarecer esta masacre, soy una ciudadana que me rebelo ante la falta de justicia, soy una argentina que me avergüenzo de la impunidad que reina en mi país.

I am the mother of an AMIA victim, I am a woman who cries for the irreparable loss of her only child, I am one more of those who struggle without rest to shed light on this massacre, I am a citizen rebelling before the lack of justice, I am an Argentine who is ashamed of the impunity that reigns in my country.

Sofía Kaplinsky de Guterman

Para nosotros/as, los socios/as-trabajadores del Hotel B.A.U.E.N., el derecho a trabajar con dignidad es el corazón de nuestra lucha. Desde que recuperamos el hotel con 20 trabajadores el 21 de marzo 2003, hemos podido reconstruir todo el edificio, ponerlo en pleno funcionamiento, creando más de 140 puestos de trabajo y convirtiendo al hotel Bauen en un espacio de solidaridad y encuentro de todas las organizaciones sociales, entidades cooperativas y mutualistas. . . . Luego de 8 años, la sociedad pudo comprobar que la autogestión de los trabajadores es posible, como una forma de gestión colectiva, solidaria y participativa. Hemos reconstruido por completo el hotel, haciendo del mismo un verdadero espacio de utilidad pública, para todas y todos.
Solidaridad y apoyo en nuestra campaña por la expropiación definitiva del Hotel B.A.U.E.N.

Ciudad Autónoma de Buenos Aires, 27 de julio de 2011

For us, the members/workers of the Hotel BAUEN, the right to work with dignity is the heart of our struggle. Since we recovered the hotel with 20 workers the 21st of March 2003, we have been able to reconstruct the entire building, putting it into full use, creating more than 140 jobs, and converting the Hotel Bauen into a space of solidarity and of gathering for all social organizations, cooperative entities and mutual associations. . . . After 8 years, society has been able to see proof that worker self-management is possible, as a form of management that is collective, participatory, and based in solidarity. We have completely reconstructed the hotel, making of it a space of true public good, for everyone.

Solidarity and support for our campaign for the definitive expropriation of the Hotel BAUEN.

Autonomous City of Buenos Aires, July 27, 2011

T HESE TWO QUOTES, one from a woman whose daughter died in the AMIA attack, the other a press release from the BAUEN Cooperative, exemplify how each group conceptualizes and uses the idea of rights in particular ways in confronting the issues that directly affect their lives. The family members of the AMIA victims denounce what they consider endemic impunity and corruption in asserting their right to justice. The BAUEN Cooperative is also concerned with achieving justice, in this case economic justice in the form of the right to work. In each case, the demand for these rights to be protected and ensured is intrinsically linked to a particular vision of the proper role of the democratic state. The members of Memoria Activa allege that the state has violated their right to equal protection and legal justice, with its failure to properly respond to the attacks and for the deliberately flawed investigations that followed them. For the members of the BAUEN Cooperative, it is their right to work that is being violated, both through the initial closure of the business and by subsequent attempts to deprive them of the material conditions for the source of work they themselves created in response. The state, in their view, has the responsibility of assuring the collective right to dignified employment over and above individual property rights. This chapter looks at these notions of judicial and economic justice, the assertions of rights that accompany them, and the nature of the state that is being envisioned and demanded in each case.

Changing the Terms of the Debate

From its inception, Memoria Activa has worked to locate its struggle within the broader context of the movements against impunity in Argentina. Almost immediately following the AMIA bombing it began to hold weekly public demonstrations (actos) in memory of the victims and in protest against the lack of effective resolution. These were held without interruption for more than ten years, and the group continues to hold yearly events on the anniversary of the attack. In developing these actos Memoria Activa drew on the language and forms of protest developed or popularized by established counterimpunity movements like the Madres de Plaza de Mayo. Adopting familiar patterns such as weekly protests in public plazas helped establish its cause as part of the generalized problem of impunity, and in the process Memoria Activa both drew on and strengthened impunity as a central and formative notion. Though the group has had little formal or technical support from organizations concerned with the Dirty War, it frequently appeals to their symbolic alliances, made visible through such actions as the presence of one of the Madres in the weekly events. By locating its demands for justice in the Israeli embassy and AMIA bombings as part of the larger counterimpunity movement, it is arguing that these attacks are not a problem for Jews or the Argentine Jewish community alone, but a problem for Argentine society as a whole.

The choice of location for these actos was in itself intended to be symbolic of Memoria Activa's claims and objectives, which centered on the notion of justice. The Plaza Lavalle sits in the downtown center of Buenos Aires, known locally as the *microcentro*. This area is recognized as the as the cultural, political, and economic heart of the city and the nation, and was historically the first stopping point for Jewish immigrants to Argentina. Located thirteen blocks from the Plaza de Mayo, this plaza extends from Avenida Córdoba to Lavalle Street, occupying the space between Talcahuano and Libertad. Its southwest corner faces the Tribunales, the imposing neoclassical building bustling with the bureaucratic activity of an overburdened legal system. To the southeast it borders the renowned Teatro Colón, the magnificent national theater whose seasonal operatic and symphonic offerings can rival those of the world's most prestigious locales. The northeast corner holds the Templo de la Congregación Israelita Argentina (Temple of the Argentine Jewish Congregation). The facade of this synagogue, whose foundation stone was laid in 1897 and which also houses a museum of Jewish immigration to Argentina, is punctuated with the spaced concrete barriers (*pilotes*) that now separate all Jewish buildings in the city from the street in front. These barriers, an icon of segregation and distance, were put in place to prevent another attack like those that destroyed the Israeli embassy in 1992 and the AMIA building in 1994. Like so many other things surrounding these attacks and the community's response to them, these barriers are a source of contention among members of the community and serve as a symbolic marker of the self-imposed divisions that these attacks have left behind.

Memoria Activa's Monday morning rituals in a corner of the Plaza Lavalle were held without fail from July 1994 to December 27, 2004. While in the initial weeks these were silent, undirected gatherings, over time a group of individuals began to take on more of a leadership role, and the format of the events changed as they began to invite speakers to address those present. The form was altered somewhat as the years passed, but the essential elements remained constant. On a typical Monday, the crowd, ranging from fifty to several hundred, would gather on the sidewalk on the western side of the Plaza, facing the Justice Building. The events always began at 9:53 am, the moment when the bomb had exploded on July 18, 1994. They would be opened with the sounding of the shofar. Three men would approach the microphone, kippas carefully in place, and fill the plaza with the loud, persistent wail of the ancient horn. Then, a central member of the movement, from what came to be known as the board of directors (*mesa directiva*), would call for a minute of silence in honor of those killed. This would be followed by some introductory words that might give an update on the status of a legal or political aspect of the case, or simply renew the call for the need for justice and serious investigation into the attack. During the introduction, the speaker would remind the listeners of the number of weeks that had passed since the attack, still without justice: 300, 400, 544 weeks. This would be followed by one to three speakers, who over the years included activists, lawyers, psychologists, performers, politicians, journalists, religious leaders, writers, artists, and other public personalities, both Jewish and non-Jewish. These speeches are published on the group's website and selections from 1997, 1998, and 1999 were compiled and published in booklet form by the newspaper *Página/12*, serving, as the cover of the 1999 edition asserts, as a "national document against impunity." The speakers would be followed by some general announcements, typically concerning upcoming community events, and the act would be closed with a demand for justice directed toward Tribunales.

The move to define the bombings and the struggle for justice as problems for all of society is not a denial or an effacement of the fact on the part of Memoria Activa that the movement arose from the Jewish community. Indeed, the movement also publicly valorizes its identity and location as based within a Jewish tradition, however diverse and multivocal the definitions of and identifications with this community may have been, in ways that simultaneously work to creatively reinterpret or reactivate that tradition. The consistent presence of children from Jewish schools brought out on these Monday mornings to attend the protest-memorials shows the interest of the group in transmitting the enacted traditions that these rituals represent.

Perhaps the most visible and cherished marker of this Jewish identification comes with the playing of the shofar. Participants frequently highlighted this moment as an emotional source of pride and a central feature of the events. The shofar is commonly used in religious ceremonies for the high holidays of Rosh Hashanah and Yom Kippur, but it also carries a biblical history as an instrument of summoning or a call to battle. The blowing of the shofar is said to have helped Joshua capture Jericho. Memoria Activa and its participants draw on and invoke this history of the shofar in adopting it as a symbol of their Jewish identity. The moment of silence is introduced with the coordinator of the acto saying, "Escuchamos el shofar, con su llamado milenario que nos acompaña y nos convoca, para que derrumbe los muros de la impunidad."[1] The shofar and its "eternal call" are thus summoned to accompany Memoria Activa's struggle, to call out against the dangers of forgetting, and to remind the community of its responsibility to struggle for justice. The age, tradition, and the symbolic power of the shofar are highlighted, with appeals for all to listen to its "ancient cry," which would help to "bring down the walls of impunity," as it brought down the walls at Jericho.

Another important and constant feature was the biblical phrase Memoria Activa uses as its closing invocation. This was recited every week at the end of the acto, with the coordinator inviting the crowd to join in the call for justice. While this feature exhibited minor variations, the formula remained constant. One typical morning the call was as follows:

We have heard the call of the shofar. We end as always with our voices:
For the 30,000 disappeared, victims of state terrorism in our country, we demand—
[crowd] JUSTICE
For the children, stolen from their homes during the last dictatorship, who are still today searching for their true identity, we demand—
    JUSTICE
For the dead in the bombing of the Israeli embassy, we demand--
    JUSTICE

For our relatives and friends, victims of the atrocious attack on the AMIA
building in our country, we demand—
JUSTICE.
justice, justice, you will seek *tze·dek tze·dek, tir·dof.*[2] (Deuteronomy 16:20)

The passage from Deuteronomy is also inscribed on the monument erected
to the dead in the Plaza Lavalle, where Memoria Activa holds its *actos*, and
frequently appears on the documents it publishes. In using this biblical passage,
Memoria Activa is affirming that the struggle for justice is a moral injunction
as well as a social responsibility. This appeal to theological justification allows
Memoria Activa to assert a religious identity, even while discursively insert-
ing itself and its struggle within a broader national context of counterimpunity
movements. The reiterated use of the phrase "our country" (*nuestro país*) also
emphasizes the assertion that the attack and the political interests that orchestrated its cover-up affect Argentina as a whole.

Neoliberal Democracy and Cultural Pluralism

While alarming moments of anti-Semitic actions still occasionally dot the
news headlines, the long record of Jewish presence within and contributions
to Argentine society were by the 1990s generally recognized by the majority
of non-Jewish Argentines. Two days after the embassy bombing, 90,000 Argentines, Jews and non-Jews, poured into Avenida 9 de Julio to repudiate the
attack.[3] After the AMIA explosion, another demonstration, this time of over
150,000 people, gathered in front of the Congress Building to denounce the
violence, with banners that read "Hoy somos todos judíos" (We are all Jews today) hanging across streets. A survey conducted at the request of the Instituto
Nacional contra la Discriminación, la Xenofobia y el Racismo (INADI), or National Institute against Discrimination, Xenophobia, and Racism, in December
2006 found that while those surveyed reported being aware of discrimination
against Jews, only 17.6 percent identified Jews as a principal category subject
to discrimination, far behind the 52.3 percent who believed that Bolivian immigrants would be most likely to face victimization. Overall, in the perception
of the interviewed, discriminatory attitudes were most often based on socioeconomic class rather than any other consideration.[4]

Yet anti-Semitism has continued to be entrenched in powerful institutions
in Argentine society, especially the military and the police. There have been
very few Jewish officers in the Argentine military, even in comparison with
other predominantly Catholic countries such as Chile, and the anti-Semitism

entrenched in the cultural milieu of the security forces is well-documented.[5] In 1990 a notorious army colonel and carapintada leader publicly remarked, "I know neither any green horses nor any decent Jews" (cited in Feierstein 1999:363). While the police force is often cited as lacking in its ability to increase the sense of public security among the populace (Hinton 2006, Kalmanowiecki 2000), this is compounded for Argentine Jews, particularly those with lesser economic resources.

More pervasive than this entrenched anti-Semitism, however, is the tendency among many non-Jewish Argentines to perceive Argentine Jews as marginal, at once a part of yet separate from the "true" Argentines. This view has remained formalized in significant legal formulations, such as the law that, until the constitutional revision of 1994, stipulated that the president and vice-president of the nation must be communicants of the Catholic Church.[6] The idea of Jews as marginal results in part from the still prevalent idea of the Argentine nation as culturally homogeneous. This has ramifications for all Argentine minority communities, including the expanding Korean, Bolivian, and Paraguayan immigrant communities.[7] Federico Pablo Feldstein and Carolina Acosta-Alzuru, in a comprehensive textual analysis of the mainstream newspaper coverage of the bombing of the AMIA building, demonstrate how the press reflected this view, by employing discursive strategies that distanced Argentine Jews from non-Jews (2003). With public attention so forcibly directed toward the Jewish collectivity following the AMIA explosion, the mass media coverage of events often depicted Argentine Jews as foreigners or Israelis. This interpretation is subtlety reinforced by the common use of the term *israelita* to mean Jew(ish), dating back to well before the establishment of the modern state of Israel. In contrast, the term *israelí* is the Spanish word for someone or something pertaining to the modern state of Israel. Feldstein and Acosta-Alzuru also found that the press consistently presented the attacks as being against Jews, who were said to ultimately bear the blame for their problems, rather than as against "Argentines," implicitly defined as not Jewish. Some of the bleakest moments in this coverage included news articles and television reports lamenting the deaths in the bombings of both "judíos e inocentes" (Jews and innocent people).[8] This phrasing implies that Jews killed in the attack were intrinsically connected to the precipitating causes of such violence and thereby not "innocent." In the words of Ricardo Feierstein, "How is it still possible—when the Argentine Jewish institutional presence has just celebrated its hundredth year—[for there to be] a confusion between 'us and the others,'

'Jews and Israelis,' 'foreigners and non-foreigners,' citizens of the same country?" (Feierstein 1999:428).

It is within this context that Memoria Activa combines elements of Jewish ritual with an insistence on the attacks as *not* being a "Jewish" issue. Rather than seeing the attacks as perpetrated against Jews, with Argentine soil being a displaced battleground for a foreign conflict, through its actions Memoria Activa locates the Jewish community as an integral part of the nation while simultaneously asserting the right to Jewish specificity and difference (see also Aizenberg 2000; Zaretsky 2008). This reveals a complex layering of multiple subject positions and identities, combining Jewish, Argentine, and, for some, Israeli identifications at the same time. The strategic deployment of multiple identities is an example of how citizenship, or what it means to be a citizen within a nation-state, is being reconfigured. As John and Jean Comaroff argue, "the fractal nature of contemporary political personhood, the fact that it is overlaid and undercut by a politics of difference and identity, does not necessarily involve the negation of national belonging, . . . merely its . . . ambiguous coexistence with other modes of being-in-the-world" (Comaroff and Comaroff 2004:191). In calling for recognition of Argentine Jews as full and integral members of the Argentine nation, the movement is proposing a redefinition of the nature of the national imaginary as essentially plural, multiethnic, and multicultural.

Memoria Activa made these assertions at a time when the idea of cultural plurality was increasingly gaining the force of political correctness. Proponents of neoliberal economic reforms also often embraced a broader set of neoliberal social policies, including a kind of "multicultural citizenship" whereby a recognition of cultural difference becomes a central (and often empty) feature of official discourse. Charles Hale has used the term "neoliberal multiculturalism" to name the phenomenon "whereby proponents of the neoliberal doctrine pro-actively endorse a substantive, if limited, version of . . . cultural rights, as a means to resolve their own problems and advance their own political agendas" (2002:485). This embrace of a "politics of recognition" (Taylor 1992) by the proponents of neoliberalism and its application in Latin America came about in large measure because of pressures from indigenous and other marginalized groups, which were becoming increasingly vocal in pushing for an expansion of their rights. The package of cultural rights often encompassed political reforms to include indigenous and other citizens, at least nominally, in the processes of government, as well as education reform, increased acceptance and promotion of indigenous languages, and antidiscrimination policies.

Though the Argentine state was, unlike other Latin American nations such as Bolivia, Colombia, Ecuador, or Peru, not contending with a large and organized indigenous population demanding change (but see Gordillo and Hirsch 2003), and though minority groups like Argentine Jews had historically enjoyed full rights as political citizens, Menemist-era Argentina nonetheless adopted a version of neoliberal multiculturalism. In Argentina this acceptance of cultural plurality was based in particular on international and local discourses of human rights and democracy. Multiculturalism and the right to difference were presented as human rights and the respect of these rights the duty of a democratic country. A limited embrace of multiculturalism thus afforded a low-risk way for the Menem administration and its allies to claim they were promoting human rights while denying demands for justice for the state-sanctioned perpetrators of Dirty War violence.

The emerging discourse of the right to difference, soon adopted across large sectors of the Argentine political spectrum, is reflected in, for example, the 1994 constitutional reforms, particularly in Article 75, Section 17, which, in response to increasing activism among several ethnic groups, for the first time explicitly recognizes indigenous Argentines as a part of the nation. Multiculturalism is also sanctified in the preamble to the 1996 constitution of the Autonomous City of Buenos Aires, following a polemical restructuring of the political terrain. The preamble defines the objectives of the city government to include "the promotion of human development in a democracy based on liberty, equality, solidarity, justice, and human rights, recognizing identity in plurality." Significant as the formal recognition of the right to difference is, and without minimizing important advances such as the 1988 passage of anti-hate-crime legislation, the adoption of neoliberal multiculturalism can be dangerous nonetheless for those demanding their own or others' cultural rights. Hale points out that

> these initiatives also come with clearly articulated limits. . . . Powerful political and economic actors use neoliberal multiculturalism to affirm cultural difference, while retaining the prerogative to discern between cultural rights consistent with the ideal of liberal, democratic pluralism, and cultural rights inimical to that ideal. In so doing, they advance a universalist ethic which constitutes a defense of the neoliberal capitalist order itself. (2002:489–490)

Hale is referring specifically to certain kinds of cultural rights that are often perceived as a threat to the basic premises of capitalist society, such as collective rights. In the case of Memoria Activa, the version of state-endorsed cultural plurality is seen as problematic not only for the nature of its content but also for its perceived use as a diversionary tactic to allow the state to rhetorically present itself as promoting human rights even while, through action and omission, it is systematically violating these rights. More than anything else, members of Memoria Activa point to the inconsistency between the government's words and actions. The preamble to the city constitution, cited above for its evocation of cultural difference as a protected feature of democratic life, has been constantly held up by members of Memoria Activa and other dissident sectors of the Jewish community as both a highly significant step and ironic in its hypocrisy. One member of Memoria Activa frequently remarked on the importance of the preamble during actos in the Plaza Lavalle, and the magazine *Convergencia*, a progressive Jewish publication deeply concerned with human rights, often published this excerpt in advertisement-style full-page layouts on the back cover of its issues. However, the inner pages of *Convergencia* and the impassioned invectives intoned by my informant affirm that its espoused ideas were not always concretized.

The community's relationship to state-sponsored visions of multiculturalism is illustrated by contrasting examples of moments when political leaders have attempted to publicly and symbolically demonstrate the state's commitment to a politics of cultural diversity. At the end of the 1980s, many in the Jewish collectivity and the broader Jewish community had reservations about the upcoming presidential election, given the growing likelihood that Menem, a nominal Peronist of Syrian descent, would win. A skilled politician who relied heavily on his charisma, Menem worked hard to gain the support of a very reluctant Jewish constituency.[9] Shortly after becoming president, Menem attended an event, held in the historical synagogue on the Calle Libertad, in repudiation of recent anti-Semitic attacks in France. As Menem approached the door to the synagogue, a member of his entourage tried to brush aside the offered kippa. Menem, however, took it into his own hands and placed it on his head. The event itself, which also included the presence of a high official from the Argentine Catholic Church, the president of the Islamic Center of Buenos Aires, and numerous local and national political figures, was meant to demonstrate the multicultural and multi-religious composition of Argentine society, and to demonstrate the harmonious relationships between the different sectors. The occasion was (somewhat confusingly) heralded by the DAIA as the first time a national president attended such an event outside of countries with a climate of anti-Semitism. In itself this was an example of political spin—here the same organization responsible for logging and denouncing acts of anti-Semitism on Argentine soil (the DAIA) was classifying Argentina as a country without anti-Semitism. However, I suspect this strange pronouncement was offered as a show of gratitude and in recognition of Menem's decision to attend. Contradictory as it seems, the claim was widely and uncritically repeated across mass media and community publications, and the moment it garnered Menem considerable (initial) support from a once reluctant community.

This moment from the early 1990s, before the AMIA bombing, can be contrasted with a similar one that took place over a decade later. In 2004, the AMIA/DAIA held an event inside the reconstructed AMIA building in the Plaza Seca to commemorate the disappeared. This event was the first of its kind held by the AMIA/DAIA in honor of the memories of the Jewish victims of the Dirty War. The official Jewish collectivity leadership had been roundly criticized for its perceived lack of intervention on behalf of the Jewish disappeared, both during the repression and in the search for justice that followed the return to democracy. Voices within the community had continued to call on the AMIA/DAIA to hold a moment of public self-reflection on accepting this perceived failing. Many remained dissatisfied with the leadership in this regard, but the staging of this and similar memorial events marked a significant shift in the public posture of these organizations.

This occasion was attended by President Kirchner, who also donned a kippa. In his case, though, the gesture resulted in an uncomfortable moment of awkwardness as he struggled to get it positioned properly in front of an expectant and tittering crowd, eventually being assisted by several senior members of the collectivity leadership. He then proceeded to light a menorah candle, and, after giving a brief speech, uncovered the new high-relief sculpture designed for the occasion by Sara Brodsky, plastic artist and mother of Fernando Brodsky, who was disappeared in 1976. While Kirchner's words were widely praised, this kind of symbolic gesture nonetheless failed to earn him the kind of uncritical support it had for Menem more than a decade before. Members of Memoria Activa whom I interviewed took the position that while his presence at such events was important, the concrete measures he might take in advancing the investigation mattered far more. Accordingly, his wife, then senator and future president Cristina Fernández de Kirchner, who chaired the Bicameral Congressional Commission that undertook an evaluation of the AMIA investigation, received a far more positive and uncritical evaluation from members of Memoria Activa. By 2004, actions counted for far more than words, and members of a deceived and distrustful community were far less likely to give politicians the benefit of the doubt based on their symbolic gestures.

Many Argentines believe this gulf between rhetoric and practice is a consequence of the generalized problems of corruption and impunity identified as pervading political and economic practice during the 1990s. Thus, by the end of the 1990s, they dismissed state-directed neoliberal multiculturalism as little more than top-down concessionary measures to placate dissidents even as public officials and powerful economic actors encouraged a climate of decision-making based more on personal interest than collective good. Diego Melamud (2000) reflects a sentiment expressed by many when he asserts that the 1990s also witnessed a "Menemization" of the Jewish collectivity, with the leaders of community institutions also paying lip service to the good of the community while undertaking fraudulent privatizations, making drastic cuts in the number of employees and in social services, and acting out of personal interests in tampering with the workings of justice. In this way, the policies and symbolic gestures of public officials under the Menemist regime came to be read as little more than bald-faced attempts to counter criticism of the implementation of Argentine-style neoliberalism.

Unlike the indigenous communities that have negotiated the new political space opened up by neoliberal multiculturalist policies (Hale 2002; Yashar 2005), the Argentine Jewish community was already formally incorporated into the political structure. Nonetheless, the Jewish community and Memoria Activa appropriated the tenor of this neoliberal discourse 1) to urge changes in the cultural sphere (Álvarez, Dagnino, and Escobar 1998) and 2) to promote reform, appealing equally to the responsibilities of a democratic state and to Jewish tradition, particularly with regard to memory and justice. Memoria Activa's insistence that the AMIA bombing and its lack of legal resolution are Argentine, rather than Jewish, problems, arises within the context of a crisis of institutionality that it considers endemic throughout society. In this way, and perhaps ironically, the vision of cultural plurality advanced by Memoria Activa is best understood as emerging in dialogue with state-directed neoliberal multiculturalism. Memoria Activa appeals to the state's own language on democratic consolidation and a nascent cultural pluralism to make its demands for the right of (cultural) citizenship (Faulk 2008b; Zaretsky 2008). Yet, looking to change the nature of the state itself, it uses this kind of "cultural citizenship" (Rosaldo 1994; Ong 1996) deliberately and productively by insisting discursively on institutional changes for the benefit of all Argentines.

Memory as an Injunction to Action

Charles Tilly has argued that citizenship is composed not only of rights and obligations but also collective memories about what these rights and obligations can and should be (1994). Referring specifically to the right to justice, he proposes that: 1) definitions of justice are culturally and historically specific, 2) people have a choice between the mnemonic and moral frames adopted in pursuing justice, and 3) an observer cannot account for the shared interest of people (a prerequisite for collective action) without looking at available mnemonic and moral frames.

The way Memoria Activa articulates its demands matters as much as their content and illustrates the relationship of mnemonic frames of justice to practices of citizenship. Memoria Activa's weekly events entwined the act of remembering the victims of the attack with a protest against the mishandling of the investigation, a demand for justice, and a reconceptualization of the nation and its citizens. The name of the group itself implies the need to remember combined with a call for justice as a social necessity, as expressed by one speaker and prominent member of the movement, Enrique Burbinski, who, commemorating the beginnings of the movement on the occasion of the 500th week of uninterrupted protest, said,

> We wanted to remember, we wanted to practice memory but we wanted to do it in an active way, exercising our rights as citizens, as members of a community, as free men who seek to live in freedom and we could only achieve that through justice. For that reason [we have] our name, to practice our memory actively; for that reason [we come] to this place, in front of the Palace of Justice that does not honor its name. (March 8, 2004)

This idea can also be seen in the inscription on the plaque describing the monument by plastic artist Mirta Kupferminc that was erected in the Plaza Lavalle in honor of those killed in the AMIA blast (see Figure 2). This bronze plaque, before it was stolen, read:

> The basic idea of this work is a protest. Not a remembrance or a homage
>
> A protest materialized through each one of its elements
>
> A circle of granite serves as the foundation of the whole and symbolizes the totality around which everything turns
>
> Stakes of quebracho wood of different sizes and textures penetrate the stone
>
> Fusing themselves in one destiny, they form a singular mass but maintain their singularity

The monument is posed expectantly facing the Palace of Justice and projected
to the world as a pillar of the search

The base, hammered and broken in one place, signals a clock stopped at 9:53 am

The biblical text etched in the granite "Justice, justice you will seek"
(Deuteronomy 16) is an appeal for active memory[10]

In addition, participants in these events often insist that coming to the plaza
and performing memory in this way has been essential in assuring that the
dead "don't die twice, once from the bomb and again from being forgotten."
Para que no mueran dos veces, or "so that they don't die twice," became a central
slogan of those that turned out every week.

Memoria Activa's use of memory as part of the struggle against impunity
must be considered within the climate of the politicization of memory in
Argentina at the time of the bombings. Many scholars have taken up ques-

Figure 2 AMIA monument, in the Plaza Lavalle. Artist: Mirta Kupferminc. Photo by
the author.

tions surrounding the relationship between memory and the construction of a national history.[11] However, what I want to pursue is not how historical memory shapes and is transformed by experience (Rappaport 1990), nor how personal or collective identity stands in a mutually constructive relationship to memory (Malkki 1992, Bardenstein 1998, 1999), but how memory of lived experience has been invoked and used in Argentina in asserting specific rights in order to promote political and legal reform. By demanding justice, counterimpunity movements have insisted on their right as citizens to protection from the abuse of power and on the enforcement of the rule of law in case of violation. In this way, these groups' struggle against impunity and corruption has become simultaneously a performance of citizenship that asserts their rights to protection from abuse. In pursuing its goals, Memoria Activa drew on (and helped to create) a mnemonic frame of justice in accordance with the practices and principles of other Argentine human rights movements. The members of Memoria Activa cast the presentation of the memory of their experiences into the molds used by other groups, reworking and presenting it in accordance with their own demands, including an assertion of Jewishness and a vision of Argentina as a nation with a plurality of different cultural, ethnic, and religious traditions.

For Memoria Activa, the responsibility to mobilize immediately following the 1994 attack was clear. Repeatedly stressing that "no one else is going to undertake this struggle for us," speeches from the early years of the group's existence make frequent reference to the need to pursue construction of a nation whose institutions would protect and provide resolution for its citizens, as seen as well in this passage from a 1997 flyer:

Memoria Activa was born to confront the impunity for the criminals and those who protect them, and to struggle against forgetting. We are a group of citizens . . . dedicated to memory, devoted to justice, lovers of peace and desiring that the institutions take the place that belongs to them within our afflicted democracy.

This quote exemplifies Memoria Activa's focus on confronting impunity and corruption as a way toward the construction of a better society. The public space of the Plaza Lavalle became the forum from which to articulate its demands and make visible its struggle.

Memoria Activa also insists that its events are as much memorials as protests and that the memory of those lost be an activator for bringing change. But what does it mean for memory to be "active"? Daniel Goldman, a highly respected politically progressive rabbi and an ally of the group, has reflected on the nature and purpose of memory as used in the Bible. He argues that the Bible proposes an essential dialectic, with one side holding the idea of "remembering" and the other holding the opposite idea, which is not an absence of memory but rather "not forgetting." Key here is the notion that "remembering" is active, while "not forgetting" is passive. The binary opposition comes not between two active acts (remembering and forgetting), but between the act of remembering versus the passive state of not forgetting. Goldman cites Yerushalmi's seminal 1982 work *Zakhor*, in which Yerushalmi argues that the repeated use in biblical texts of the word "zakhor," which can encompass meanings including to remember, to memorize, and to commemorate, attests to the importance the concept holds as a religious mandate. Finally, Goldman argues that

> the other central axis of the Bible is rooted in the practice of denouncement as a permanent activity, in opposition to the submission of humanity to mediocre conformativism and the authoritarianism exercised by the powerful in particular moments of history who through corrupt mechanisms have obstructed the capacity of the people to be outraged by the unjust ways in which humanity has been oppressed as a creature of God.[12]

Memoria Activa's idea of active memory resonates with Goldman's analysis. The conception of memory Memoria Activa deploys contains the insistence by participants in the actos that the memory of the attack serve as a catalyst and constant reminder of the need and obligation to pursue justice. The participants in these events frequently expressed their continued participation in terms of their obligation to continue this struggle. As a group, Memoria Activa insists on the pursuit of justice as a basic right of citizenship, and a moral, social, and religious obligation. Attention to the way members of Memoria Activa talk about memory reveals a common appeal to the idea that the behavior of the Argentine state led them to feel pressured to take on new roles. Members assert that not only did the state not fulfill its constitutional obligation to provide justice but in fact obstructed justice, and that this is what led them to feel that they were left the unwelcome obligation to take up the fight against corrupt and inefficient government institutions. In this way, they understand their actions not just as a search for justice, but for justice as the path toward the construction of a better nation, one in which the state upholds and protects the rights of citizens rather than violates them. As expressed by Goldman at Memoria Activa's event on the sixteenth anniversary of the AMIA attack:

> The 18th of July caused the word "citizenship" to change course for those of us who are here, for those who inhabit our city, this city, its houses, its streets, and its plazas. Until this date, the dominant concept of citizenship insisted on the idea that "to be a citizen is something that is granted, as it implies the explicit recognition of a body of civil, political, and social rights." In this sense, the concept of citizenship was . . . passive. . . . [Since the 18th of July 1994] to be a citizen means to inhabit the city . . . as a concrete place that pledges me to my identity. . . . This "to be a citizen" is constructed and reconstructed in the territory of memory. For this reason, the opposite of citizenship is forgetting. . . . To be a citizen is in essence to be an individual with an identity of resistance and a supporter of active memory.

Another, related aspect of the idea of memory used by Memoria Activa concerns the social and emotional effects of uncertainty following the traumatic loss of a loved one or an irruptive moment of violence. The participants in these events argue that not until a social recognition of the deaths of the victims through a serious pursuit of justice has been achieved will their memories be able to become part of a past, completing a kind of social death to accompany the physical one already suffered. To give one example, I quote the words of Laura Ginsberg, whose husband died in the AMIA:

> And, because that morning they left their homes as they did every morning, they deserve justice. And because we will not forget, we demand justice. . . . And because they believed that they lived in a country that was free and safe, we demand justice. And because their voices call out from the very center of the earth, we insist on justice. And because we reject terrorism in any and all of its manifestations, violence, hate between peoples and discrimination, and *because shedding light on the attack is an inescapable responsibility, we take up the struggle for justice. And they deserve justice, because from the place in the universe in which they are, or from inside of us, only after justice has been served can our dead rest in peace.* The dead from the AMIA: present.[13]

This social recognition of death is taken here to be the result of a kind of knowledge produced through the workings of a competent and effective legal system. Central members of Memoria Activa place great importance on the production of knowledge through its certification by credible legal institutions, and this vision has influenced their course of action. They feel the appeal to justice is also a necessary route toward social and emotional healing after a moment of traumatic loss, in ways intimately related to the broader counter-impunity discourse that gained widespread public acceptance in the decade prior to the AMIA and Israeli embassy attacks.

This need for closure, but only through and after a full accounting of what happened, has become a key aspect of public discourse and source of contention in the political field in recent years. Memoria Activa's insistence on the importance of justice in allowing for the social death of loved ones resonates with that of one of the best-known counterimpunity movements, the Madres of Plaza de Mayo. Even years after all hope of finding survivors still imprisoned in military detention centers had been abandoned, the Mothers still demanded the *aparición con vida* (reappearance with life) of those missing, arguing that their children could only pass from sites of living struggle into points of remembrance once their deaths were recognized as acts of state violence and the perpetrators brought to justice. This position is powerfully expressed in their oft-repeated chant that has left an almost tangible residue on the cityscape surrounding the plaza, "Con vida los llevaron, con vida los queremos" (They were alive when they were taken, we want them back alive) (Fisher 1989).

For survivors as well the remembrance of the past is a focal point for action. One unwavering participant in Memoria Activa's actos in the Plaza Lavalle was a survivor of the Olimpo, a clandestine detention center used by the last military dictatorship. The Olimpo (Olympus) was cruelly and ironically nicknamed after the home of the gods by those who considered themselves the all-powerful controllers of life and history. Until 2005, the Federal Police ran the car registration center for the capital (the city of Buenos Aires) out of this building. That is, if you bought a car or needed to renew your registration, you had to go to the Olimpo. During the four months she spent inside its infernal walls in 1978, this woman, Tita, was tortured by the infamous Julian the Turk, eventually imprisoned for his role in the repression. As Tita was inviting us to an acto at the Olimpo one evening, another participant began talking about Simón Radowitzky and how we "should never forget that it was a Jew who had the courage to kill the repressor Falcón." The connection was immediately apparent to those present (though not to me). They patiently explained that the Olimpo is located precisely on Calle Ramón Falcón (Ramón Falcón Street). The past breathes out of the walls at you in Buenos Aires

Tita tells of the "special treatment" she received for being Jewish. One night, El Turco Julián made her stay up and sing the national anthem all night long, saying that "this Jew probably doesn't even know our anthem." Tita recalls how she had at that time been a schoolteacher for over thirty years and thus had personally taught the national anthem to hundreds of children, but this reality counted for nothing inside the Olimpo. We later learned through a well-connected friend that El Turco Julián, in jail awaiting trial, had been abandoned by his former allies and was not enjoying the pampered life in prison that these former incarcerators often have. Tita's response, without a trace of sarcasm, was, "Oh, poor thing, I'll have to take him some food." And she probably would. On December 21, 2010, El Turco Julián was sentenced to life in prison.

Justice and the State

Following the lead of many other counterimpunity organizations, Memoria Activa has set justice at the center of its demands and the goal for which the memory of the victims is to be mobilized. In spite of the divisions among them, this demand is shared by all of the organized groups of family members of victims of the bombings. The idea is expressed in an attention-grabbing method designed by the AMIA for the thirteenth anniversary of the AMIA bombing. In the days leading up to July 18, AMIA members handed out paperboard boxes made to resemble the package of commonly available medicines, with the label JUSTICE printed in bold across the front (see Figure 3). Inside each box was a flyer announcing the memorial/protest to be held on the anniversary, along with a list of the names of those killed in the attack and an empty pill sheet. The boxes were distributed, according to the AMIA website, "so that society as a whole can continue to reflect on all the victims that, in different cases, our country has because of the lack of justice."

Figure 3 Medicine box, advertising "Justice" pills as a "fast-acting" way to fight off impunity. Distributed by AMIA, 2007.

As with the human rights organizations demanding legal justice in the wake of state terrorism, the organized groups of family members of victims of the AMIA bombing seek a justice that rests on state-organized juridical resolution of the event (i.e., an officially sanctioned accounting of what happened) and condemnation and punishment of those responsible following procedures prescribed in a preexisting democratic code of law. In this way, these groups both draw from and bolster the emphasis on accountability within transnational human rights (Tate 2007). That is, what they seek is not, for example, an ultimate goal of peace or reconciliation and forgiveness, but rather accountability and punishment through formal legal channels. What are the assumptions behind the desire for legal accountability for the perpetrators? First, the search for legal accountability looks to the state as the appropriate and necessary source of justice. Second, this justice should take the form of the trial of alleged offenders in an impartial court, where guilt or innocence is to be established according to accepted and established legal procedures through the presentation of credible evidence. Third, legal investigation and trial must evaluate and validate "knowledge" surrounding the events. Ideally, the court must be the arbiter of the truth, and thus produce knowledge about the events. Fourth, the legal system must follow the "rule of law." In Argentina, this term is used to express a fundamental difference between democratic and authoritarian modes of governance. This is especially significant in a place like Argentina, where the value accorded democratic institutions and the rule of law, in contrast to authoritarianism, is continually reinforced in public discourse. Finally, upon condemnation the guilty are to be incarcerated in a state-run or state-approved prison, and thus denied certain basic liberties or rights of all citizens. Members of these groups frequently insist that the planners and perpetrators must "rot in jail" ("pudrirse en la cárcel") for their crimes. The demand that the offenders, which in the case of the AMIA bombing includes both those responsible for the original violence and those who prevented its juridical resolution, should and in fact must be imprisoned in order for the event to be resolved is an expression of this idea of justice. Each of these features entails a particular vision of the state and its role as well as a particular valuation of and expectation for democracy.

Nonetheless, this conception of justice is not the only one readily available the family members of the AMIA bombing. Local circumstances in Argentina in recent years have led to other notions of justice gaining rhetorical force. As a result of many years of trying to change government policy without success, and given the distrust and perception of the judiciary as corrupt, inefficient, and (for many years) beholden to the executive branch of government, some counterimpunity organizations began to explore avenues for achieving justice that did not rely on the (Argentine) state. These included initiating and participating in trials of alleged offenders in foreign courts as well as expanding the idea of justice to include forms of social approbation that did not rely on formal judicial proceedings. This is the case with, for example, the group HIJOS, which undertakes *escraches* or public outings of former repressors. HIJOS (Hijos por la Identidad y la Justicia contra el Olvido y el Silencio, or Children for Identity and Justice against Forgetting and Silence) comprises the children of those disappeared during the last dictatorship. Its outings consist of groups of supporters gathering at former repressors' homes or places of work and publicly denouncing them and decrying the abuses they allegedly committed during the Dirty War. Their targets are exposed both vocally, through chants and shouts, and visually, by painting *asesinos* (murderers) or other epitaphs on the sidewalk and walls and by holding signs that would be widely seen though news coverage of the events. They define the escrache as "a tool to denounce the impunity that keeps afflicting us. It publicly 'marks' the house of the perpetrator of genocide, to show society where the assassins of our people hide. Since there is no justice [here], at least they should not have peace, at least they should be pointed out on the street for what they are: criminals."[14] This exposure equals a kind of exhibition of knowledge, the forced imposition of a public face, the ultimate act of "appearing" those who first disappeared others and then tried to effect their own anonymity. HIJOS's slogan *a donde vayan los iremos a buscar* deploys grammatical ambiguity both to affirm its dedication to society as a whole ("wherever they go, we will find them") and threaten those who would be its targets ("wherever you [plural] go, we will find you"). Starting in 1995, HIJOS's escraches became well-known both within the counterimpunity movement and throughout the broader society thanks to the media attention they received. The word *escrache* has become part of popular parlance, and the tactic has been adopted by other groups on numerous occasions. Though many people considered it a complement to, and not a replacement for, legal prosecution, it did present a model for an alternative in the quest for justice and an expanded understanding of what justice could entail. These escraches are a local version of the recent emphasis in a number of Latin American contexts on alternative forms of community justice, such as lynchings (Goldstein 2003).

Given this context, to emphasize legal accountability is a deliberate choice from within a field of options. The difficulties and frustrations of using the legal system (*recurrir a la justicia*) have not deterred the members of Memoria Activa. In this, they fit within a broader pattern in Argentine society of seeking the judicialization of conflicts in spite of negative and even worsening perceptions of the judiciary (Smulovitz 2010). The increased recourse to the judicial system has grown out of the long process of resistance to the dictatorship and the search for condemnation of the perpetrators of the violence. As such, it is "not related to ex ante changes in legal culture, but rather to the combined effects of changes in opportunity structures for claim making and the earlier emergence of a support structure for legal mobilization consisting of labor lawyers and a new rights advocacy network of NGOs" (Smulovitz 2010:234).

The appeal of judicial reckoning for members of Memoria Activa, even though they acknowledge the route through the legal system has been long and torturously winding, lies in its connection to the notion of (re)building a particular kind of Argentine state. They believe that achieving justice is a means of strengthening (*fortalecer*) democracy and democratic institutions.[15] Noteworthy in this respect is the positive evaluation they gave the TOF3 (the judicial panel that heard the AMIA case) in the trial of Telleldín and the Buenos Aires police officers. Though the trial ended in the condemnation of the judge (Galeano) and not the defendants, Memoria Activa felt that the court acted appropriately in exposing the investigation's irregularities. In making the construction of strong and accountable institutions one of its primary concerns, Memoria Activa envisions and works to bring about an Argentine state that conforms to the rubric for a modern democracy. Memoria Activa's demands and denunciations continue because of the failure of the state to fulfill its obligations within this vision of democracy. The state it imagines would consistently and effectively confront head-on the problems they signal as endemic to the system—impunity and corruption—through the medium of a strong and functional legal system. While Memoria Activa draws on Jewish cultural and religious traditions in highlighting the moral obligation to seek justice, its goal is the establishment of state institutions committed to and capable of providing justice and equality for all Argentines.

From the Plaza Lavalle to Callao and Corrientes

Walking away from the Plaza Lavalle, in front of Tribunales and down Talcahuano Street, you enter a narrow passage lined by many *locutorios* (telephone, and now also internet, stations), photocopy shops, and book-stores specializing in legal texts. Almost immediately Avenida Corrientes comes into view, a major artery of the city's *microcentro*. On the corner is El Banchero, one of a chain of cafes where a subgroup of participants in Memoria Activa's *actos* would gather for coffee and conversation. Heading right, there are countless small bookstores, performance venues, and restaurants, catering to the local lunchtime business crowd and people seeking nighttime entertainment in this never-sleeping metropolis. Two blocks up is the Centro Cultural de la Cooperación (Cooperation Cultural Center), which hosts films, theater productions, and academic events in the spirit of a continuously reconstructed cooperativist tradition. Shortly after, you come to the intersection with Callao Street, filled with subway passengers descending or emerging from the ground below, pedestrians, cars, buses, trucks, and motorcycles. On the left, looming above the other buildings on the block and nestled between the strands of concrete Parisian ornamentation that characterize so much of central *porteño* architecture stands the bleak modernist tower that is the Hotel Bauen. I walked this route many times, both as one of a multitude of daily pedestrians in this heavily transited district and, down the very center of the road, as part of the marches that the BAUEN Cooperative and its allies often organized in demanding recognition of their right to hold on to the source of labor they had created for themselves. Although BAUEN Cooperative's struggle is different from that of Memoria Activa in focus and objectives, both groups insist that the problems they confront spring from the joint malady of impunity and corruption. Furthermore, they assert that justice, in BAUEN's case economic justice through the right to dignified work, is an essential part of a functional social and political system and must be the basis of an effective and responsive state.

Economic Justice and the Right to Work

Born out of necessity, the BAUEN Cooperative has since its inception been engaged in a never-ending struggle for survival against the legal and economic pressures mounted against it. In making its defense, the cooperative asserts that the state must promote and protect access to dignified employment as a fundamental right. In doing so, the cooperative adopts the language of human rights employed by the Argentine human rights community as well as drawing on and reformulating notions of the right to work with historical resonance in Argentine society.

Work as a Right

According to data collected by the Ministry of Labor, as of 2010 there were an estimated 280 recuperated factories/businesses throughout Argentina, involving approximately 15,000 workers. The appearance of the recuperated businesses movement in the late 1990s and early 2000s has come on the heels of a protracted succession of changes in the formal rights and actual possibilities for protected and stable employment in Argentina. Though such rights have been formally guaranteed by the Argentine constitution since 1949, the second half of the twentieth century saw a long decline in protections of workers both legally and through formal organizations such as unions and government ministries and agencies.[16]

During much of the twentieth century Argentina was characterized by high employment rates in the formal sector, and this has been a lasting source of pride and identity. This history has made Argentina notable among Latin American countries for a deeply engrained sense of work as a right, to be enjoyed by all (adult) members of society. A long and vibrant history of labor activism imbued the idea of labor with its associations to dignity and located it as the anchor and ultimate source of social justice. As Argentine anthropologist Mariano Perelman has argued, "In general terms, it is possible to say that 'work' has constituted one of the most powerful disciplinary discourses of modernity, and in Argentina, it was one of the principal forms of social integration, and one that also reached those that were outside of the market of formal work" (Perelman 2011:5; 2007a).

Built in a weak sense into classical liberalism, the notion of the right to work in Argentina has roots in the socialist, anarchist, and syndicalist movements at the turn of the twentieth century. Early state policies, such as those instating universal education, supported a belief in upward mobility and social integration. In the first Peronist administrations (1946–1955), under a state-supported "model of integration" (Svampa 2005b), the working class won a broad range of social rights, including strong protections for workers, state-run or state-supported health-care systems, and pensions. The importance of classical Peronist ideology in establishing the notion of work as a right should not be underestimated, even given the drastic and contradictory changes that the party has undergone. "Peronism did not only represent higher wages, its historical meaning for workers was embodied also in a political vision which entailed an expanded notion of the meaning of citizenship and the workers' relations with the state, and a 'heretical' social component which spoke to working-class claims to greater social status, dignity within the workplace and beyond, and a denial of the elite's social and cultural pretensions" (James 1988b:263).

Guillermo O'Donnell's article "¿Y a mí, qué mierda me importa?" playfully details the notion of work as a right (O'Donnell 1997). In it, O'Donnell contrasts a hypothetical interaction between an Argentine service worker and a customer/client from a higher class, to a similar encounter in Brazil. He argues that, upon feeling disrespected, the Brazilian may assay the worker with the phrase "Você sabe com quem está falando?" (Do you know who you're talking to?) as a way of demanding the deference s/he expects to receive. An Argentine worker, O'Donnell says, endowed with a firmly embedded sense of rights, rather than accepting that deference is owed to a person of a higher class, is more likely to believe that s/he is doing a favor to the customer by providing service. Thus, the client's reprimand would receive as a reply something akin to the title phrase, "What the hell do I care?"

The idea that the state is responsible for ensuring access to stable jobs continued to hold force and provide impetus to workers' organizations even as the conditions of labor came under threat both from state forces and union bureaucracies. The historically essential role for the state was eroded over the second half of the twentieth century, beginning with the military coup against Perón in 1955 and the overturning of the short-lived constitution of 1949, which guaranteed social and economic rights. In spite of moments of intense resistance during the following decade (James 1988b), the weakening of organized labor and the rolling back of the gains acquired in decades of struggle were to continue. The brutal repression and crippling of the worker's movement during the dictatorship era set the stage for the later economic policies, which would have been much more difficult to implement had the workers' movement maintained its previous strength and vitality.[17] Repression, the erosion of rights, and state policies that failed to adequately consider the dire poverty in which so many millions of Argentines find themselves are intimately interconnected.

Neoliberal Workers

Neoliberal reforms in Argentina reached their peak in the 1990s. Structural adjustment policies led to a marked increase in irregular and black-market work devoid of traditional protections in a nation that had always prided itself on stable, regularized employment as a fundamental aspect of identity. The 1991 National Employment Law, which established the possibility of short-term labor contracts, marked a change from previous legislation that emphasized job stability. Later laws, in 1994 and 1995, further eroded protections to workers' rights, limiting the compensation due injured workers, instituting a "trial period" for new workers, reducing the amount and situations under which employers must pay social security, and eventually eliminating all together the obligation to give severance pay to many workers.[18]

The rewriting of the Law of Insolvency and Bankruptcy (discussed in Chapter 2) was a clear expression of the neoliberal determination to redefine the role of workers and remake the political economic system. The law was altered through reforms in 1995 (under President Menem and Minister Cavallo) and 2002 (under Duhalde and his Economic Minister, Roberto Lavagna). Both reforms were demanded by the IMF and closely follow its prescriptions. The new law dealt with the rights of the thousands of workers affected by the roughly five thousand factory closures that ensued in the 1990s. Although it made workers creditors of bankrupt businesses, alongside investors and lenders, workers have rarely been able to collect on any of what is owed them since the law puts them last on the list of creditors (and entitles them to only 50 percent—without interest—of the debt owed to them, while other creditors are able to recover 100 percent plus interest). Furthermore, the latter are paid first, which in practice means that workers rarely if ever receive even a tiny percentage of what is owed to them (in accumulated arrearages, contract provisions for termination of employment, shares in the company, etc.), thereby relieving owners of many of the obligations toward workers under the old law. A modification presented under the Kirchner administration and approved in 2006 (Moro 2006) returned jurisdiction of bankruptcy cases to the local judicial circuits for labor disputes (the 1995 Menem–Cavallo reforms had placed these cases under federal commercial and civil courts). However, this did not fundamentally alter the basic structure of the law, which continued to greatly favor creditors over workers.

Against this background the recuperated businesses movement began to emerge and formulate its demands. Argentine anthropologist María Inés Fernández Álvarez elaborates on the notion of work as understood and promoted particularly within this movement (2004). She notes that the primary sense of work among these workers (though I would add, not necessarily among the promoters) is often that of labor as daily experience, as the means of social reproduction. This sense is expressed by many workers when they highlight their participation in the cooperatives as a means to "llevar el pan a nuestras casas" (to bring home the bread) or the fundamental condition of life that guarantees their subsistence and that of their families. This, she argues, is "a key element from which a resource for political action is constructed, and from which protest is legitimated, both before the state and before their own families" (Fernández Álvarez 2004:353–354).

However, this is not the only sense in which work is understood and protest legitimated. Workers in the recuperated businesses movement assert work as a right that should be available to all. This sense involves several interrelated aspects, all of which relate to how the recuperadas workers envisage their relationship to the state. One of these contrasts work to unemployment. In this aspect, holding a job is strongly linked to the idea of dignity. Workers insist that they do not want to simply receive their means of subsistence from the state (as was being promoted through a number of state plans, such as *Jefes y Jefas de Hogares*, which provided monthly payments to unemployed heads of households). Rather, they contend that the state should take responsibility for ensuring jobs for those who need them instead of than simply providing handouts. Work in this sense is a regulated source of stability and protection. The workers hold the state accountable for guaranteeing a set of basic rights, "instituted as rights beginning in the 1940s and considered as fruits of the struggles of the working class" (Fernández Álvarez 2004:358). These include limits on the hours of the workday, fair pay, yearly bonuses, standards of production, safe working conditions, and access to social security and health benefits. The workers also assert their own legitimacy, highlighting their effort (*esfuerzo*) to create their own source of jobs while the state remained unwilling and unable to do so. By insisting on the state's responsibility to provide work, they demand that it treat them as rights-bearing participants in the life and economy of the nation (*portadores de derechos*) rather than as passive recipients of state programs (*beneficiarios*), that is, they demand to be treated as active citizens, not passive subjects.

In the recuperated businesses movement the notion of work as a right, although clearly drawing on historically resonant notions of the right to work in Argentine society, is not a simple reassertion of an earlier principle. Rather, the idea of work has taken on the added dimension of being something that has been realized by the workers themselves. The practice of factory occupation has historical precedent in Argentina. In 1959 workers occupied the meatpacking plant Lisandro de la Torre in response to its privatization under Frondizi (see James 1988b:113–118). And workers facing imminent personnel reductions occupied and took over production at the Ford plant in General Pacheco in 1985.[19] These occupations and others like them were generally part of a defensive strategy designed to apply pressure, and not considered a permanent measure. The more recent occupations differ from these earlier experiences in their focus on workers owning and controlling both the process and the product of their labor. Rather than seeing worker control primarily as a defensive response to a dire situation, in its more recent manifestation "the occupation of the factory is not just a form of protest but itself constitutes an affirmation" (García Allegrone et al. 2004:341).

The implications of worker control are explored further in the following chapter. Here, in relation to the cooperative members' assertion of work as a right, I note one feature of worker-controlled management, namely, its fundamental difference from neoliberal ideas of autonomy. The idea of worker-controlled businesses may seem to be similar to the kind of autonomy embedded in the neoliberal model of citizenship, based in part on the notion of community assistance/participation, as a way of displacing responsibilities formerly assumed by the state onto local groups in the name of community self-reliance. However, I argue that the kind of autonomy the workers are promoting is moving toward an alternative political construction, in building the kind of "other world" made possible "through the potentiality found in the collective actions that emerge from and are rooted in society" (Thwaites Rey 2004:14). Thus, though the idea of self-management may bear a resemblance in practice to that promoted under neoliberalism, both the intention and the effects are quite different. Rather than being empowering, the kind of community autonomy promoted by neoliberalism generally led either to a dire lack of basic services or restrictive modes of participation, often carried out under the strict guidance of international NGOs. The BAUEN workers argue that the business class sees *worker self-management*, on the other hand, as a threat rather than a way of relieving a burden, and interpret the constant attempts to have the hotel under their management shut down in this way. As a member of the cooperative declared, "They can't leave things as they are, because we are showing the people that we *negros* can also be, not bosses, but create sources of labor."[20] As such, they see their struggle as more than a rhetorical challenge to the individualism of (neo)liberalist philosophy. By having demonstrated their capacity, as workers, to run and manage businesses and factories without the managing class or financial backing from banks or other lending institutions, they consider their achievements a practical challenge to the very premise of how work is organized under the current economic system.

This reassertion of the right to work as a fundamental right is apparent in the rhetoric and actions of the BAUEN Cooperative. The centrality of the right to work in its struggle was eloquently exhibited during a protest in 2005. A mix of cultural centers, theaters, bookstores, and local, national, and provincial government institutions all coexist around the heavily transited corner of Callao and Corrientes. This location lends the protests held by BAUEN Cooperative vitality and visibility. As they had done on numerous previous occasions, during this protest the workers cut off the block of Callao Street that ran in front of the hotel. However, this time, the agreement reached with the police forces that quickly arrived was that one lane of Callao would remain open to traffic. In visible symbolic demonstration of "work" as a central notion of their struggle, during this protest the workers brought a representation of their labor into the street, setting up elaborate dinner tables and beds in the lanes closed to traffic (see Figure 4). The physical evidence of the work of the cooperative was dramatically displayed directly on the grey pavement, with delicate wine glasses and flowered bedspreads providing a striking contrast to the cars, buses, and pedestrians that never ceased to pass by.

Figure 4 Beds set up on Callao Street. Photo by the author.

Property Rights Versus the Right to Meaningful Equality

Embedded in this idea of work is an assertion of a particular role for government. The idea that the state must guarantee the right to dignified employment is central to the movement's demand for further changes to the Law of Insolvency and Bankruptcy. Modifying this law has been a priority for many of the recuperadas and has been a focal point for their activism as they have sought to alter the terms that govern their possibilities upon the closure of a business or factory.[21] The movement has proposed a rewriting of the law that includes the possibility for the workers to recuperate 100 percent of what is owed to them and gives priority to maintaining the source of labor. The 1995 law dictated that in the case of a bankruptcy the judge should shut down and clear out the factory or business within four months, even though this meant leaving the workers out of a job. The proposed reforms, presented for the first time in 2004, would allow workers to operate these enterprises as a cooperative immediately and without having to pass through the *síndico* or judge. In addition, the proposal would allow the workers to use what is owed to them to purchase the machinery, raw materials, brand names, patents, and whatever else is necessary for taking over the operation of the factory or business. A supporter of the proposed modifications has argued:

> What began in the 1990s as struggles against factory closures and the defense of jobs within the neoliberal model, where the basis was financial speculation, is today consolidated after a decade within a model that puts production and work at its center. To make it so that the workers have priority in the process of liquidation and bankruptcy is to break with the perverse business practice of emptying the installation and the denial of rights and of the recourse the justice system that was and is practiced by owners in order to continue concentrating earnings and socializing losses. Giving [the workers] the possibility to acquire ownership of the means and physical spaces of production through forming a cooperative dignifies the role of the workers and recognizes their most essential rights, insuring the continuity of their jobs. (Federico Ugo, Subsecretario de Acción Cooperativas, Secretaría de Participación Ciudadana, Gobierno de la Provincia de Buenos Aires [Subsecretary of Cooperative Action and Secretary of Citizen Participation, Buenos Aires Provincial Government])[22]

Through symbolic demonstrations of their work and proposals such as the attempt to amend the Bankruptcy Law, the words and actions of the workers insist on their constitutionally guaranteed basic rights to economic justice in the form of dignified employment, the right to a wage that meets their basic needs, and access to social benefits such as retirement support and health care.[23] In their view, the state as representative of the people is obligated to protect the rights of workers. The workers' argument for the state's responsibility to uphold the right to work is buttressed, perhaps ironically, by the 1994 constitution, which affords constitutional status to treaties and conventions Argentina has ratified. Article 23 of the UDHR stipulates that "Everyone has the right to work, to free choice of employment, to just and favorable conditions of work and to protection against unemployment." Conversely, the business owners, operating under the logic of neoliberal capitalism, emphasize their moral responsibility to shareholders and to the maximization of profit. The state in this view has the responsibility to defend the right to private property and the free operation of business.

Fundamentally, these differences can be classified according to the basic split between giving primacy to the right to property (the owners) versus to the right to meaningful equality (the cooperative). This tension, inherent in classical liberal political philosophy, has reasserted itself at the heart of the debates left in the wake of neoliberal restructuring, and may even be considered a central axis of initial and subsequent debates over human rights. The right to work has long been at the center of this tension. Almost two centuries ago the French philosopher Pierre-Joseph Proudhon declared that "property is theft" and advocated mutualism through cooperative associations. His contemporary Louis Blanc proposed the formation of "National Workshops" and attacked liberal ideology for excluding the right to work, arguing that this right is fundamental and should be protected by the state. He wrote in 1848, "That which the proletariat needs in order to liberate himself are the tools of work; these the government must provide" (Blanc 1848, cited in Ishay 2008:140, 332).Utopian philosopher Charles Fourier likewise wrote of "the futility of wrangling over the rights of man, without thinking of the most essential, that of labor, without which the others are nothing" (Ishay 2008:140).

In spite of these early critiques, the right to private property, though not codified in key international documents or covenants like the UDHR, ICCPR, or ICESCR, remains a foundation of legal practice in many places, Argentina included. In making their claims to legitimacy, the BAUEN Cooperative builds on conventional notions of human rights, which, as I have shown in Chapter 1, tend to emphasize civil and political over social and economic rights. Yet in doing so, they underscore the right to work as a fundamental and protected economic right. Furthermore, they frame their demands in ways that do not contradict the right to private property. That is, by emphasizing the illegal methods of the former owners (i.e., illegal even under the laws as modified by neoliberal reforms) and in asserting the workers' right to operate the hotel, the BAUEN Cooperative is not denying the right to private property. Rather, by highlighting the illegality of the owners' actions, including the non-payment of taxes and the failure to repay the government for the initial loan for the hotel's construction, it is arguing that, even under neoliberal-era laws, the hotel can legitimately be expropriated by the government and, in recognition of the (human) right to employment, turned over to the cooperative. The importance of establishing that the right to work as not inherently in contradiction to the right to private property is reflected in how the leadership of the recuperadas movements criticized Naomi Klein and Ari Lewis's 2004 documentary *The Take*. Many felt that the film missed the point for not differentiating between the violation of the right to private property, which in their eyes the filmmakers glorify, and the constitutional right of the workers to maintain their source of work.

I am not arguing that the cooperative has purposefully framed their claims in the way they have so as to challenge transnational discourses of human rights, but that it has done so deliberately in negotiating the sociopolitical field in Argentina. This sociopolitical field was (and still is) strongly influenced by the neoliberalist discourses of democracy and human rights. Though transnational codifications of human rights and neoliberal doctrines are in many ways opposed to one another, each also, through their contemporaneous oppositionality, came to bear features of the other, and to modify or highlight its elements through a complex process of mutually transformative interaction. Exemplifying this, the BAUEN's claims carefully attend to private property, even as neoliberal and post-neoliberal government administrations phrase their policies in terms of protecting human rights, including rights to justice, cultural equality, and work.

Looking at the concrete changes in the nature and practice of work and the legal and economic forces that influence and regulate it, as well as contemporary forms of social protest, reveals that the idea of work is being conceptualized and deployed in new ways in Argentina (Battistini 2004). Key to this transformation is the way workers define themselves as such, after having been pushed out of the traditional labor market. The figure of the worker as a social identity provides the members of the BAUEN Cooperative and the rest of the recuperated businesses movement with an argument for legitimacy that resonates with previous notions and contradicts the primacy of highly mobile financial capital and labor "flexibilization" in neoliberalist philosophy. Their reactions to and defenses in the face of the legal and discursive challenges mounted against them forefront stable and regular work as a fundamental right, rather than a benefit or a privilege. Thus, the cooperative draws on and attracts people committed to historically prominent ideologies in Argentina, including leftist and center-leftist Peronism as well as traditional socialism. The members of the cooperative, however, seek to adapt these inherited ideologies to the current political situation: a post-neoliberalist, post-crisis Argentina now infused with an ineludible discourse of human rights. Their insistence on work as a right thus cannot be read as either an entirely new phenomenon or as a return to the thinking of a previous era. Rather, their the actions and words reveal the way they have innovatively revitalized historical patterns and trajectories.

Conclusion

In advancing their demands, both Memoria Activa and the BAUEN Cooperative express particular visions justice, and each uses the language of rights to articulate what it believes the role of the state should be in protecting and assuring these rights. Memoria Activa draws on the tradition of human rights activism in Argentina in demanding justice through legal accountability for the perpetrators of the attacks. It also demands legal prosecution of the state agents involved in covering up or obstructing the investigation. Drawing on notions of active memory and invoking Jewish traditions, it asserts a vision of state and nation based on the rhetorical foundations of modern democracy through strong legal institutions and an effective justice system. In doing so, it insists on justice as a fundamental right of all Argentines. Similarly, the BAUEN appeals to the need for economic justice, forefronting work as both a right of citizenship and a human right. It rejects the privileging of rights to private property over workers' rights, yet it delegitimizes the former business owners, who seek to displace the workers, by highlighting the illegality of the business failures and by seeking to restructure laws favoring capital over workers. In the next chapter, I turn to another aspect of the idea of rights embedded in the demands made by these groups: the right to collective well-being.

Chapter 4

The Right to Collective Well-being

THE MOST RECENT MILITARY DICTATORSHIP, through its isolation of individuals and undermining of the capacity for constructive interaction, was a destructive force on social life in Argentina. Neoliberalism, rather than opening a space for social reconstruction, had many of the same effects.[1] Though the methods and aims were different, the atomization of individuals and the dismantling or discrediting of the structures for participation in public life were a legacy and a continuation of a process begun with the violence around the 1976 coup. As Carlos Forment has argued, "Neoliberal policies took aim against the 'social,' understood as the relations, interdependencies, and trust among citizens which serve to sustain public life" (Forment, n.d.). Corruption and impunity, which for many people and organizations, including groups like Memoria Activa and the BAUEN Cooperative, are the anchors for the country's contemporary maladies, play a major role in this corrosion of the social. By undermining trust in the government, public officials, the justice system, big business, and the employer-employee relationship, the attitudes and patterns summarized in the figures of impunity and corruption are deemed the source and ultimate determiner of today's ills, lying at the heart of issues as diverse and yet connected as police brutality and extrajudicial killings (*gatillo fácil*), the ineffectiveness of the judicial system, and the recent spate of discoveries of Bolivian and Paraguayan immigrants forced to live and work under conditions of modern urban slavery in the heart of Buenos Aires. Corruption's effects are taken as pervasive and destabilizing, eroding society from within: "Both the everyday practices and the moral critiques of 'corruption' were bound up in the construction of an evaluative framework that not only expressed the untrustworthiness of specific institutions, but also went so far as to question the very possibility of sociality" (Muir 2011:196).

By identifying corruption and impunity as the key issues, Memoria Activa and the BAUEN Cooperative work against their effects, insisting on forms of social solidarity that counteract the individualistic tendencies inherent in Argentine neoliberalism. This chapter examines how they conceptualize and enact social solidarity, arguing that symbolic acts performed at the international, national, and local levels reconfigure the possibilities and premises for social interaction. The tendency to work for social betterment rather than individual retribution is a common feature, I argue, across many Argentine human rights organizations, and can be seen in a case brought by Memoria Activa in 1997 before the Inter-American Commission on Human Rights in the OAS. This case accuses the Argentine state of violating the rights of its citizens by failing to bring justice and security in the wake of the AMIA bombing. The emphasis on sociality and solidarity can also be seen in the logic of cooperativism embraced by the BAUEN Cooperative and the recuperated businesses movement. In each case, the demands made by Memoria Activa and the BAUEN argue for a more inclusive sense of the social and an alternative moral framework than that are embodied in (neo)liberalism and the normative transnational frameworks of human rights. Like those discussed in earlier chapters, each of these acts centers on ideas of human rights, the role of the state, and the meaning of democracy.

A New Politics of Memory

La memoria no se construye en los museos sino en las calles, luchando para cambiar la historia.

Memory is not constructed in museums, but in the streets, in the struggle to change history.

> From a plaque on the corner of A. Gallardo St. and Corrientes Ave.,
> by the neighborhood assembly of Almagro

The political crisis of December 19–20, 2001, which spawned a rapid succession of five presidents in a span of two weeks and record levels of unemployment, reaching over 50 percent in some areas, was a durable symbol of the impoverishment that gripped the population. In 2003, a little-known governor from the Patagonian province of Santa Cruz was ushered in as the newly elected president. Néstor Carlos Kirchner soon proved himself a formidable politician, and gained solid national popularity and high approval ratings, based in large part on his immediate adoption of a new policy of human rights. His wife, Cristina

Fernández de Kirchner, a national senator at the time of her husband's election and herself elected president in 2007, has likewise advocated the prosecution of human rights offenders throughout her political career, and her presidential administration has continued and built upon the policies they enacted during the 2003–2007 era.

In spite of Alfonsín's attempt to achieve a viable transitional justice through military and later civil trials of the leaders of the military government, the prosecution of perpetrators of state-enacted violence was forestalled and remembrance of the era officially subsumed under the "theory of the two demons." The government's stance on the dictatorship era and issues of memory and impunity changed drastically with the assumption of power of Néstor Kirchner on May 25, 2003. Kirchner came to the presidency in a political climate in which it made sense to demonstrate symbolically a radical difference with previous administrations. Though elected with a mere 23 percent of the vote,[2] Kirchner garnered considerable public support during his tenure as president, maintaining high approval ratings from across numerous social sectors. This success, which allowed him to consolidate *kircherismo* as a formidable political force, was based at least in part and initially on his adopting a strategy regarding the memory of the dictatorship era different from than of his predecessors.

Kirchner worked to dismantle the earlier politics of forgetting. His first actions once in office were to force high-ranking military and police officials to retire in order to bring about a change of command in these institutions. He also made immediate reforms to the judicial system, which was vital in bringing about the processing and disrobing of members of the Menemist Supreme Court on charges of corruption. These steps, perhaps one of his most important legacies, have led to the previous immunity/impunity laws of Due Obedience and Full Stop being declared unconstitutional, allowing the perpetrators of the state-sponsored violence to be tried in Argentine courts.[3]

In addition to engineering these moves, Kirchner proved adept at performing powerful symbolic gestures that resonate with many Argentines. The March 24, 2004, anniversary of the 1976 coup that inaugurated the most recent dictatorial regime was like no previous one. Counterimpunity groups had for years observed this date with acts of remembrance for the Dirty War's victims and renewed calls for justice. These events, through their codification of memory, in many ways set the stage on which Kirchner chose to perform. The events had in general not been actively supported by the different national administrations in the post-dictatorship years. But in 2004, Kirchner joined in this time of remembrance by carrying out evocative public spectacles that symbolically justified rather than minimized the counterimpunity groups' insistence on the need for their voices to be part of the narrative of national history. As was triumphantly noted by the center-leftist (and eventually Kirchnerist) newspaper *Página/12*, this was the first time the commemoration was organized by the national government and the first time the state organized an official act of repudiation of the military coup.[4]

In addition to the massive march and numerous cultural activities organized by human rights organizations, Kirchner orchestrated two additional actos for the 2004 anniversary. In the first, Kirchner and nearly his entire cabinet went to the Colegio Militar, or Military College, where he ordered the head of the army, Roberto Bendini, to take down the portraits of Jorge Rafael Videla and Reynaldo Benito Bignone, two of the principal junta leaders from the dictatorship. Kirchner then addressed the assembled cadets, demanding that they leave behind "the hell" into which state terrorism had plunged them. He also invited them to reencounter "their San Martinian history" and their role as the armed branch of the people, and thus a part of and not separate from it.[5] By forcing the head of the army to publicly remove these portraits, Kirchner was both reaffirming the civilian government's dominance over the armed forces and eliciting a moment of public self-criticism from the army.

Yet even a time as radically new as this moment of submission was eclipsed by the other government-organized event of the day. Kirchner left the Colegio Militar for the Escuela Mecánica de la Armada (ESMA, Naval School of Mechanics). The ESMA was known to be one of the largest detention centers where for years during the repression the disappeared where held and tortured. Over five thousand people are thought to have passed through the ESMA, most never to be seen again. Those who did survive have described the horror and raw brutality that was unleashed within its walls. Located in the neighborhood of Núñez, within sight of El Monumental, the stadium of the soccer club River, the ESMA remained under the control of the navy after the end of the dictatorship era. El Monumental was the site of the championship game in the final round of the 1978 World Cup, in which Argentina secured the nation's first World Cup victory. Survivors of the ESMA relate the contradictory experience of living this moment of national glory from inside the walls of a prison camp, hearing the cheers of those on the outside as the Argentine national team scored its goals only meters away. For survivors and the victims' loved ones, its continued presence as a naval institution was yet another haunting reminder of the void disappearance had left behind. The ESMA had become a symbol of state terrorism, a site for demonstrations or exhibitions of the continued call for truth and justice for those responsible. For years counterimpunity groups had been demanding that it be taken from the navy and turned into a museum.

It was this site that Kirchner chose to publicly demonstrate an official break with the past. After spending several months consulting with a committee of representatives from several counterimpunity organizations, that March 24 Kirchner and Aníbal Ibarra, then head of government for the City of Buenos Aires, publicly signed an agreement that in effect removed the grounds and buildings that made up the ESMA from the navy and restored them to the City of Buenos Aires. The agreement also established that the site would be remade into "A Space for Memory and the Promotion and Defense of Human Rights" (*Espacio para la Memoria y para la Promoción y Defensa de los Derechos Humanos*). Tens of thousands of people attend the event, which included musical performances by León Gieco, Víctor Heredia, and Joan Manuel Serrat, and speeches by children of the disappeared who had been born in the ESMA.

After signing the agreement, Kirchner spoke, stressing a dual identity for himself in addressing the crowd. On the one hand, he presented himself as a leftist militant from the 1970s, from the same generation as the disappeared, continuing the struggle to construct a better nation. "Just now when I saw your hands, when you sang the National Anthem, I saw the arms of my *compañeros*, of those from the generation that believed and those of us left who still believe that this country can change." But he also spoke as President of the Nation, and in doing so, apologized in the name of the state for the lack of justice following the dictatorship era.

> Things have to be called as they are, so here, if you will permit me, not now as the *compañero* and brother of all those of us who shared that past era, but as President of the Argentine Nation, I come to ask forgiveness on behalf of the National State for the shame of having kept quiet so many atrocities during twenty years of democracy.[6]

He also, as he had with the act in the Colegio Militar, unequivocally repudiated the actions of the dictatorship:

> Let us speak clearly: It is neither a grudge nor hate that guides us. I am guided by justice and the struggle against impunity. Those responsible for the horrid and macabre act of having these many detention centers, like the ESMA was, have only one name: they are assassins rejected by the Argentine people.

Using the word "assassins" (*asesinos*) is in itself a political act in Argentina, denying the military's assertion that its actions were just(ified). Doing so was a clear adoption of the discursive language of the human rights organizations. Kirchner also achieved an initial popularity though attempts to include the opinions and voices of these groups in the planning of human rights policies. For example, the nature of the Museum of Memory planned for the ESMA was neither decided by the government nor in place at the time of the March 24, 2004 act. Rather, there was a convocation for proposals, and the final use of the space was to be decided in cooperation between the city and national governments, survivors, the victims' families, human rights groups, and other "representative organizations of civil society."[7]

Michel-Rolph Trouillot has written about the conditions of possibility for this kind of public ritual, with actors making apologies for historical wrongs in which they personally were not implicated. As he notes, these apologies depend on the attribution of aspects of the liberal subject to collective actors, such as, in the case discussed here, the state. Furthermore, "the moral or legal case . . . for an admission of guilt can be made only . . . on a particular composition of the subjects involved and on a particular interpretation of history" (2000:174). Kirchner here was, as president, speaking in the name of the state, which, he asserted, bears the responsibility for the wrongs (now defined as crimes) committed in the ESMA. This places Kirchner firmly on the discursive side of the counterimpunity organizations, and forcefully distances him from the theory of the two demons propagated by earlier administrations.

But, as Trouillot also observes, the postulation of a collective actor that can take responsibility and express repentance rests on a problematic assumption of historical continuity. The state that Kirchner purported to personify is hardly the same as that imagined or that which functioned under the dictatorship. But while Trouillot says this makes these performances abortive rituals, unable to act tranformatively (2000:184–185), I argue that even given Kirchner's dubious assumption of the continuity of the state, this speech *could* act as a transformative ritual, or at least the beginning of one. Trouillot is correct in saying that, given the complicated nature of collective subject identification temporally removed from the events, an apology in itself can do little to bring about reconciliation between offenders and offended. However, to declare as Kirchner did that impunity exists necessarily assumes that a wrong has been committed. In apologizing, Kirchner was asserting a view of history that categorically denies any interpretation that justifies the dictatorship's actions or, importantly, state policies that either deny that wrongs had been committed or allow these crimes to remain unpunished, unrecognized, and unresolved. To the extent that it was followed by concrete actions to attend to the sense that impunity reigns, this moment has had the potential to bring real change in Argentine social and political life. In this way, Kirchner's words resonate with the quote that opens this section, which notes that the construction of memory is more about the future than the past. Thus, whether or not Kirchner could speak in the name of previous incarnations of the state, he could alter the future by altering the official historical memory of the past. But importantly, as the quote highlights, Kirchner's act only had the force that it did because it came in response to the prolonged activism of those who sought such a change.

While Kirchner's collective apology garnered strong popular support and copious attention—some people considered the apology (literally) "monumental"—it was not uniformly well received. Numerous counterimpunity organizations and individuals feel that Kirchner's actions and rhetoric functioned as part of a political strategy to co-opt or placate opposition through symbolic public spectacles while avoiding real reform. Many of these accuse Kirchner of trying to appropriate for himself the issue of human rights while failing to act concretely to undo the impunity or dismantle the economic system that they argue is inherently related to the injustices committed under the dictatorship and after. These criticisms, voiced at the time of the ESMA event, became even more acute three years later when Kirchner made a similar gesture and commemorated the thirty-first anniversary of the coup by announcing the creation of another museum in La Perla, an infamous former detention center in the interior city of Córdoba. The leftist opposition points to continuing police brutality, torture inside state-run prisons, stalled legal actions against former repressors, and recent acts of repression against workers as incongruencies in Kirchner's "politics of human rights."[8] As one critic expressed it, "Kirchner took a new path, articulating a discourse favorable to human rights, at least formally, [but] to the human rights of the past, not current ones" (Rodríguez 2010:306).

On the other side of the spectrum lie those who reject these gestures on the grounds of their symbolic meaning. One of sources of the continued strength of the counterimpunity groups is precisely the fact that there is still active opposition to the negative characterization of the military dictatorship from both inside the military and other social groups. In spite of official denials, rumors abounded in the days before March 24 that the portrait of Bignone to be removed had been stolen and replaced by an imitation, thus symbolically preventing its removal under Kirchner's orders. On the day of the event, two generals and a colonel requested retirement in protest. An apartment complex in front of the ESMA proudly displayed a "Long Live the Navy" banner while Kirchner signed the agreement, and shortly after the anniversary an organization known as Complete Memory (Memoria Completa), demanding a "revision of the past in both senses," called for a mass to be held in rejection of the March 24 event. A graffiti I observed in the porteño neighborhood of Once in 2006 likewise expressed opposition to the Kirchner government through reference to his past as an activist (Figure 5). The use here as well of the term *asesino* rhetorically references the actions of the militarized left in the lead-up to the dictatorship as criminal.

The desire of some in the military to avoid the kind of delegitimation of their actions through legal condemnation should not be underestimated. In December 2007, former navy officer Héctor Febres poisoned himself or was poisoned four days before he could be sentenced for human rights violations during the Dirty War.[9] This act is perhaps less momentous in its effects than

Figure 5 Graffiti reading "If you are a murderer and guerilla, you will be president," a derogatory reference to Néstor Kirchner's self-identification with the leftist struggle of the 1970s. Photo by the author.

other attempts to influence the outcome of the trials of former repressors that followed Congress's overturning of the impunity laws in 2003, such as the disappearance of key witness Julio López in 2006 in another case. Nonetheless, it is significant in revealing the symbolic weight these trials hold for certain members of the military. Many of those who suspect Febres' death was not accidental argue that it was intended to prevent his implication of other members of the military in crimes. However, and regardless of the intentions of those involved, avoiding his condemnation functioned as a deliberate and meaningful act in the struggle over historical memory. Disputes over the meaning and memory of the dictatorship era and its place in Argentine history hold continuing relevance.

The new space of remembering opened by the Kirchner administration's stance has also enabled other kinds of reflection previously suppressed to be more freely expressed. Attempts to solidify an oppositional memory carry the danger of silencing other voices, in part because of the need to contest official versions (Jelin 1994:53). This has been a source of contention and has contributed to the lack of unity among the counterimpunity organizations. This new moment of reflection has led to the publication in recent years of a number of books, articles, and editorials, and the staging of public forums such as talks and conferences by former left-wing activists on the activities of these groups in the 1960s and 1970s. Without justifying the dictatorship's actions, the new climate of acknowledgment of past violence has allowed ex-guerrilleros and their supporters to publically reconsider their role in and response to the bloodshed leading up to and during the dictatorship era. In this way, official condemnation of the era of state terrorism has made possible a more nuanced and multivocal understanding of the era.[10]

Alison Brysk noted in 1994, "To the extent that human rights movements . . . in Argentina fall short of their goals, it is because they fail to capture and transform the state: military, police, judiciary, and Executive" (1994:xiii). Ten years later, it was precisely changes throughout these spheres that brought a new official approach to human rights. The shift in the official discourse on human rights initiated under Néstor Kirchner has led to a profound change in how groups seeking change interact with the government, both in language and in action. Through its policy of protecting human rights and prosecuting offenders, the government has contributed to a discursive reconstruction of the social, based on mutual trust, solidarity, and the rule of law. This is not to say that this reconstruction has always been fully effected in practice. However, groups using the language of human rights in articulating their claims now operate within a profoundly different climate. The administrations of Néstor Kirchner and Cristina Fernández de Kirchner have adopted policies aligned with transnational normative frameworks for human rights in their insistence on justice through prosecution of perpetrators of crimes like torture and disappearance. The trials of those involved in the repression continue as of this writing, with several significant sentences having already been handed down. The administrations have also relied upon richly symbolic acts like the ones described here, placing an importance on memory that many argue has contributed to a broader social healing. Groups like Memoria Activa and the BAUEN Cooperative likewise embody a vision of rights that gives primacy to social reparation and collective well-being. For Memoria Activa, this is most evident in a case it brought against the Argentine state in the Inter-American Commission on Human Rights (IACHR).

An Unharmonious Accord: The Caso AMIA in the IACHR

Faced with a continued lack of progress in the AMIA case locally, in July 1999, five years after the AMIA attack, Memoria Activa filed suit with the IACHR against the state of Argentina. The IACHR and the Inter-American Court of Human Rights, part of the Organization of American States, are the organs within the OAS for the promotion and protection of human rights. Functioning since 1979, they operate according to legal instruments, principally pacts or conventions, as well as a small but significant set of established precedents, to which their signatory members are bound. By this time, the IACHR had a strong reputation among Argentine human rights groups for its rulings on several cases, including one in 1992 finding the laws of Full Stop and Due Obedience and the amnesties granted by Menem to be incompatible with the 1978 Convention on Human Rights. However, its rulings were often largely symbolic and unlikely to lead to concrete changes, at least in the short term (Farer 1997).

Memoria Activa was initially supported and accompanied in its case by CELS and the Center for Justice and International Law (CEJIL), an international NGO dedicated to "achiev[ing] the full implementation of international human rights norms in the member States of the Organization of American States (OAS) through the use of the Inter-American System for the Protection of Human Rights and other international protection mechanisms."[11] In addition, it was represented by a private lawyer, Alberto Zuppi (with the later addition of another private lawyer, Pablo Jacoby).

Memoria Activa accused the state of Argentina on two major counts, each for violating the state's obligations as a signatory of the American Convention on Human Rights, or the Pact of San José, which Argentina ratified in September 1984 upon the official return to democracy. The first accusation concerned the right to life and physical integrity of the victims of the AMIA, as guaranteed under Articles 4 and 5 of this convention. Memoria Activa argued that, following the 1992 bombing of the Israeli embassy, the Argentine state had the obligation to foresee the possibility of another attack and respond appropriately in order to prevent such an occurrence. It contended that the Argentine state "failed to adopt the necessary measures to prevent the attack," charging that the police protection of local Jewish institutions was inadequate and noting the intelligence services' lack of attention to indications and warnings of a second attack.[12]

The second count concerned the violation of the rights of the victims and their families to obtain justice through local tribunals, as guaranteed by Articles 8 and 25. It denounced numerous irregularities in the investigation carried out by Judge Galeano and his office (*juzgado*), claiming that the Argentine state had "violated to the detriment of the relatives of the victims the right to the judicial guarantees that ensure that the causes of the events that produced the damage be effectively investigated, the right that a regular process be followed against those responsible for having produced the damage, and that as part of this process the guilty be sanctioned and the victims compensated."

In taking its case to the OAS, Memoria Activa effectively removed the question of citizenship rights from a closed state–citizen relationship and drew on the international codification of human rights in bodies like the IACHR. This set of laws and precedents has historically been intimately connected to a globalized and homogenizing discourse on the nature of human rights. There are two seemingly contradictory but in fact inherently linked elements of the normative notion of human rights as initially formalized in the international sphere. First, rights were generally assumed to pertain to individuals (rather than groups). Furthermore, they were necessarily meant to be universal, by definition valid only if and as applicable to all individuals equally, regardless of nationality, ethnicity, race, or religion.

The idea of the universality of rights, and their location in the individual, has come under scrutiny. The assumed universality is based on cultural assumptions that are themselves far from universal. In addition, as Harri Englund has shown, human rights discourse requires that we pay close consideration to who has the authority to participate in it (2006:193). The very nature of the appeal to the notion of human rights can carry with it a recourse to elitist notions of the nature of rights. In the case Englund studied, "squabbling over political and civil freedoms, the ruling elite and its non-governmental watchdogs effectively silenced public debates on social and economic rights" (2006:10).

As early as 1843, Marx condemned the French Declaration of the Rights of Man and Citizen for failing to "go beyond the egoistic man" (1977:43). The Declaration and its twentieth-century counterparts contemplated rights as pertaining to individuals, not to classes or communities. The core conception of human rights remained fundamentally based on an individualized notion of the person in ways inherently tied to the Lockean idea of democracy founded on the inherent abilities of free individuals to act and interact as the basis for society.

This individualist orientation came into conflict with collectivist notions of rights, especially with regard to indigenous modes of conflict resolution and property ownership. Increasing recognition of collective rights as essential to the worldview and full protection of non-Western cultures has been a key development in international human rights law in recent years. Movements from across the world have challenged the individual bias in international conceptualizations of human rights leading to, for example, the 1989 ILO convention on the rights of indigenous and tribal people (Postero 2007; Speed and Collier 2000; Yashar 2005). Ángel Oquendo has argued that Latin America as a whole has "launched a true revolution on collective rights, moving beyond the paradigm of group entitlements . . . to that of comprehensive entitlements which generally pertain to society as a whole" but can be claimed by a single litigant (Oquendo 2008, cited in Couso, Huneeus, and Sieder 2010:10–11). Such entitlements include not only indigenous rights but in many cases rights in the name of a collective good, such as environmental protection.[13]

The IACHR, although retaining a focus on civil and political rights over social or economic ones (Huneeus 2010:133), and without fundamentally challenging the individualist orientation embedded in its legal procedures, does allow for certain kinds of collective claims. It accepts claims seeking to redress wrongs committed against entire communities, and it has recognized organizations such as Amnesty International and Human Rights Watch as "individuals" competent to bring claims against the state (Farer 1997:546). However, while the Memoria Activa case is concerned with collective over individual rights, the issues at stake are not about securing the right to appeal as a collective to gain collective retribution or to maintain cultural autonomy through the protection of collective rights. Rather, Memoria Activa is concerned with the need for broader institutional changes that will lead to greater security for society as a whole. Specifically, it demands structural and institutional changes designed to build a particular vision of democracy and benefit the nation as a whole (through unification rather than separation into particular collectivities within it). In keeping with these goals, Memoria Activa's insistence that the attacks and their mishandling are problems that affect all Argentines extends to its legal efforts to achieve resolution. OAS observer Claudio Grossman argued in his report to the IACHR that Memoria Activa's petition should be considered admissible not only under the articles it proposed but also under Article 24 of the American Convention, which guarantees the right to equal protection before the law for all persons without distinction. The report states that "the Observer recommends that the case be declared admissible in function of Article 24 of the American Convention on Human Rights to the extent that this attack could reveal a discriminatory content of anti-Semitic character" (Grossman 2005:96). Memoria Activa refused. It did not make its demands in these terms or under this article initially, nor has it done so subsequently. By choosing not to appeal on these grounds, it remains committed to the idea that the failures of the Argentine state lie not solely or even principally in its treatment of a specific minority community. This open definition of the problem echoes the insistence by many within and outside the Jewish community that the attacks and their lack of resolution are problems affecting all Argentines. The desire to foster the social by strengthening democratic institutions and thus benefit all Argentine society holds embedded within it an alternate form of justice, one inextricable from the kind of resolution Memoria Activa seeks.

Memoria Activa's devotion to institutional changes of benefit to all of society springs from culturally embedded notions of the social, which value community solidarity and collective benefit. This is not to argue for a fixed (and certainly not an inherent) idea of Argentine "culture." Rather, I want to highlight how notions of rights and justice in Argentina are formulated in the interaction between local context and meanings and the ideas that circulate within transnational regimes of rights (Goodale 2007b). Even as Argentina has played a foundational role in the development of transnational rights and institutions, the understandings of rights expressed and understood locally often challenge or deviate from the normative forms. The logic and procedural imperatives of the legal system at the foundation of transnational regimes of human rights form a kind of legal instrumentalism (itself a cultural artifact), and as such are not always easily reconciled with the varieties of local goals and understandings (Riles 2006).

An example is the use of the term "genocide" to refer to the state terrorism of the most recent military dictatorship. Within the Argentine human rights community and the broad sectors of the populace that have adopted the idea of human rights as the foundation for their democracy, it is common to classify the violence as genocide. The establishment of concentration camps and the abduction, torture, and killing of youths lend support to this interpretation. However, under the standard international definition, based in the 1948 Convention on the Prevention and Punishment of the Crime of Genocide, what occurred in Argentina is not technically genocide. "The very conception and legal definition of genocide was forged in a highly politicized atmosphere, one that resulted in inclusions and exclusions and a moral gradation of atrocity. The destruction of political groups, while abhorrent, was written out of the convention and became something else, an implicitly lesser crime" (Hinton and O'Neill 2009). Given that the Argentine dictatorship targeted those whose only resemblance to one another was that the regime considered them a potential threat, and that the violence lacked an ethnic or racial basis, it is hard to apply the term genocide to this case under international law. This is not to say that one interpretation is correct and the other erroneous, but rather to underscore the discordance that can exist between valid and meaningful local definitions and formal codifications within the international legal sphere, the construction of which is itself fraught with cultural assumptions and political interests.

Another example of this discordance played out one morning in the Plaza Lavalle. Some supporters who had gathered that morning criticized Memoria Activa's petition to the IACHR. The formal petition was presented in representation of only four individuals rather than all the victims. A bitter argument ensued between the critics and a relative of one of the group's lawyers. She vehemently denied the charge that the wording of Memoria Activa's demands showed that it was acting only in its own interest. Instead, she insisted that the formalized language required for these documents did not allow Memoria Activa to appeal on behalf of all the victims, and she made a point of bringing a photocopy of the legal document and the guidelines for filing the petition the following week.

Nonetheless, the intention of Memoria Activa in making its appeal to the IACHR and the specific acts of restitution it demands in response reveal its commitment to collective well-being through the construction of a specifically imagined kind of democratic institutionality. At the first audience of the AMIA case in the IACHR in Washington, D.C., in 2001, the Argentine state under

President de la Rúa argued that the decision should be postponed until after the trial of Telleldín and the police officers, which was about to begin. Furthermore, it proposed that the IACHR appoint an observer to report on its proceedings. This was accepted, and Chilean lawyer Claudio Grossman was designated as the observer. The verdict in the trial was announced in 2001, and Grossman presented his report recommending that the IACHR accept Memoria Activa's accusations on February 25, 2005. With this report, it was clear the Argentine state faced condemnation, and in March 2005, the IACHR called for an audience of the AMIA case. Even before the audience was held, the government announced it would assume responsibility for the deprivation of justice following the AMIA bombing. This extraordinary announcement marked an absolute reversal of the position of the state in the AMIA case. In place of the denials and claims of good management offered by previous administrations, the Kirchner government chose to publicly announce the state's guilt. In their declaration in front of the IACHR on March 4, 2005, the representatives of the state accepted the terms of Memoria Activa's original denouncement, saying:

> The government recognizes the responsibility of the Argentine State for the violation of human rights as denounced by the petitioners . . . as there existed a failure to fulfill the function of prevention by not having adopted the necessary and effective measures to avoid the attack. . . . There existed a covering up of the facts, due to a serious and deliberate failure to fulfill the function of investigation . . . and because this failure to follow through with regard to an adequate investigation produced a clear deprivation of justice. (From the Acta CIDH [IACHR Record], March 4, 2005, case 12.204)

The government went even further, formally asking Memoria Activa and all family members of AMIA and embassy victims for forgiveness,[14] reminiscent of Kirchner's public apology for the actions of the dictatorship. This admission of guilt was also subject to the same evaluation by those receiving it— though highly significant symbolically, its transformative power would rest on whether it would be followed by concrete institutional changes.

This admission of guilt avoided the state's condemnation by the IACHR in 2005, and allowed for Memoria Activa and the Argentine state to enter into a process of "friendly resolution" (*solución amistosa*). The drafting of the terms for this process, which continues under the oversight of the IACHR at the time of this writing, resulted in a detailed list of measures the state would agree to undertake. The first of these, and one of the few to have been fulfilled to date, was the publication of the Grossman Report (which validated Memoria Activa's position regarding the trial and the actions of the state) and the formalization and dissemination of the state's acceptance of guilt. The Grossman Report was subsequently published on the website of the Ministry of Justice. The public acceptance of guilt was finally formalized through Presidential Decree 812/05, though its release was delayed six months, until July 2005. In the eyes of many, this was a bald-faced PR move, designed to follow a long pattern of the government showing "advances" in answer to the public clamor that peaks around each July 18 anniversary. However, the content of the decree was well received by Memoria Activa.

The majority of Memoria Activa's principal concerns have not been similarly addressed. These are not based on individual reparations or even on judicial proceedings. Rather, they were drawn out of the experience of the AMIA bombing but are designed to better, as frequently expressed by a key member of Memoria Activa in our conversations, "the institutionality of Argentina as a whole" (*la institucionalidad de la República*). For example, Memoria Activa insists on the strengthening of the Special Investigating Unit for the AMIA attack (a part of the Ministry of Justice and Human Rights), the improvement of the system of registry in the Department of Migrations, the creation of a special catastrophe unit, and the reform of the use of funds by the Secretariat of National Intelligence to make it more transparent. These points have proven considerably harder to implement. The lack of a system of coordination between the different public emergency services undoubtedly led to the destruction of valuable evidence and perhaps increased the loss of life in the AMIA attack. Neoliberal outsourcing of security and emergency functions did not improve the situation. Ten years later, in December 2004, a nightclub fire just blocks from the AMIA site left 194 dead, mostly youth. The lack of a coordinating unit of emergency response, which had never been implemented despite the need so tragically evidenced after the AMIA attack, was once again widely considered to have led to a substantial increase in mortality, compounded by corruption among the officials responsible for safety inspections of the building.

Ultimately, taking the case before the IACHR secured for Memoria Activa international confirmation of the legitimacy of its claims (the right to justice and protection by the state) and led to the Argentine state's proclaimed recognition of the state's responsibility in this regard. Memoria Activa's definition of justice contributes to a critique of the lingering individualist bias in normative regimes of human rights. Individual reparations and even accountability for those responsible are not sufficient in reconciling the wrong wrought upon the social body by (in Memoria Activa's eyes) the inadequate functioning of democratic institutions. Rather, Memoria Activa is concerned with a collective form of justice. This entails ending impunity and corruption and strengthening democratic institutions, and hence addressing and redressing the causes of the failures in the case. In honing in on the strengthening of institutions and state mechanisms for the protection of citizens, Memoria Activa is advocating one form of collective well-being. This contributes to a growing tendency in the discourse circulating around international bodies like the IACHR for the protection of human rights. The individualist bias in human rights has been increasingly challenged in recent years as collective rights have gained greater recognition. In this, Memoria Activa's case is significant since it is not about collective rights for any particular group alone but instead rights like those to a clean environment that promote a holistic, collective well-being, one that, in this case, is joined to a specific vision of institutional democracy. I now turn to a closer consideration of the idea of collective well-being.

Sociality and the Limits of Liberalism

The actions of Memoria Activa and the Cooperativa BAUEN carry an embedded concern for collective well-being in opposition to the primacy of the individual within both neoliberalism and the normative international framework of human rights. Each of these derives its basis in the individual from lingering and entrenched percepts of the historical phenomenon of liberal ontology. The relationship of individualism to liberalism is expressed by Ileana Rodríguez:

> Individualism is the solid and unswerving bedrock upon which liberalism firmly rests and to which all other concepts of liberalism refer; all liberal concepts flow from individualism, and nothing can be understood outside of it. In actuality, human and natural rights are coterminous with the rights of the individual. Together they constitute a synergy that holds together the edifice of liberalism and that underwrites its particular claims to universality. Hence, if this core concept is flawed or insufficient, as historians of colonialism have strongly demonstrated, the whole theoretical edifice is tremulous, ready to collapse under the weight of its own tacit assumptions and presuppositions. (2009:12)

Walter Mignolo makes a similar point in exploring the history of the idea of Latin America. He argues that the history of modernity, along with the liberal philosophy that enabled and accompanied it, is also the history of coloniality. That is to say, coloniality and modernity are two sides of the same thing (Mignolo 2005). This is not to cast all "Latin Americans" as subscribers to non-liberal philosophy, but rather to excavate the underpinnings of the tenets that governed the terms of the debate under neoliberalism. Activists in Argentina in the years surrounding the turn of the twenty-first century have contested these terms, drawing on their geographical and historical positionality in rejecting what they cast as neoimperialism. Their rationale bears much in common with communitarian critiques of liberalism, which aspire to redirect attention from autonomous individuals to the notion of social responsibility.[15] Yet this rejection of individualism does not come out of a predisposed adherence to anti-liberal philosophies, but in reaction to the daily experience of people living under neoliberal reforms in a postcolonial world. Furthermore, this world is one in which liberalism had always been subject to modification and local adaptation. The kind of sociality advanced by Memoria Activa and the Cooperativa BAUEN, in advocating a particular kind of human rights in Argentina, challenges the limits of liberalism by rejecting its premises. Even more, this sociality has, in the aftermath of the last military dictatorship, become tied to notions of democracy as the opposite of authoritarianism. Democracy in the eyes of these groups is based not on individual freedoms but on government working for the benefit of society. As such, both neoliberalism and authoritarianism are rejected as attacks on the common good. Corruption and impunity are the focal points that categorize violations of rights under this actually existing, individualistic democracy.

A clear and poignant example of the way the importance of the social is highlighted and integrated into an alternative notion of democracy is evident in a No Smoking sign that I chanced to see hung on the wall of the Centro de Salud Mental y Acción Comunitaria No 7 (Center for Mental Health and Community Action Number 7), in the northern Buenos Aires neighborhood of Núñez. The serendipity of discoveries like this, where a particular aspect of cultural life is so clearly and elegantly encapsulated in ways an anthropologist can only hope for, was for me an essential feature of and rationale for extended fieldwork. This faded and slightly yellowed sign, poorly printed out on a piece of office paper and taped up at the bottom of the stairwell, admonished visitors that:

Fumar en el hospital atenta contra la convivencia. La Ordenanza 47.667 del Honorable Consejo Deliberante lo prohíbe. Si ud. [sic], a pesar de ello, fuma

aquí, da muestra de su propio autoritarismo, de su desprecio a la salud ajena
y de su descuido por el hospital, que es público, lo que quiere decir "de todos".

To consider this warning line by line: The first thing we are told is that smoking in this hospital is an attack on social living. *Convivencia* denotes basic rules for coexisting with others, like those taught to kindergarten children. The next line informs us that Rule or Decree number 47,677, an appropriately obscure number relying in all its weighty importance on assured levels of bureaucratic efficiency, is the precise rule that we would be breaking. Furthermore, this rule was decreed by the Honorable Deliberating Council, carrying the lexical connotation of having been fairly and morally decided by a group, which carefully considered the matter and made a joint decision. The next line begins with an injunction to *Ud.*, the formal third-person singular for "you," which should grammatically be capitalized, but here is not, which could be seen as a denigration of the figure of the individual. If this demoted "you" chooses, in spite of Honorable decrees, to smoke there, "you" are showing your "authoritarianism," or your own tendency to act in a dictatorial, and thus inherently undemocratic, fashion. The use of words like "authoritarianism" in contemporary Argentina cannot escape from an implied reference to the most recent military dictatorship. To use this term is to invoke the widespread discursive condemnation of Dirty War violence by the military and of those who would impose their will on society. Finally, we are told that you the smoker are acting selfishly, by "showing your lack of respect for the health of others" and failing to properly care for the hospital, which "is public, which means belonging to everyone." The appeal to the public, the social, and the condemnation of any who would act in a way that imposes their will over others and over the good of the group is the central logic by which this sign makes its injunction.

It is, however, worth noting that smoking in public places was still a widespread and commonly accepted practice in Argentina, and such a strong condemnation of such a frequent and generally tolerated act rings as being both noteworthy and somewhat out of place. The injunction was also, in my observation, nearly entirely ignored. However, the rationale it uses in making its appeal to its viewers fits the notions of the public good that underlie the motives of many protest organizations. For the rest of this chapter, I look at how the members of the Cooperativa BAUEN stress and express the notions of collectivity and democracy in their words and actions. Specifically, I consider how the concern for collective well-being is expressed is in the notion of *compañerismo*.

Cooperativism and Solidarity[16]

In her book *Ordinary Affects*, Kathleen Stewart writes that "modes of attending to scenes and events spawn socialities, identities, dream worlds, bodily states and public feelings of all kinds" (2007:10). Such "modes of attending" or ways of seeing not only spawn socialities etc., but are also informed by them. This dialogic process, by which ways of understanding and interpreting situations are both determined by and productive of social relationships, applies as well to collective practices of resistance. Barbara Sutton, in her work on women activists' narratives in Argentina, observes that these narratives "also suggested that poner el cuerpo [lit., "putting forth the body," used to express dedication to a cause] is about togetherness, about engaging other bodies in the project of creating social change, of building power together from the bottom up. From this perspective, poner el cuerpo as a practice of resistance is not a lonely or individual task, but a collective, embodied process that sprouts solidarity and valuable knowledge" (Sutton 2010:176). Likewise, Jeffrey Juris has drawn attention how the act of protesting can be productive of what he terms "affective solidarity" among those engaged in protests. He relates how "the ritualized inversion of established hierarchies during political protests generates new visions and powerful feelings of affective solidarity" (2008:77). In the case of the BAUEN, the act of protesting (understood broadly) has been productive of both affect and solidarity among its members. The socialities created through, in this case, a prolonged protest contradict and dispute the individualism and atomization propelled by neoliberal capitalism. However, affect and solidarity, though in many ways spawned by the act of protest, also, as in the case of Memoria Activa, draw on deep-seated and partially submerged ideas of sociality.

Reactions to the notion of collective well-being are reflected in the choice of words to describe this phenomenon (Rebón 2004:34–36). Names can be not only descriptive but also potentially productive of understandings and interpretations. There are a few sectors that refer to the businesses and factories in what I have been calling the recuperadas movement as *usurpadas* or usurped. This term is typically restricted to the right-wing press and to those who perceive and wish to code the workers' actions as a crime. In alleging the workers' actions are inherently illegal, they argue for the moral superiority of restoring the property to its "rightful" owners. The name *reconvertidas* or reconverted is preferred by certain agents of the state, particularly those within the Ministry of Labor, who hope to reinitiate production within the businesses without expropriating them. Some within the movement choose to call these businesses *ocupadas* (occupied). In doing so, they emphasize the method of struggle, drawing a connection between these takeovers and earlier, union-directed takeovers as a mechanism for putting pressure on the owners. The term *auto-gestionadas*, or self-managed businesses, highlights instead the workers' ability to operate the establishments on their own. This name is often used by those who wish to draw connections and alliances with other worker-controlled projects, like the *autogestionados* in Brazil. Likewise, this term has also been adopted by ANTA, the Asociación Nacional de Trabajadores Autogestionados (National Association of Self-managed Workers, or ANTA), formed in 2005 by some eighty cooperatives as a section of the CTA (Argentine Workers Central Union, or CTA), an umbrella union group that split off from the Confederación General de Trabajo (General Confederation of Labor, or CGT) in 1992. ANTA includes neighborhood-based and farming cooperatives as well as some recuperadas.

Despite these variations, I found *recuperada* to be the word most commonly used by the workers' themselves. The meaning of the word *recuperada* is compactly expressed in the words of one BAUEN Cooperative member:

> Our dedication is unshakable. We are caring for a different Argentina (*estamos cuidando una Argentina distinta*). Our conflict with the Iurcovich family [the former owners] is a reproduction of the one that exists between the business-people who sunk this country and the workers, who generate work and not inflation. We are doing everything that an ordinary businessperson has not done: we pay taxes, we pay our suppliers in full and on time, we reinvest in the installation and [for this] we suffer chronic attacks, because we believe that those who produce, the honest ones, those that think of businesses as social goods are those who save the country.[17]

As reflected in these words, a dominant meaning of having "recuperated" a factory or other business is of having recuperated a source of labor. In this view, it is the nation's productivity that is being recuperated after the crisis, one business at a time, a reversal of the long decline of Argentina's self-identity as an industrialized country. Workers often cite how the word "Bauen" itself carries the meaning "to build" or "to construct" in its original German, drawing a symbolic connection between their struggle and the rebuilding of the nation. They also reflect this in the naming of the cooperative. The very name BAUEN, which stands for *B*uenos *A*ires, *U*na *E*mpresa

Nacional (Buenos Aires, a National Company), encapsulates the fundamental message of the workers in insisting the hotel is in the service of the public, national good. Their moral injunction to collective well-being refers to the need for a kind of sociality and moral consideration that places the viability of a national business, which by nature enmeshes workers, suppliers, and owners in a unified system of interests, over an individualized concern with earning money or responding only to the interests of a limited set of individuals, such as stockholders or investors.

Cooperativismo

The notion of *trabajo sin patrón*, or worker-self management, lies at the core of the recuperated businesses movement. No longer workers in a relationship of dependency to the owners of the business, cooperative members collectively own the business and can shape its direction, purpose, and future. They often cite what is referred to as the *costo patrón*, or the cost to the business of having an owner. The exorbitant salaries that businesses executives might take for themselves, the common practice of siphoning profits from one business to invest in another or placing them in off-shore accounts, and the weight of a bureaucracy of managers earning considerably more than the workers engaged in direct production or operation are all frequently mentioned as factors leading to business insolvency. Under cooperative management, the members argue, decisions are made collectively on how to reinvest or distribute the profits they themselves generate. Collective ownership allows for equal or equitable distribution of resources and strengthening of the business.

Although there are many issues yet to be resolved in the implementation and practice of worker control, the notion of cooperativism has become central to the recuperated businesses movements. The word *cooperativismo* refers to labor being organized collectively and oriented toward the benefit of all. It also includes a moral sense of cooperation, both between the members of a cooperative and with society at large (Faulk 2008a; Reed and McMurtry 2009).

Cooperativism itself in various forms has a long history in Argentina, beginning with the mutual aid societies (like the AMIA) created by immigrant groups around the turn of the twentieth century (Munck 1998; Sábato 2004). In the second half of the twentieth century cooperativist groups produced several important institutions, including cooperative credit unions and educational institutes.[18] These went through numerous vicissitudes as they contended with the various military dictatorships, which often imposed restrictive laws, reducing their possibilities for action. Forming workers' cooperatives was also a union strategy for placing pressure on owners during the 1980s, most notably in the case of the metalworkers union (Rebón 2004:29–30; Fajn et al. 2003:185–219).

Though this history undeniably has affected the form of cooperativism in the recuperated businesses movement, the relationship between these earlier or already-established supportive organizations and the recuperated businesses movement is not direct. The impulse behind the current recuperated businesses movement comes from a mixture of political ideologies, with its principal promoters coming from traditional Peronist, militant unionist, and organized leftist political backgrounds. Some of these promoters came from or initially worked with existing organizations devoted to cooperatives, but these organizations were ultimately unable to adapt to the needs and realities of the workers recuperating businesses. In an important way, these recuperated businesses adopted cooperativism in response to the particular historical moment at the time they emerged. It is these workers' lived experience that has been key in the formation of a discourse of cooperativism and work as a right, more so than the influence of political ideologies. The history of these workers, and the cooperativism they have embraced, cannot be separated from the era that produced them and was a direct challenge to the neoliberalist ideas that led to the dissolution of their source of regularized labor. The disenchantment intensified by the sense of entrenched impunity and corruption in the political and economic system produced the prominence of *autogestión* (self-management) as the central rationale of post-neoliberal cooperatives.

In what follows, I discuss what I see as three different though complementary aspects of the logic of cooperativism being expressed in the BAUEN Cooperative and the broader recuperated businesses movement. I distinguish analytically between what I call formal cooperativism and affective cooperativism, or *compañerismo*. By formal cooperativism, I refer to the association of workers into legal or otherwise formalized cooperatives as a means of organizing management and production within the workplace. This differs from what is generally called compañerismo, which connotes working together for the benefit of the group. In addition to these two aspects, I consider the community support that the BAUEN has garnered through its self-definition as a community resource dedicated to protecting and promoting "culture" as an essential feature of community life.

Compañerismo

The Other Bauen   The importance of compañerismo or affective cooperativism among the workers of the Bauen was clearly expressed one October day, immediately following a protest march against a city judge who had ordered the hotel's closure. This order accused the cooperative of failing to have the proper safety authorizations to operate a business, and was based on formal complaints (*denuncias*) filed by individuals directly connected to, and acting in the interests of, the former owners of the Bauen. While technically true, cooperative members argue that this overlooked the numerous papers they had filed attempting to address the problems cited and regularize their situation. Not having legal tenancy of the hotel, their attempts were thwarted at every step in the convoluted process. The protest march, which had noisily installed itself outside the judge's office for more than an hour, was heading back to the Bauen when a few of those in the lead decided not to stop in front of the doors of the hotel. Instead, they continued to lead the march up Callao Street to Corrientes, where they turned left and stopped in front of the Bauen Suites, a former partner hotel to the Bauen, which had not been closed at the same time and which remained in the hands of the Iurcovich family.

This decision was spontaneous as far as I was able to discern, and was suggested and led by a few of the core male members of the cooperative (though none of those that held office, nor those who were typically responsible for designing the cooperative's political strategy and protest tactics). Initially the idea of taking the march in front of the Bauen Suites seemed to center on the figure of the former owner, who was considered responsible for the dilemma that had precipitated the day's activities. Indeed, in other moments marches had paused briefly in front of a restaurant that Iurcovich owned only a few blocks away. However, once in front of the Suites and directly facing the workers of that hotel, many of whom had been former coworkers of those now organized into the cooperative, emotions ran higher than in any of the many marches that came before or after. One member of the cooperative, the head chef, whose rotund figure was encased as always in his entirely white work clothes, took hold of the megaphone. In an increasingly impassioned manner he called out against those inside, asking them why they had not had the courage to join in their struggle nor had demonstrated solidarity with them when the hotel had been closed and their jobs liquidated. His words seemed to give voice to feelings of rage and pain shared by many of his compañeros. For the first and only time in any of the many marches I accompanied, some members became violent and began to break minor exterior features of the Suites, including smashing a standing sign and ripping out the plants that decorated the entranceway. The doors had been locked upon our arrival, though I doubt anyone would have tried to enter, and the confused and frightened faces of hotel guests were visible from behind several layers of glass. (Later the story circulated that one Suites guest, afraid to leave the hotel while the marchers were outside, had missed his flight out of Buenos Aires. The workers' response was to offer him a room in the Bauen—"Y bueno, lo podemos poner acá" (Okay, well, we can just put him up here). More poignant, though, was the observant but pained expression of one Suites' security guards, who faced unflinchingly but with obvious distress the accusations ardently hurled from the other side of the glass.

This event reveals the utmost importance that compañerismo had taken on for the members of the BAUEN Cooperative. Though their struggle for survival was with the institutions of the state and members of the business elite, emotions ran highest when they confronted what they considered a betrayal of their cause by other workers who could have but chose not to either take the same risks as they had or to renounce their job in solidarity with those who had lost them. It was the failure to act in concert with the group, and to join in their struggle and sacrifice, that produced the strongest and least controlled or calculated emotion.

Singing for Solidarity The emphasis on compañerismo also rings out clearly in the chants that the workers improvise and sing during the marches. Chants have a long history in public demonstrations throughout Latin America and are famously employed as rallying cries and points of enjoyment during soccer matches, with fans of opposing teams competing to outdo each other with the volume and creativity of their songs (Archetti 1997). The chants taken up during protest marches are generally patterned after a standard set of rhythmic tunes, and often draw on traditional forms in their construction, changing only a few words to fit the situation. For example, "El BAUEN/unido/jamás será vencido" (the BAUEN/united/will never be defeated) is a basic modification of the widespread "el pueblo/unido/jamás será vencido" (the people/united/will never be defeated). Another telling example has excited chanters calling upon the observer to participate: "borom bom bom/borom bom bom/el que no salta/tiene un patrón" (borom bom bom/borom bom bom/whoever doesn't jump/has a boss). This chant has a simple elegance in encapsulating the essence of *trabajo sin patrón*. It serves as a powerful interpellation to those accompanying the marchers from other organizations, whether from political parties, neighborhood assemblies, or even unemployed workers, to truly join in their movement and embrace this new logic of organizing production. For this reason, though frequently used, it often produced a moment of tension, with only a core group of workers joining in the circle of jumping chanters. At one of these marches a member of an alternative press organization covering the event looked around a little sheepishly and jokingly explained, "Well, I do have a boss." He jumped anyway, in solidarity, but that particular chant served to potently mark and remind everyone of the essential nature of these workers' struggle.

The sense of play and creative invention that often accompanies these marches comes through in the way these songs are crafted and transmitted. Many times I walked alongside groups of two or three workers as they bantered back and forth suggested lyrics, which would then quickly be taught to and carried on by the marchers as a whole. This process gave rise to another popular example: "vamos compañeros/hay que poner un poco más de huevo/ estamos todos juntos nuevamente/la dignidad del BAUEN no se vende, se defiende" (come on, compañeros, we've got to try a little harder [lit., put our balls into it]/we're all together again/the dignity of the BAUEN is not to be sold, but defended). By calling on those assembled to work together harder, this chant expresses the essence of compañerismo.

Affective Kinship   For many members of the cooperative, compañerismo and a sense of solidarity with other workers are both literally and figuratively expressed through the idea of the family. In the BAUEN, as in many other recuperated businesses, once the business began to function again, the original small group of workers who had occupied the installation needed to incorporate others into the cooperative. Many of these were former coworkers, but as the need for more hands increased, the offer of work was frequently extended to family members of the workers. The presence of actual family members within the cooperative added another dimension to the way compañerismo was felt and expressed among many in the cooperative. As one member said:

> Here, really with all that we've done, all the sacrifices, together with our compañeros, here we have practically the entire family of each compañero. If one doesn't have a child here, they have a sibling, and if not, a cousin. Here we are, practically the whole family, and so it's for that reason perhaps that we're more united than ever because when they touch one of us it's as if they touch all of us. When the compañeros saw that they were hitting us women it nearly turned

into a massacre, but we tried to stop those compañeros because there weren't many of us there. How were we going to let them, with all the assault vehicles there, when there were like five hundred police officers and only ten of us?

Here, she slips between talking about actual family members and the way the members of the cooperative would see each other as family. The conflation of real and figurative family adds another dimension to the cultural context that must be taken into account in considering corruption. I have never heard of giving preference to family in incorporating new cooperative members described as a form of corruption. Though the decision to incorporate family members was contentious, the debate centered on whether the cooperative would be better served by adding the most qualified personnel available rather than those most in need of work or already implicated in the struggle, as family members were seen to be.

Formal Cooperativism

A cooperative is "an autonomous association of persons united voluntarily to meet their common economic, social and cultural needs and aspirations through a jointly owned and democratically controlled enterprise" (ILO R193, art. 2A).

From the 1995 International Cooperative Alliance, Declaration on Identity and Cooperative Principles, Manchester, England, adopted by INAES

Affective cooperativism has its counterpart in the formal cooperativism that is the mode of organization for the majority of the recuperated businesses. While the idea of compañerismo is strongly expressed throughout the recuperated businesses movement, the level of formal cooperativism varies widely and in practice takes on numerous forms. These differences typically depend on the history and circumstances of the factory or business and the internal organization and political stance that, given these factors, the factory or business has chosen to adopt.

Though the procedure and some details vary according to provincial laws, presently forming a workers' cooperative in Argentina requires registration with the Instituto Nacional de Asociativismo y Economía Social (National Institute of Associations and Social Economics, or INAES). Created by presidential decree in 2000, the INAES centralized the laws on cooperatives.[19] Legally registering a cooperative provides workers with certain rights and protections and gives them legal standing. For this reason, many involved in recuperating their source of labor chose to formally organize and register as a cooperative.

A few recuperated businesses decided to register as *sociedades anónimas,* or corporations. Although providing a legal status, a corporation is both more expensive to form and ineligible for the tax benefits enjoyed by cooperatives. In practice, forming a corporation has perhaps afforded these businesses a more stable and lucrative place within the capitalist market. Nonetheless, legal organization within a structure that embraces the values of cooperation has been a powerful discursive tool for the recuperated businesses movement.

The adoption of the cooperative format in not interpreted uniformly, however, and even among businesses that choose cooperativism there are significant differences in their plans of action and internal organization. Considering these differences and the reasons cooperative members give for their choices reveals some of the fundamental contradictions at the heart of the recuperated business movement, the BAUEN included.

There are two main visions of the ideal solution to the legal uncertainty surrounding the majority of the recuperated businesses. For the BAUEN, the formation of a workers' cooperative was an essential and desirable step in designing the internal organization of the hotel under worker control. The BAUEN ultimately seeks to have the state expropriate the hotel, which it argues is the principal creditor of the millions of dollars of debt left by the former owners. The state would then either cede or concede the building and its installations to the cooperative. Thus, for the BAUEN and many other recuperated businesses, the workers' cooperative is attractive not merely as a temporary expediency, since it provides legal standing during the period of uncertainty and a method of formal internal organization, but is also desirable as a permanent institution. "Property is a relationship embedded in a cultural and moral framework that produces a particular vision of community" (Postero 2007:89). The BAUEN sees collective ownership of the business by its workers as the basis for the organization of a community that embodies cooperativismo and social responsibility through collective accountability for the source of wealth.

Some other recuperated businesses, however, intend their organization as a formal cooperative to be a temporary measure rather than a desired permanent outcome. The largest and best recognized of the recuperated businesses that fall into this category is the ceramic factory formerly called and still widely referred to as Zanón, now operated by the cooperative FaSinPat (Fábrica Sin Patrón). Unlike their allies at the BAUEN, the Zanón workers demand that the state expropriate and maintain the title to the factory, which would be run under worker control but remain public property, not owned by the cooperative.

The underlying issue in this debate revolves around one of the central predicaments faced by workers in recuperated businesses: how can a cooperative, dedicated to solidarity and the collective good, fit into (and survive in) a capitalist market? For FaSinPat, this quandary is one more reason to demand state control of the factory, as a means of protection. FaSinPat member Raúl Godoy, at the time also secretary general of the Ceramics Workers Union of Neuquén, explains:

> For us, the cooperative isn't the end solution, because one has to compete against enormous conglomerates that set prices, like San Lorenzo or Alberdi, groups that export, have foreign capital, international credits, that lobby. . . . We're vulnerable. If they lower prices for four months to kill us, they'll take us out of the game.[20]

The danger to cooperatives is real, but many have been viable as businesses and have even expanded production and created additional jobs. Therefore, debates over desired final solutions often take a backseat to the more urgent questions of day-to-day operation and survival.

In addition to facing the issue of ultimate goals, the cooperatives also confront more immediate questions over how to interpret and adhere to cooperativist principles within a neoliberal capitalist climate. One of these concerns how new members are incorporated into the cooperatives as production resumes and additional labor is needed. In some cooperatives, members of local unemployed organizations have given the first available jobs. In the case of the BAUEN, the need for additional labor grew quickly, and the cooperative prides itself on having created around 150 jobs. The initial expansion from the 32 people who entered the hotel in 2003 to the creation of a stable workforce was not without debate, however. Both within the BAUEN and in other recuperated businesses, there are some who believe that it is more important to select the most skilled workers in order to preserve and enhance the productivity and profitability of the business. Others argue for the importance of offering jobs to those who most need them. As shown above, the BAUEN eventually decided to first offer positions to family members, as they "are the ones already paying the price of our being here." For the BAUEN, the concept of work is not purely rationalistic, but includes an affective dimension.

Debates over remuneration and distribution of profits have also arisen within the recuperated businesses. The laws on cooperatives under INAES stipulate only that, rather than receive wages (*salarios*), the cooperative members deal in the distribution of earnings among themselves (*reparto*). Many of the recuperated businesses follow an ethic of equal distribution among all members, without gradations for position or seniority. In these cases, an agreed upon amount is usually also set aside for investment in the business. However, in the early and difficult days of many cooperatives, the scant earnings would be either entirely dedicated to putting the business in operation again or given to workers whose need was considered greatest due to their personal circumstances. Within the BAUEN, during the initial days of operation the distribution of pay was equal, but as the need for labor increased and new workers were incorporated into the cooperative or hired on a temporary basis some members began to feel the need to distribute earnings on a gradated scale, one that included a recognition of time with the cooperative.

In all of these debates, the resolution in practice is rarely fixed and unchanging or devoid of internal contradictions. The legal uncertainty surrounding many recuperated businesses, including the BAUEN, forced the construction of an internally coherent practice to be to some degree postponed, with attention focused squarely on the sheer survival of their efforts.

One way of mitigating the contradictions has been to direct production or the provision of service toward the benefit of the community. Thus, although some businesses have, through either choice or necessity, concentrated on the money-making aspects of production, others have decided and been able to direct more effort to community service. One way of doing so has been the donation of goods or services to local community organizations or the establishment of community programs, including secondary schools and health clinics. Cooperatives such as FaSinPat emphasize putting the factory in the service of the community as part of the goal of turning the installations into state-owned, worker-operated enterprises devoted exclusively to the needs of society as a whole. The BAUEN differs from FaSinPat in embracing formal cooperativism as a permanent solution, but shares the core ideal that business should serve the community.

Building a Community: Trabajo Lucha Cultura

The final aspect of the logic of cooperativism that has particular relevance for the BAUEN is the nature and extent of the collaboration among recuperated businesses and the relationship of these businesses with the broader community. As a large hotel with nearly two hundred functioning rooms and ample meeting space, the Bauen is able to comfortably host conferences, workshops, and exhibitions, as well as events such as wedding receptions and parties. This has allowed the cooperative to develop as a central player and referent in the recuperated businesses movement, as well as among the community of people and organizations concerned with social justice from a variety of perspectives.

From the beginning, the cooperative counted on the support it received from neighbors, university groups, and other individuals and organizations sympathetic to its cause. As one member explains:

> Then, when we began to go to the neighborhood assemblies to tell what was happening, what was really [happening], that we were fighting for our source of work, that we were [in] here, they came from the university, they helped us, they decided to bring yerba, sugar, so we could drink mate, eh, they brought a bit of rice, and they came from over there, from the food bank, they helped us a lot, so after that we began to move a little, we began to learn from this, what it is, what work is.

Her narrative relates not only how the cooperative both cultivated and received support from numerous groups, but also how she sees the change in the concept of work emerging from the possibilities opened to the BAUEN Cooperative through this support.

Collaboration between recuperated businesses has also been important and has taken a variety of forms. These have included organizing umbrella movements, cultivating individual mutual aid or trade relationships between recuperated businesses, and staging recuperated businesses expositions.[21] The BAUEN has played a central role in this collaboration by lending event space and by providing material and other forms of support to many other cooperatives. It also helped organize and hosted one of the expositions, which was designed to promote cooperation between and publicize the recuperated businesses and their products/services.

From the time it reopened its doors, the Bauen has also provided meeting space, often free of charge, to a wide variety of groups beyond the recuperated businesses movement. A few of the many examples of this include its use by subway workers on strike, workers from Garrahan State Hospital during their extended conflict with the government over compensation and working conditions, international anarchist groups, piqueteros (street picketers), HIJOS, and those concerned over the Dirty War–style disappearance of a man who was to testify against a former repressor.[22]

In providing a space for the issues and agendas of other groups, the BAUEN Cooperative attests to the idea of the hotel as a space for building community, belonging, first and foremost, to the people. The cooperative recognizes the need to disseminate the idea of work based on cooperation, and as such insists that all workers are welcome in the Bauen, both those from the recuperated businesses movement and those "in relationships of dependence" (*recuperados o en relación de dependencia*). It also provides assistance to individuals and groups in need, such as offering free lodging to patients from the interior provinces who come to Buenos Aires to receive operations at state hospitals. In this way, to quote the words of one cooperative president, the workers of the BAUEN have transformed the space "de cuna de la burocracia a cuna de la sociedad," from the cradle of the bureaucracy into the cradle of society.

The BAUEN Cooperative also highlights the importance of artistic expression as fundamental to the construction and expression of citizenship. The hotel has a constant run of movies and theater productions, and its marches and protests are frequently accompanied by performances from major cultural figures, such as the director of the Teatro Colón, or popular countercultural rock bands, who volunteer their support. The BAUEN Cooperative adopted *Trabajo Lucha Cultura* (Work, Struggle, and Culture) as its motto, brandished on the enormous banners that proclaim its identity in street protests. The attention to artistic expression integrates an element of playfulness into the BAUEN's struggle, with its protests often being as full of festiveness as they are of determination. The interweaving of work with artistic expression at once draws in further support for the BAUEN's cause, especially among youth, and adds another dimension to the reconfigured idea of work based on ideas of social well-being and cooperation over and above profitability.

The articulation of the Bauen as a space of popular cultural expression establishes links with broader struggles in contemporary Argentina over the use of public spaces and their recuperation from private hands. This reappropriation and resignification of public space encompasses a wide range of interests, including human rights and memory activists and street artisans. As one group expressed it, as part of their struggle to keep their community center open in spite of government attempts to close it down:

> The refusal to recognize that cultural and social spaces fulfill the function of articulating the participation of neighbors with the production of our local artists within a context of values of solidarity and of collective work is to refuse to recognize that cultural spaces are the builders of citizenship and of social, collective, and democratic participation.[23]

In the same way, by emphasizing Work, Struggle, and Culture, the BAUEN insists that the opening of a space where events can be planned and held fulfills an important function within society, one that goes beyond the articulation of the interests of any one group or faction within the movement or the community as a whole. The conflation of public and private undermines the division inherent in liberalism itself (Pateman 1983). This adds another element to the concept of citizenship as advanced and practiced (and advanced through practice) by the BAUEN Cooperative. Such alternative practices of citizenship differ strongly from neoliberal models of civic engagement and are closely related to how the BAUEN Cooperative understands democracy.

Democracy Inside and Out: The Role of Social Responsibility

For the members of the BAUEN Cooperative, as for Memoria Activa, the idea of collective well-being is embedded in a particular understanding of democracy. Like corruption, impunity, and human rights, "democracy" is not a neutral category, but is culturally imbued with multiple meanings and manifestations. As a continuum of political practices encompassing a seemingly endless diversity of forms, what democracy entails, and the extent to which any particular political system can be fairly categorized as democratic, is open to widely varying definitions and interpretations. For many, the idea of democracy in postdictatorship Argentina is discursively linked to social accountability, in the sense of recognition of the self as part of a larger group (in this case, democratic society) to which the self bears a responsibility for the proper functioning and well-being of the collective. This sense of the group, and the importance of solidarity, has a resonance in Argentina that reverberates through society across and across class lines. Though political formulations from a variety of angles interpret and address what solidarity implies in different ways, it is a constant feature of social discourse.[24] This linkage of the democratic to the social, inflected according to local socio-historical particularities, draws on deep-seated notions of social responsibility and solidarity and has recently been forcefully asserted in opposition to and rejection of authoritarian governance on the one hand, and the individualism of neoliberal citizenship on the other.

Though the discourse of democracy in Argentina inevitably invokes its rejected counterpart, dictatorship, the widespread sense that the existing democratic political system is unfair has proved the most difficult challenge for groups organized in recent years. A crisis of legitimacy has besieged the Argentina government at least since the 1990s, culminating in the social eruption of December 2001 (see, for example, Colectivo Situaciones 2002; Svampa 2002). The recent lack of faith in all politicians has certainly affected the way electoral democracy is perceived and talked about in Argentina.[25] Regardless, and apart from the complications that arise from their continued insertion within a capitalist market, recuperadas must also continue to operate within an established system of public administration. The practical implications of this, and its effects on members' notions of democracy, can be seen in the interactions the BAUEN Cooperative has had with the Buenos Aires City Legislature.

Part of the legal strategy the BAUEN Cooperative has pursued in fighting for the legal right to operate the hotel has involved putting pressure on the national and local governments to get them to pass laws of expropriation (*leyes de expropiación*) that would firmly place the hotel in the hands of the workers. While a permanent expropriation would be their ideal solution, the cooperative has also tried to push a temporary expropriation law through the Buenos Aires legislature. In consultation with the BAUEN, Congressman Diego Kravetz, a lawyer and founding member of the MNER, introduced legislation that would have given the cooperative legal protection to operate the hotel. Similar laws had been passed for a few other recuperated businesses in the city, notably the 2004 law that authorized the temporary expropriation of thirteen factories. However, though this law stipulated that the state indemnify the former owners, Congress has failed to pass the accompanying budgetary legislation that would provide the funds to do so. This lack of funding poses a real danger to recuperadas pursuing this form of legal protection and validation.

The project proposed by Kravetz asked specifically that the hotel be considered of public utility (*utilidad pública*). Like eminent domain, this juridical notion, most often invoked for the appropriation of privately owned lands for public works projects such as highways, implies that the Argentine state has the right and obligation to put to public use that which can benefit the people as a whole. Granting this status to the Hotel Bauen would provide the legal grounds for its expropriation by the state. The BAUEN Cooperative's forceful appeal to this juridical principle places the right of citizens to collective well-being over private property rights.

The temporary expropriation law presented by Kravetz on behalf of the BAUEN passed through the Congress's Development Commission and, in August of 2005, was passed by the Comisión de Presupuesto (Budgetary Commission), which meant that it was then eligible to be voted on by the legislature as a whole. However, a counterproposal was suddenly presented by Congressman Jorge Morando, an ally of the right-wing politician Mauricio Macri (in 2007 elected head of the government of the Autonomous City of Buenos Aires). This counterproposal, though it entailed numerous legal irregularities such as not having passed through the Development Commission as is mandatory, was passed by majority vote in the Comisión de Presupuesto also in August 2005. The project proposed recognizing the Iurcovich family's claim to ownership of the hotel through the firm Mercoteles and creating a negotiating commission, which would include such cooperative members as had been formally employed by the Iurcovichs (i.e., and not those contracted under the hotel's subsequent management by Solari, S.A.), to discuss the terms of their continued employment, to take place once again under the Iurcovich family.[26]

The workers were forced to wait under continuing legal uncertainty for these projects to come up for a vote. Early on November 3 they finally heard that the projects were on the agenda for that day. They quickly called for support, and hundreds gathered in front of the legislature building on Peru Street to urge against the passing of the Morando bill, as it was known. Approximately seventy members of the cooperative had gained permission to attend the session as part of the viewing public. In spite of this, though allowed inside the building, they were prevented from entering the floor itself. After waiting seven hours in the cold white stone passages that led to the symbolic center of political decision-making, the gathered workers listened anxiously to Congressman Kravetz as he updated them on the situation. The hard truth was that the cooperative's project did not have the votes to pass, but the Morando project did. Therefore, Kravetz proposed accepting some of the terms of the Morando project, which would allow the cooperative the right to negotiate a settlement. At any rate, he argued, it would buy the cooperative time, during which it could lobby the head of the city government, Aníbal Ibarra, to veto the law. A discussion was quickly held. Many workers expressed why accepting this proposal was so difficult. For the workers, accepting Iurcovich as the owner meant ignoring the layers of corruption that surrounded the selling of the hotel and the process of its bankruptcy. One member shouted out, "If Iurcovich wants to be recognized as the owner then let him show the papers proving it!" Furthermore, the project at its best would result in a return to working for a boss, "trabajo con patrón." And lastly, the project provoked resistance by putting the right to private property ahead of the right to work. The MNER and the Cooperativa BAUEN argued, "Businesses are not exclusively private property, but rather social goods. They are built with a lot of human capital and the labor of the workers."[27]

With their own project for temporary expropriation as good as dead, the workers understood that they had limited options at this critical juncture. Should the Morando bill pass, the former owners and right-wing political forces would have a potent tool to use against the cooperative's fight to hold onto the hotel. Should the legislature act, the workers' situation would become all the more precarious. The frustration of the cooperative members was visible. MNER and certain members of the cooperative had spent months meeting with legislators, visiting their offices, lobbying, trying to win votes for their proposal. Now, suddenly, they could seemingly do little to stop a vote against them. Within moments of the impromptu debate spawned by Kravetz's explanations, Fabio Resino, from the MNER and an integral figure within the BAUEN, shouted out over the din, "Okay, raise of hands, all those in favor of accepting this proposal?" No one moved. "All those in favor of bursting onto the legislature floor and preventing a vote on the Morando law?" Cheers erupted, and the workers moved off toward the inner doors leading to the session hall.

No longer content to accept their restriction from the session floor, the workers pushed through the human barrier of police and congressional security and won their way through the doors. They burst into the circular depressed cavity ringed by polished wooden benches where the legislators were gathered in small groups. From the public seating areas in the highest level of the hall, the workers rained down cries of "Bauen es, de los trabajadores, y él que no le gusta, se jode, se jode" (Bauen belongs to the workers, and whoever doesn't like it can go to hell), and other cries against those who refused, through action or omission, to support their efforts. Pounding, clapping, yelling, their objective was simply to make it impossible for this government body to continue the proceedings. After a while, the legislators accepted the inevitable and closed the session. The vote on the Morando proposal had not come, and the workers left.

How can these events be interpreted? What kind of democracy can the members of the cooperative have believed in? It would perhaps be possible to view the actions of the BAUEN Cooperative as undemocratic, since the protestors purposefully prevented a freely elected body of Congress from conducting its business and did so to prevent a vote they were likely to lose. Yet this was not their interpretation. As many of members insisted in the lead up to and following this event, it was the actions of the legislature that were undemocratic. This was in part because of an overwhelming sense among members of the cooperative that the kind of "democracy" offered by and practiced within the legislature was one already heavily stacked against them. The BAUEN workers, even and often especially those not intimately connected with planning and implementing the cooperative's political strategies, repeatedly mentioned to me their impression that the legislature was not playing by the rules, that they were up against an unresponsive and unfair system.

Their allegations were both general, directed against the political system as a whole, and particular. They cited in minute detail the numerous irregularities presented by the Morando proposal, including its failure to follow the proper channels (which the BAUEN proposal did follow, and which in practice meant months of stressful waiting) and its granting legal recognition of ownership when this was still disputed in court. Furthermore, many were convinced that Morando had himself been paid to present the proposal against them. Several members mentioned to me how it was certain that Morando had received his little suitcase of money (*valijita de plata*) for having brought the law to the floor.

For the members of the BAUEN Cooperative, the question became, how can you play their game if they don't play by their own rules? For the BAUEN workers, the answer lies in their practice. Their interruption of the legislature session that day reveals two aspects of this practice. On the one hand, their forced entry into the floor of the session was a literal irruption of those affected by the laws being debated into the sphere of debate. Their physical presence forced onto the scene a visual reminder, at least, of their actual existence as noise-making, bodily entities, in contrast to the sterilization and flattening of existence effected through the inscription onto sheets of paper of language that codified, but failed to recognize, their position as stakeholders in the process. Furthermore, their prevention of the vote on the Morando proposal, and their accusations against the measure and those supporting it, challenged the workings of politics as usual within the chamber. Their presence exposed the nature of political practice within the body, defying the legislature and legislators to live up to their own rules.

On the other hand, the actions of the cooperative that day were also an example of an alternative to this kind of practice. The space outside the legislature session hall witnessed a moment of direct democracy, of the kind that rallied the workers around a position rather than isolating them from the process. This is not to allege that democracy as practiced within the BAUEN is strictly egalitarian or devoid of hierarchy. Indeed, debates over the nature and practice of democratic decision-making within the recuperated businesses are some of the most hotly contested. Nonetheless, the existence of these debates seems to give workers a sense of confidence in the way democracy is practiced in the recuperadas, a confidence that workers do not have in governmental institutions. The significant difference lies in that democracy as practiced within the BAUEN Cooperative inspires confidence rather than distrust among its members. Furthermore, its members believe that democracy should be practiced in a way that fulfills the obligations of social responsibility and collective good, something the actions of the legislature, they contend, frequently fail to achieve.

The struggle has also led to a change in some cooperative members' understanding of their role in the political system. Rather than feeling alienated from the workings of politics, some now feel empowered to try to change the system itself. One member pointed to her experiences with the cooperative for her newfound understanding of workers' rights as citizens, rights both to protest the corrupt politics of elected officials and to influence the governmental policies that most directly affect their lives:

> Yeah, this has totally changed my life, the fact of having seen this, and I've never, as I always say, I've never gone in for any political party, I'd never known what it was, never entered a legislature building or stepped into the National Congress. And I more or less was a little afraid of the politics . . . of these people, like, legislators. Maybe I was a little afraid because I'd say "I'm going to go talk to a legislator? Why?" Now it's like, "No, we're the ones who vote for them. They have to receive us. And, why wouldn't they receive us?" It's thanks to us that they are there, so they really have to provide us with a solution. Not us going to ask them for a favor, when it's they who are representing us. That's why we gave them our vote. So, I'm totally different now than what I was before, no?

Conclusion

The official discourse on human rights in Argentina was fundamentally changed with the inauguration of the Kirchner administrations. With the actions of the Kirchners, human rights gained the official recognition that many human rights organizations saw as an essential step in renewed social cohesion and healing. In this new climate, the axis of debate has been reoriented, and the principle of collective well-being, always present in the demands of many groups advocating the full realization of rights, has taken center stage. Collective well-being, as an issue of citizenship and human rights, is deeply implicated in the way members of these groups think about the practice and promises of democracy. Any attempt to satisfy the demands of groups like these that does not take into account their commitment to collective well-being will ultimately be incomplete. It remains to be seen if the notion of collective well-being, which emerged strengthened precisely because of the attempts to undermine it during the neoliberal era, will gain full and concrete legal and administrative expression in the years to come.

Chapter 5

Conclusion

Rethinking Citizenship and Human Rights

H ISTORICALLY, state and capital have been closely intertwined in Latin America. The very production of the modern state in Argentina in the early 1800s sprang from the need of the entrepreneurial class to formalize and regulate property rights and commerce (Adelman 1999). The role of government officials throughout the next two centuries in facilitating the penetration of foreign capital illustrates the porous boundaries between the state and the evolving interests of transnational capitalist accumulation (Romero 2002; Striffler 2002). Even though the most recent dictatorship continued rather than invented the collusion of government and capital in Argentina, it dramatically dismantled forces favoring economic stability based on sustainable and equitable principles. The horrific scale and methods of the repression that enabled the economic restructuring led the figures of torture and disappearance to take center stage in defining violations of rights. The imperatives of the neoliberal experiment and its implementation and consequences in Argentina precipitated the shift of attention to ideas of impunity and corruption, which capture the source of the abuses in the nexus between government institutions, the local political and economic elite, international lending agencies, and multinational corporations (Teubal 2004; Vilas 2004). This book has provided a historically grounded, ethnographic exploration of how notions of impunity and corruption are the principal interpretive trope for groups currently engaged in petitioning the government to attend to their rights. The articulation of this demand through words and actions not only addresses the particular issues around which protest groups have organized, but also presents concrete visions of the state and society. These groups draw on historically resonant notions of sociality and an expanded discourse of human rights in challenging dominant conceptions of the role of the state and of its citizens. In this concluding chapter, I reflect on some major themes that have run throughout this book.

Performing Memory and the Nation

Memory, commemoration, and the invocation of history constitute one of these themes. Public enactments and visual displays have been essential to the performance of memory and history in Argentina. These multifarious displays can be thought of as "spectacles." Daniel Goldstein uses the word "spectacle" to describe certain forms of public performance, defining it as "a form of political action based on visual display, undertaken by specifically positioned social groups and actors attempting to stamp society with their own agenda" (2004:18). The actions and actos of groups like Memoria Activa and the BAUEN Cooperative and the many exhibitions of the politics of memory utilized by different national governments and social sectors—from the staging of the 1978 World Cup to Menem's visible enactment of multiculturalism to the carapintada rebellions to Kirchner's removal of military portraits—rely on this kind of spectacular performance in invoking and constructing specific notions of memory, of national history, of national identity, and of rights. These elements were powerfully intertwined and their importance reasserted on May 25, 2010, when Argentina celebrated its bicentennial. The many events around this day included concerts, lectures, exhibits, parades, and a rally in the Plaza de Mayo, hosted by President Cristina Fernández de Kirchner and attended by heads of state from across the region, including Hugo Chávez of Venezuela, Luiz Inácio Lula da Silva of Brazil, Rafael Correa of Ecuador, and Evo Morales of Bolivia.

The bicentennial celebrations took place over a span of months, culminating on May 25. They were attended by hundreds of thousands. Commentators from across the political spectrum remarked on the impressive outpouring of bodies in the collective festivities. They described the turnout as the largest since the December 19–20 protests, with which I opened this book. Some compared the events to the moment when Argentina won the World Cup, or the demonstrations in support of democracy following Alfonsín's resolution of the 1987 carapintadas military rebellion. Many saw the moment as marking a deep and renewed faith and pride in the nation, particularly among youth. For the many who filled the plazas and lined the streets, the nation became a vehicle for fulfilling the need for collective expression.

Two of the events around the bicentennial are especially significant in looking at the public performance of memory and nation and for thinking about the
construction of collective understandings of self and community. Elements of
each of these events powerfully echo the issues that animate and direct the spectacular performances of rights described in the preceding chapters. One of these
events was an 11-minute video projection that was displayed on exterior wall of
the Cabildo, on the southwestern corner of the Plaza de Mayo. This compilation
of music and images provided the packed crowd of onlookers with a compacted
trip through Argentine history since the May Revolution of 1810. Perhaps the
most noteworthy feature of this overview was how much historical knowledge it
required of its viewers, itself a testament to the country's traditionally high levels
of literacy and successful universal public education system. It is also a testament
to the importance of history (understood in this context as the linear progression of transformative temporal events) in public discourse in Argentina. This
history was indisputably partial and directed, reflecting through its imagery and
sound effects highlights and dark periods of national historical progression. Yet
it was enthusiastically received by the crowd and the many in the media.

The sequence of images in the projection could be, I think fairly, read as
telling a story of oscillation between the expansion/protection of rights and
their systemic violation. The great flourishing of lights, music, entertainment,
and escalating construction used to depict the period following the centennial
(1910) was dramatically cut down by an abrupt short circuit representing the
military coup of 1930, the tragedy of which the crowd responded to with respectful silence. The arrival of Perón, indicated on screen through a slow and
emotive buildup of silences and hopeful notes, was accompanied by chants of
"Per-ón, Per-ón, Per-ón" that emanated not from the projection, but from the
observing crowd. Images from the most recent military regime were received
with hisses, and Alfonsín and the original trials of the repressors with respectful whistles. A cacophony of events from the last twenty years, including a picture of the AMIA building in ruins, flashed across the walls of the colonial
town hall in rapid-fire succession, culminating in a simple yet picturesque gi-
gantic Argentine flag, eliciting a explosion of applause and cheers.

Though it would be possible to speculate on how this projection might have
looked different had there been a Radical (UCR) and not a Peronist government in power, overall the narrative as portrayed was not a political one but
one that highlighted ideas of rights and democracy. This was echoed as well
in the other principal event held on May 25. The *Desfile del Bicenenario*, or

Bicentennial Parade, was touted as "a scenic journey through the 200 years" of the nation. It included over two thousand performers to "interpret distinctive moments in local history."[1] The parade consisted of lines of *murgas*, or themed blocks of performers (also prevalent in Carnaval celebrations), each organized to represent a different theme from national history. From the crossing of the Andes and the Vuelta de Obligado, to a *murga* of taxicabs with tango dancers on their roofs, period costumes and symbolism provocatively evoked key moments. Argentina's numerous military coups were represented by a float carrying an enlarged copy of the constitution in flames. The Madres of Plaza de Mayo were greeted with a resonating cry of "el pueblo las abraza" (the people embrace you), and the War of the Malvinas inspired a revival of the chant "él que no salta/es un inglés" (whoever doesn't jump is an Englishman).

The parade also contained folkloric and ethnic floats dedicated to cultures from the interior of the country and national groups. Though invited to participate, the leaders of the organized Jewish community refused. The DAIA defended its decision on the grounds that the invitation was extended to national organizations, like Russians, Ukrainians, or Poles, and not to religious communities. They emphasized that neither the Muslim community nor Catholics nor Evangelicals had been invited to participate as such. Instead, they argued, many members of the Jewish collectivity would be able, if they chose, to march with a German, Austrian, or other such community, but that to have Jews, by sole virtue of being such, march behind an Israeli flag would only create confusion. "We are not foreigners, we are Argentine," a member of the DAIA directive board clarified once again to a local Jewish news organization.[2]

These performances of memory and nation, spectacularly on stage and in the streets for the bicentennial celebration, were opportunities for the consolidation of an official narrative of history and the nation in the aftermath of neoliberal restructuring and the politics of forgetting. The protection and strengthening of citizenship and human rights were the underlying theme that unified these performances and provided a coherent vision of national direction and collective aims.

Citizenship and Human Rights

Another theme that has run throughout this book is the relationship between citizenship and human rights. On the most basic level, human rights is a concept that allows the discussion of rights to leave the national sphere. Citizenship is fundamentally a relationship between the state and its subjects. In theory, human rights are not limited by state boundaries, age, gender, ethnicity, disability, or any other criterion, but, again in theory, apply to all members of the human species. Such a (utopian) universalist vision allows for the transcendence of the question of rights from the nexus of state and subject.[3] This is partially what was put in play with Memoria Activa's IACHR case against the Argentine state for failing to protect the victims' human/citizenship rights. And yet, even this appeal to the international protectors of human rights does not remove the state as one of the principal actors. Indeed, the state remains the (purported) guarantor of ultimate rights, as it is in the last instance responsible ensuring and upholding these rights.

Given this importance of the state in citizenship and human rights, part of what this book highlights is how demands for rights are often about defining the very nature of the state itself. That is, when Memoria Activa demands that the Argentine state defend citizens' right to protection from attack and their right to justice, it is equally demanding that the state be democratic, which, as Memoria Activa defines it, means being willing and capable of upholding and enforcing the rule of law and ensuring collective well-being. Similarly, when the BAUEN Cooperative demands that the state expropriate the hotel in protection of the workers' right to work, it is equally demanding that the state uphold the right to collective well-being over and above the right to private property.

As these cases show, if we separate rights of citizenship from human rights we risk reducing rights of citizenship primarily to their civil and political components, thus losing their social, economic, and cultural aspects (Marshall 1950; Caldeira and Holston 1999). By adhering to this division, the state becomes simply a defender of rights rather than also a guardian of the economic well-being of its citizens. The neoliberal state withdrew from its role to protect the right to economic welfare by placing the burden on autonomous neighborhood organizations or NGOs (Ferguson and Gupta 2002; Postero 2007). As this book has shown, citizens have mobilized against this withdrawal, utilizing the language of human rights to bolster their claims. Full rights of citizenship, including economic, social, and cultural rights, are, in this formulation, the responsibility of all states. States thus bear the responsibility not just to protect rights, but to be an active agent in their realization. The demands of these groups reorient the focus away from individual rights and limits (as persons or as nations) and toward cooperation as the basis for communal well-being.

The tension between the individual and the collective is resolved in part through a notion of citizenship and the role of the citizen that includes an absorption of the sense of collective responsibility into the individual. More than a "bundle of rights" or a "legal condition," citizenship is also fundamentally "a social process of mediated production of values" (Ong 2003:xvii, cited in Feldman 2007:149). While Ong's work is primarily concerned with citizenship as the site for the production of the values of freedom, autonomy, and security, in the case of Memoria Activa and the Cooperative BAUEN, I argue that they invest citizenship with values of sociality and accountability. Accountability, both for the state and for citizens, who are called upon to be participants in the construction of communal values, is the antithesis and the resolution of the impunity and corruption that this book has highlighted as central concerns of recent movements in Argentina.

Elizabeth Jelin sees the Argentine human rights movement, through resorting to universal ethical appeals, as having taken a leading role in creating a sense of social responsibility among its members. She traces the history of the human rights movement in Latin America, arguing that in the 1970s and 1980s the struggles for democracy and against human rights violations by the region's military dictatorships also led to demands for the rights and responsibilities of citizenship, which include in her view demanding and enforcing accountability and responsibility on the part of the state. The state itself in her formulation is not above and beyond its citizens, but actively constructed, defined, resisted, and improved through a responsible, duty-bound, and engaged citizenry. This kind of engaged citizenry, she argues, must be fundamentally based in an ethics of solidarity, a concern for rights and reciprocal recognition, and "a human concern for others" (1996:115n6). Furthermore, for Jelin, a sense of community is essential to the formation of this kind of citizenry: "It is the sense of community that promotes the consciousness of being a subject with the right to have rights. The civic dimension of citizenship is anchored in the subjective feelings that unite or bind a community, in contrast to the seemingly more rational elements of civil and social rights" (1996:106). This legacy of the human rights movement can be seen in the concern of groups like Memoria Activa and the Cooperativa BAUEN for constructing an active and engaged citizenry, one invested not just in making demands on the state to fulfill immediate needs but also in serving as agents in the construction of a society attuned to the needs of the collective.

Practicing Citizenship in the Streets

Is it fair to speak of Argentina as being now in a post-neoliberal moment? I suggest that there are both continuities with the past and evidence that it may be useful to mark some significant differences. It is possible to argue that the poli-cies of the Kirchner administrations represent a departure from Argentine neo-liberalist economics of the 1990s. The immediate repayment of IMF loans in 2005 and the commitment to avoid taking on further debt to international lend-ing agencies certainly marks a change in direction. Other aspects of the Kirch-ners' administrations also seem to depart from neoliberal ideals, such as Cristina Fernández de Kirchner's attempt to fund redistributive policies through a tax on agricultural exports in 2008, and the reform of the Media Law in 2009, which, if adhered to, would weaken the existing monopoly of media outlets. Some observ-ers, however, point to corruption in the government and accuse the administra-tion of continuing clientalist and corporate politics.[4]

Regardless of many ambiguities, one legacy of neoliberalism that is evident, I argue, is the shift in the discourse of rights. Impunity and corruption have become the principal tropes through which rights of citizenship and human rights are seen as being stifled, violated, and unrealized. Throughout this book I have emphasized the importance of the emerging language of rights, and I have shown how this shift in discourse has been expressed through public symbolic action and popular mobilization. Taking to the streets is also a form of commu-nity building and identity formation or reinforcement. The appropriation and re-presentation of symbols of identity is often a vehicle for this expression. The Madres de Plaza de Mayo chose the white *pañuelos* to emphasize their identity as mothers, embodying this role through its material artifacts. A local neigh-borhood organization announces its monthly "olla popular y cultural" (cultural event and public soup kitchen) with a call that plays on the lyrics of a tradi-tional tango to assert the importance of street mobilization: "¡¡Que no se abolle la olla, que no se calle la calle!!" (That the pot shall not be dented, and the street not be silent!). When Memoria Activa invokes Jewish symbols and traditions, or the Cooperativa BAUEN appeals to the notion of the worker as a form of political subjectivity, they do so through public demonstrations that proclaim and fortify these notions among the participants.

Expressing public will and exerting pressure on government officials through street protest is a practice of citizenship with a long history in Ar-gentina. Hilda Sábato has shown how in Buenos Aries in the second half of the nineteenth century the performance of citizenship was based far more on participation or support of public demonstrations than on the formal mecha-nism of voting (Sábato 1992, 2004). Notwithstanding the differences in histori-cal moments, many of the most momentous events in Argentine history have been based in public demonstration. The 17th and 18th of October 1945, when hundreds of thousands filled the streets to protest the resignation and imprisonment of Juan Domingo Perón, signaled a decisive shift in Argentine politics. They also became key moments from which the Peronist regime traced its legitimacy, as proof of the leader's intimate connection to the people (James 1988a; Plotkin 1995, 2003). The Madres made public demonstration a cornerstone of their actions, to this day making their Thursday afternoon rounds in the Plaza de Mayo without exception. The protests of December 19–20, 2001, were sparked when President de la Rúa declared a state of siege, ordering Argentines to stay indoors, that is, not to take to the streets. Once and again fundamental change in Argentina has depended on groups (clubs, unions, political parties, or social movements) or issues having the capacity to mobilize the public to exert pressure through public demonstrations.

The use of the language of rights, forcefully expressed during mobilizations and which first gained prominence in the movements that took to the streets to protest the violence of the most recent military dictatorship, has continued to spread and has been adopted by groups from across the social and political spectrum. This is the case, for example, in the adoption of the language of "security" as a right. The call for security, perhaps expressed most visibly and viscerally in the marches led by Juan Carlos Blumberg, whose son was killed in an act of violent crime in 2004. The marches he convened followed a pattern throughout much of Latin America where some sectors of society have demanded stricter laws and more intensive policing in response to (real or perceived) heightened levels of urban insecurity (Goldstein 2007; Marquardt, in press). While Blumberg's protagonism was short-lived, the massive marches he led reinforced the traditional formula of street protest combined with the rhetoric of rights. The difference with this protest, and later demonstrations such as those organized by the leaders of the agroindustrial sector opposed to Cristina Fernández de Kirchner's attempt to increase export tariffs, was the use of the language of rights and street protest tactics (such as the blockading of major highways) by members of the economic elite. That the sectors of society more frequently the objects rather than the subjects of street protest have also adopted these practices underscores the ubiquity of the language of rights and tactics of protest in contemporary political action.

A further, and very different, example of the continued relevance of street mobilization as a form of political expression comes from a funeral, namely that of former president Raúl Alfonsín. Alfonsín died March 31, 2009, after a well-attended vigil in front of his house by supporters from across social and political lines. The years directly preceding his death had seen a recuperation of his image as a respected political figure and militant, and numerous awards and honors were bestowed upon him, even by his political opponents. That so many people came into the streets to honor Alfonsín upon his death points to the importance that the struggle for human rights has come to take in Argentina, as Alfonsín was commemorated primarily for his attempt to bring military leaders to trial. Some also read the mobilization around his funeral as a positive step in the consolidation of democracy. Having political or ideological rivals publicly share common ground and honor one another for their contribution to the good of the nation was seen by many commentators as indicating a level of stability and maturity in the democratic system.

A year and a half later, another funeral also brought many into the streets. A spontaneous and massive crowd turned out the night following Néstor Kirchner's sudden death from heart failure on October 27, 2010. That day happened to be the date of the national census, and the streets were eerily bare as the population kept to their homes in anticipation of the census official who would count them. It was there that the news of Kirchner's death was received. At 8 pm, after the mandatory period of bureaucratic confinement had ended, multitudes filled the Plaza de Mayo to express their shock at his passing. At the time of his death Néstor Kirchner was still a highly influential figure, widely considered a leading contender in the next presidential election, and the secretary general of the Latin American organization UNASUR (Unión de Naciones Suramericanas, or Union of South American Nations). Of course, stories also circulated of census workers arriving at houses where ecstatic festivities were going on among those who couldn't have been happier by the unexpected news. But even reports in the mainstream press, whose relationship with the Kirchners and especially Cristina Fernández has been bitterly antagonistic following the reforms to the Media Law, generally took a subdued (though sensationalistic) tone. Chants of "argentino/argentino/soy soldado del pingüino" (I'm a soldier of Néstor's—"penguin" being a nickname for the Patagonian politician) were heard throughout the plaza that night. The participation of the youth during the bicentennial celebration was repeated during these enormous demonstrations of support that followed his death. Many people regarded the strong turnout of young Argentines on this night as evidence of the success of Kirchner's attempt to reengage the youth in politics, resisting the apathy left in the wake of neoliberal social restructuring.[5]

While not a protest, this massive taking to the streets was once again how many expressed their feelings and made their voices heard. In the words of one commentator:

> Argentine society has the healthy custom of taking to the streets when something moves them. It is good that this occurs, because the growing presence of the media, across the globe, tends toward the isolation of consumer-citizens in their private worlds. But what is happening in these days of commemoration of Néstor Kirchner goes beyond this generalized vocation to occupy public space. . . . The organized columns are swallowed by the thousands of small groups— families, friends, neighbors, and co-workers—and spontaneous participants. This dispersion . . . offers the best image of what we may today call the Argentine people. . . . Some of the measures of this government have struck deep and this sense of gratitude, that isn't for concessions, as some think, but for the recognition of rights, can be transformed into a very powerful social energy to sustain this process of change.[6]

By considering, as I have throughout this book, mobilizations from across the political spectrum as practices of citizenship, I want to emphasize how the "repertoires of contention" in Argentina both draw upon previous forms of action and continuously undergo innovation in form and content (Tilly 1994). These public actions also demonstrate the level of penetration of the discourse of rights into the political and social realms. A poll by the Center for the Study of Public Opinion at the University of Buenos Aires taken the day of the 2011 presidential election found that 93 percent of the respondents who voted for Cristina Fernández de Kirchner approved of the trials of the military personnel accused of crimes during the dictatorship. Of the respondents who did not vote for Fernández, 79 percent nonetheless stated that they approved of the trials. That the vast majority of those polled reported agreeing with the policy shows how essential and ineludible the official discourse of human rights has become. The language of rights and democracy has become an inescapable currency for articulating demands in post-neoliberal Argentina.

Living with Indeterminacy
Cooperativa BAUEN

The final theme that I want to highlight is the degree to which all players are forced to live with indeterminacy, even as they pursue highly specific goals.

Indeed, in many cases the groups discussed in these pages have not just learned to live with indeterminacy but have managed to use it to their advantage.

Following the workers' initial success in preventing the passage of the Morando bill, the City Legislature eventually passed the law at two o'clock in the morning during a later session. The workers frequently emphasize how this kind of maneuvering leaves them in a constant state of uncertainty, never knowing where and when the next threat will arrive, denying them the ability to "work in peace" (*laburar en paz*). Though this law recognized the Iurcovich family as the owners of the Bauen and stipulated the creation of a legislative committee to oversee its return to them, the cooperative managed to exert enough pressure on the new head of the city government, Jorge Telerman, to prevent the law from taking effect. The cooperative demanded that the law be vetoed. However Telerman, whose position on the recuperated businesses was more moderate than that of the recently deposed Aníbal Ibarra, was not willing to antagonize the opposition political forces by doing so.[7] Falling short of this, closed-door negotiations between leaders of the BAUEN Cooperative and members of the executive led to the law being effectively set aside. Though Telerman refused to veto it, he also did not sign it, an irregular but not uncommon legal procedure that left it without effect while allowing him to avoid taking a public position. In this case, the BAUEN Cooperative was able to prevent the implementation of the Morando law by capitalizing on the popular support its efforts commanded—it would not serve the political interests of even the right-wing head of city government to forcibly and violently evict the workers, even when there was a law that demanded it, given that public opinion would likely be strongly against such an action.

Amid this kind of uncertainty, the workers have continued to go about the multifarious daily tasks involved in running the hotel. Hosting many events, theater productions, conferences, and a constant stream of guests, the Bauen continues to operate as a cooperative in providing clean, efficient, and affordable service to the public, while offering support to organizations and individuals in need. In 2009, FACTA (Federación Argentina de Cooperativas de Trabajadores Autogestionados, or Argentine Federation of Self-managed Workers' Cooperatives) produced a play reenacting the trial of the Italian immigrant anarchists Nicola Sacco and Bartolomeo Vanzetti as part of its promotion of art in the service of popular education. This was one of the cooperative's steps to make the hotel a space for the construction of communal social values. For now, the hotel remains in the hands of the workers, but without legal definition or protection. The workers cannot yet *laburar en paz*, as they so ardently have sought, but they have maintained control of the hotel and have successfully managed it in accordance with the principles of solidarity and cooperation.

Nationally, this kind of indeterminacy plagues many of the recuperadas. To a degree, this is true even in the one example that may on the surface seem to be an exception. After a long and arduous struggle by the workers, on August 12, 2009, the legislature of Neuquén voted to expropriate the Zanón ceramics factory and formally turn it over to the cooperative FaSinPat, which has controlled the factory since 2001.[8] The governor soon signed the law and it was published in the Official Bulletin. However, the conditions stated by the law, which require the state to pay a still undetermined amount to the holders of the debt amassed under the factory's former owners, have yet to be fulfilled.

After years of pressure, a new bankruptcy law, proposed by one of the recuperadas umbrella organizations and put forth by the ruling Kirchnerist party, was approved by the Argentine Senate on June 2, 2011. It prioritizes the solvency of the business, giving the workers legal protection to operate the establishment as a cooperative and to use all credits, indemnizations, back pay, and other unmet obligations to the workers as payment for the business. While the law is likely to face legal challenges, its passage represents a significant shift in the prioritization of state responsibility in cases of insolvency or bankruptcy. On the other hand, in July 2011 the Supreme Court rejected a motion by the BAUEN Cooperative to review the lower court rulings on ownership of the hotel and to countermand its eviction, ordered by Commercial Circuit Judge Hualde. The decision effectively exhausted its options for a judicial solution. Since that time and as of this writing, the workers have mobilized in defense of a potential eviction while pursuing with renewed vigor a national law of expropriation for recuperated businesses. The Law of Expropriation was presented in 2008 by legislator Victoria Donda, one of the more than a hundred recuperated children of parents disappeared during the last military dictatorship. It stipulates that expropriation of recuperated businesses should occur where doing so would "secure the fulfillment of the common good, be this of material or spiritual nature." As workers say, "la lucha continúa" (the struggle continues).

Memoria Activa

In February 2011, the newspaper *Página/12* published some the content of classified US embassy cables, which they had obtained through the organization WikiLeaks. These cables confirmed what many had already suspected—that the US government, particularly after the post-September-11–2001 Iraq War, had an interest in the development of the AMIA investigations in Argentina. In 2008, the head of the AMIA Investigative Unit, Alberto Nisman, resuscitated the arrest warrants originally issued by Galeano against eleven high-ranking Iranian officials accused of planning the attack. The original warrants had been cancelled by Interpol following the 2004 trial that invalidated Galeano's investigation. However, after taking charge of the case, Nisman asked for and was granted their reissue. The US government, the leaked cables show, advised Nisman to neglect the case into the mishandling of the investigation of the attacks in order to not, in its eyes, weaken the case against the Iranians by questioning the investigation. The cables also show a key member of the DAIA working closely with the US embassy and supporting its position, a fact that Memoria Activa publicly denounced.[9]

This investigation of the investigation led federal Judge Ariel Lijo to order in May 2008 that key players in the alleged cover-up be called in to provide testimony, including ex-president Carlos Menem, his brother Munir, former police commissioner Jorge "Fino" Palacios, and ex-judge Galeano. The uncovering of mismanagement of the AMIA case and the political and personal pressures that led to the destruction of evidence and neglect of major leads had been a principal concern of family members almost since the case's inception and had been a fundamental part of the IACHR case. The trials against Menem and others may or may not begin in 2012.[10] In the meantime, Menem remains the ranking national senator from the province of La Rioja. The international capture requests for the Iranian officials are mentioned every year in Cristina Fernández's speech to the United Nations, reiterating that Iran should collaborate with the Argentine justice system. Until recently, offers to hold trials in an impartial third country had achieved little in the way of results, though in 2011 President Ahmadinejad made an offer of Iranian assistance in investigating the AMIA attack. What this will mean concretely remains to be seen. The accused former police commissioner Jorge Palacios, who allegedly played a key role in misdirecting the AMIA investigation, was chosen by Telerman's successor in the position of Buenos Aires Head of Government, Mauricio Macri, to direct the New Metropolitan Police Force, though his nomination eventually had to be rescinded following an outcry from family members of victims and many others with reasons to object.

Memoria Activa has accepted in many ways the state's definition of the guilty parties in the AMIA attack, even as the "friendly resolution" process drags on with only sporadic signs of results. Memoria Activa believes the trials that have been held have been conducted under the kind of impartial and effective legal system it wants, and in each case have tended to confirm Memoria Activa's accusations and demands. As such, Memoria Activa considers the national and international justice systems credible, and it is willing to accept the knowledge about the attack that they have produced. Yet this is not a simple acceptance of what is said or done. The truth becomes subsumed under institutionally sound knowledge, and most live with the recognition of truth in one realm being contradictory with truth in another. Justice in the form of punishment of the guilty has not, or has only partially, been achieved. The investigations continue, painfully slow and inconclusive, but not inconsequential.

It seems clear that living with indeterminacy will continue as part of the post-neoliberal milieu in Argentina, a dance that Partha Chatterjee has described as a "constantly shifting compromise between the normative values of modernity and the moral assertions of popular demands" (2004:41). Yet it seems equally clear that groups like Memoria Activa and the BAUEN Cooperative, or those that they inspire, will not relinquish their demands nor cease their struggles. The language of rights that they embody and have helped to construct, with its basis in sociality and an emphasis on the collective good, has changed the terms of the debate and conditioned the new limits of the possible in the future of the country.

REFERENCE MATTER

Notes

Introduction

1. Similar challenges are made by groups in other Latin American nations. The focus on the collective resonates with the focus integrated into the discourse and practice of citizenship among residents of El Alto, as studied by Sian Lazar (2008). A main difference among the Argentine groups discussed here is that the notion of the collective does not draw upon or reference indigenous forms of social organization.

2. Caldeira and Holston define citizenship as "prerogatives and encumbrances of membership in the modern political community" (1999:693).

3. For more on gated communities, see Caldeira 2000; Low 2003; in Argentina Svampa 2001.

4. 1 USD = 1 Argentine peso throughout the 1990s.

5. See, for example, *Informe Latinobarómetro 1995–2005: 10 años de opinión pública*, www.latinobarometro.org (accessed Jan. 15, 2006).

6. A survey from July 2004 identified the justice system as the institution with the worst image, with only 18 percent of respondents granting it a positive rating, while 78 percent said they viewed it negatively. This same survey reported only 23 percent of those surveyed holding a positive image of the Supreme Court. The survey was conducted by Analogías, directed by Analía del Franco. Reported in "Encuesta sobre imagen de sectores del país," *Página/12*, July 11, 2004. However, and arguably reflecting a degree of renewed confidence following the Kirchner administration's directed reforms, the numbers cited here for the 2004 survey were in fact better than those of the preceding year, when the Supreme Court had garnered only a 9.5 percent approval rating, and the judicial system as a whole had received only 4 percent.

Chapter 1

1. Ley no. 215, de ocupación de la tierra, August 1867.

2. Statistics from Dirección General de Estadística, República Argentina. Cited in Feierstein 1999: 399.

3. Immigrants to Argentina from the later 1980s onward have been mainly come from the surrounding Latin American nations, and from Asia, mostly Korea and China. See, for example, Courtis 2000.

4. As mentioned above, earlier foundational documents and the 1853 constitution formally gave voting rights to all males born in Argentina or naturalized. However, vot-

ing was restricted in practice to upper-class white males until the passage of these reforms in 1912. See Sábato 2004: esp. 12–15; Adelman 1999:82.

5. See www.escuelafalcon.edu.ar (accessed Sept. 16, 2006).

6. The term "liberal consensus" is adopted from Mariano Ben Plotkin (2003).

7. Yrigoyen would serve part of a second term, from 1928 to 1930, but by this time
he had largely abandoned the working classes and struggled to maintain support even
among the urban middle class, his traditional base. He was deposed by a military coup
on September 6, 1930.

8. See Mirelman 1975; Feierstein 1999:197–203 on the Semana Trágica; Moya 2004
for a discussion of the association of Jews with anarchism in the early twentieth century.
Moya makes the argument that this association, which led to the martyrization of Radowitzky, contributed to the low levels of anti-Semitism among the working class during
this era.

9. From the ILO website, www.ilo.org/global/About_the_ILO/lang—en/index.htm
(accessed May 25, 2009). The ILO also held as a stated intention the effort to enforce
labor standards as a way to reduce the motives for war, emphasizing the fundamental
role attributed to economic well-being and self-realization.

10. This return to the 1853 constitution included maintaining the earlier reforms of
1860, 1866, and 1898. These had been largely concerned with the relationship of Buenos
Aires to the rest of the country, and to modifications in procedures for establishing the
number of legislators and government ministries in response to the changing needs of
a growing nation. Any reference in this book to the later use of the 1853 constitution
should be understood as containing these modifications, which have remained intact.

11. A poignant illustration of this era and the fighting between Peronist factions can
be found in Osvaldo Soriano's novel *No habrá más pena ni olvido* (published in English
under the potentially confusing title *A Funny, Dirty Little War*). Written in 1974 and first
published in 1978, the book was not printed in Buenos Aires until 1983, the same year
the acclaimed film adaptation by Héctor Olivera was made.

12. The CONADEP report (*Nunca Más*) cites 8,960 documented cases of disappearance, but acknowledges that this number is far below the actual figure. The number
30,000 is based on a rough multiplication of the available evidence on disappearances
across the nation. Though the number is only an estimate, it has been adopted broadly
within Argentina, and holds significant symbolic value. In this case, the estimated number is far more resonant than the more "official" number established through documented research by an investigative body.

13. *La Nación*, Dec. 14, 1976, cited in Robben 2005:171.

14. For example, in Videla's first speech to the nation as junta leader, he appealed
to the public: "Citizens, assume your obligations as Reserve Soldiers. Your information
is always useful. Bring it to us." Published in all the major newspapers, March 27, 1976,
and cited in Feitlowitz 1998:23.

15. Spoken at a press conference, Dec. 18, 1977, quoted in Feitlowitz 1998:24.

16. I use the term "state terrorism" both as a literal translation of the phrase "terrorismo del estado" commonly used by human rights groups in Argentina and as a techni-

cal term. Jeffrey Sluka has argued that while state violence is conventionally referred to as "terror" and the word "terrorism" reserved for anti-state violence, this distinction is "more political and ideological than empirical" and serves as an "ideological subterfuge" (2000:1). Practices of political intimidation by violence or its threat thus get elided from the category "terrorism" when practiced by the state, which, paradoxically, commands a greater ability to commit such acts than most non-state actors. As he points out, "even small states . . . have the ability to deprive large numbers of people of subsistence requirements and produce hunger, malnutrition, high infant mortality rates, and other chronic diseases of poverty and neglect, as [a] means of political intimidation and control" (2000:2).

17. Examples of human rights organizations in Argentina include SERPAJ (Servicio de Paz y Justicia, or Peace and Justice Service), APDH (Asamblea Permanente para Derechos Humanos, or Permanent Assembly for Human Rights), founded in 1975, and CELS (Centro de Estudios Legales y Sociales, or Center for Legal and Social Studies). CELS is an off-shoot of APDH that has become a respected organization for the defense of human rights on a wide variety of fronts reaching well beyond the issue of Dirty War justice. For further information and analysis of these groups and of other Argentine human rights organizations, see Arditti 1999; Bonner 2007; Brysk 1994; Fisher 1989; Guzman Bouvard 1994; Jelin 1994, 1995; Navarro 1989; Schirmer 1994; Taylor 1998; Torre 1996.

18. See Informe Rattenbach, www.casarosada.gov.ar/component/content/article/108-gobierno-informa/25773-informe-rattenbach (accessed April 2, 2012).

19. Alfonsín's electoral campaign was surprisingly successful. Even Radical leaders had expected a Peronist victory in the election. Alfonsín's campaign sought to present above all a message of peace and the importance of democracy, and some have argued that this focus on democracy and the lingering effects of Peronist revolutionary politics led to his success (see, for example, Cucchetti 2007).

20. For further discussion of the CONADEP report and the legacy of the military trials in Argentina, see Hayner 1995; and Nino 1996.

21. For a detailed discussion of the mechanics of the legal prosecutions of Dirty War repressors during this era, see Maris Ageitos 2002.

22. In any discussion of this era, is important not to downplay the real divisions within the military. Some had opposed the repressive violence from the start (many of whom either left or were forced out of the armed forces) (Mittbach 1986); others were themselves disappeared (Izaguirre 1998). Other factions, particularly those placed in command after the return to democracy, advocated a more reconciliatory stance toward the democratic government. However, particularly with this last group, the argument can be made that the discourse of history was shared, even if they settled for a different course of action. Whether cases like the 1995 public apology for abuses pronounced by then head of the army Martín Balza (later ambassador to Colombia under the Néstor Kirchner administration) are due to genuine repentance or political opportunism is open to debate, but they were in any case rare until after the end of the 1990s. As always, class divisions among officers and enlisted men led to substantial divergences in perspective.

Chapter 2

1. In thinking with the idea of a counterpoint, I am indebted to Fernando Coronil's insightful analysis of Fernando Ortiz's classic work, *Cuban Counterpoint*. For Ortiz, treating sugar and tobacco as points in a contrapuntal relationship involved their identification in terms of binary oppositions that were, if one dug deeply enough, as unified as they were distinct. That is, Ortiz treated these oppositions "not as fixities, but as hybrid and productive, reflecting their transcultural formation and their transitional value in the flow of Cuban history" (Coronil 1999:xiv). Disappearance and impunity are not constructed solely in terms of contrasting attributes, for though the first is primarily a violation of physical integrity and the latter a violation of a more abstract form of a right to justice, they share a fundamental unity in being identified through the social wounds they produce. As such, the relationship between the two is similar to how Ortiz analyzes sugar and tobacco in Cuba in that, at their core, the two are intimately interconnected in terms of their impact on social and political life. The power in Ortiz's work comes with the realization of the convergences between the two commodities as they become subject to capitalist forces. Impunity in Argentina, understood as a violation of rights, is only explicable when contextualized as the counterpoint to disappearance.

2. This concept was expressed in Hitler's decree of December 7, 1941.

3. The military was particularly keen to avoid any visible acts or declarations of anti-Semitism so as not jeopardize the arms trade with Israel. Israel provided at least 13 percent of the weapons imported by Argentina between 1976 and 1981.

4. Recently declassified CIA documents have provided irrefutable evidence of the long-suspected tacit and active support the dictatorship received from the US government, in particular Secretary of State Henry Kissinger (Kornbluh 2003). These documents also demonstrate US support for the Plan Condor, which linked repressive dictatorships throughout the Southern Cone. However, the Carter administration pressured the dictatorship to improve its human rights record. Overall, US support of the military's economic plans limited the effectiveness of human rights networks and the protection they could offer. See Escudé 1991.

5. Carina Perelli claims that this statement is from 1977 (Perelli 1994:43); however, though widely disseminated and repeated in months to come, the statement first appears in May 1976, only shortly after the coup. In showing this, Antonius Robben points out that by 1977 Saint Jean denied having said it, accusing the Montoneros of fabricating the quote (*Somos* 1977 38: 19, cited in Robben 2005:394). However, Robben is astute in observing that whether or not the original and highly quoted statement is authentic, it clearly reflected military thinking of the time and is echoed in other public statements by high military officials from 1976 to 1977 (See Robben 2005:394 for further references). The version in Spanish reads: "Primero matamos a los subversivos; después a los colaboradores, a los simpatizantes, a los indiferentes, y finalmente a quienes no reaccionan."

6. Some of the phone calls and temporary releases of the disappeared are also likely the result of the human dynamics of repressive machinery; the captors held their own

particular relationships and interests with regard to their captives. A recent portrayal of this theme is in the 1999 film by Marco Bechis, *Garage Olimpo*.

7. Author's interview, June 8, 2000, Reconquista, Santa Fe.

8. The confirmation of this public secret by navy captain Adolfo Scilingo to journalist and Horacio Verbitsky in 1995 sent shock waves throughout Argentine society and gave further impetus to the demands for justice for all perpetrators of the repression. See Verbitsky 1995. In a public spectacle that included Scilingo's insistence on his own victimization, a dubious hunger strike, and performed courtroom faintings, the former navy captain, who had admitted to personally throwing some thirty drugged but still living individuals out of an airplane into the Río de la Plata, was tried in a Spanish court in 2005 and sentenced to 640 years in prison.

9. For further discussion of the logistics of impunity and its effects within Argentina, see Abregú 2000; Arditti 1999; Balaban and Megged 2003; Hayner 1995; Izaguirre 1998; Kordon 1995; Lozada 1999; Nino 1996, Pérez Aguirre 1992; Roht-Arriaza 1995; SERPAJ 1992; Sveaass 1994a, 1994b.

10. I am indebted to Carlos Forment for these observations on the importance of scandals in Argentine neoliberal politics.

11. See, for example, www.lebanon.com/news/local/2003/3/20.htm; "Hezbolá niega," *Página/12*, Aug. 27, 2006.

12. Mughniyah appeared on George Bush's list of 22 most-wanted terrorists on October 10, 2001. He was assassinated in Damascus in February 2008.

13. The Supreme Court, after its renovation under President Kirchner, later ruled that the case be revisited. In 2005 a new prosecutor was assigned to the investigation. As of this writing, practical advances remain elusive.

14. See Gargarella 2004:196. My thanks to Leticia Barrera and her work on the Argentine Supreme Court for drawing my attention to this source.

15. In addition to the four new members, two Supreme Court justices resigned, one in protest over the new plan, allowing Menem to hand pick six out of nine justices.

16. Polling done by Graciela Romer y Asociados.

17. Gurevich 2005b gives an overview of how concerns over international terrorism and international political relationships influenced the AMIA investigation(s).

18. These include Caballero 2005; Goobar 1996; Guterman 1999, 2004; Lanata and Goldman 1994; Levinas 1998; Poritzker and Salgado 2005; Salinas 1997. See also the websites of Memoria Activa (www.memoriaactiva.com), AMIA (www.amia.org.ar), and the DAIA (www.daia.org.ar) for documents listing the various allegations of irregularities that these organizations have made over the years. The DAIA website also includes video and press archives of media coverage of the attacks and the trial. In English, the American Jewish Committee put out a series of yearly reports on the investigation and trial, written by Sergio Kiernan and available at www.ajc.org.

19. Retired police commissioner Carlos Castañeda was eventually sentenced to four years in prison for his role in the destruction of some sixty audio recordings of wire-tapped phone lines made as part of the AMIA investigation. This conviction, upheld by the Court of Appeals in October 2007, marked the first criminal conviction in

any AMIA-related case. Nonetheless, even this case was concerned only with the cover-up that accompanied Galeano's investigation and not with the attack itself. Casteñeda was neither tried for nor is suspected of having had any role in the planning or execution of the bombing, only with having failed to preserve evidence that fell under his jurisdiction.

20. "Patricio Irala. Paraguayo, según denunciara su concubina había empezado a trabajar como chofer de la AMIA ese mismo día. Solo fueron encontrados restos." From the presentation of Fiscales Mullen and Barbaccia, number 64579. Mullen and Barbaccia were later removed from the trial for their alleged complicity in the illegal procedures used by the investigating judge, Galeano.

21. See "Fraude con la tragedia de la AMIA," *Clarín*, April 20, 2001.

22. From a speech given in the Plaza Lavalle during Memoria Activa's acto for the 353rd week following the AMIA bombing, April 23, 2001. Available at www.memoria activa.com/anteriores2001abril1.htm.

23. The original reads: "[Galeano] orientó su actuación en 'construir' una hipótesis incriminatoria, pretendiendo atender, de eso modo, las lógicas demandas de la sociedad, a la vez que satisfacer oscuros intereses de gobernantes inescrupulosos." From the press release of the TOF3, causa n° 487/00, 496/00, 501/01, 502/03, origen Jdo. Fed. n° 9, sec. n°17, registro n° 1/04, Sept. 2, 2004. See the complete verdict of the judges of the Federal Justice at http://sursur.com/files/veredicto%20AMIA.pdf.

24. As with the embassy bombing, the claim that the explosion was the result of a car bomb remains disputed, and conflicting reports of evidence and its interpretation serve to confound rather than clarify what happened. The theory of the car bomb was verified by the TOF3 (Tribunal Oral Federal 3), the judicial panel that heard the AMIA case, and confirmed by the Court of Appeals that upheld the sentence. For the members of Memoria Activa, this evidence was decisive, and their faith in the careful application of legal principles allowed them to feel secure on this point at least. But critics remain, citing contradictory evidence and laboratory reports that indicate otherwise. This provides an example of the way facts and knowledge are produced, verified, and accepted by different actors.

25. The mafia-like operations and structure of the Provincial Police force is common knowledge in Argentina. Recent treatments include Caballero 2005; Hinton 2006. The 2002 film by Pablo Trapero, *El Bonaerense*, provides a compelling cinematographic account. The low pay for police officers and the tendency toward the privatization of security that has led to job instability are undoubtedly in part to blame for the predisposition of some officials to use the authority provided by their uniform for illicit personal gain.

26. From the verdict of the TOF3, causa n° 487/00, 496/00, 501/01, 502/03, origen Jdo. Fed. n° 9, sec. n° 17, registro n° 1/04.

27. Galeano had been removed from the AMIA investigation in December 2003. The trial against Telleldín and the Buenos Aires police officers continued under federal prosecutors who had worked under Galeano and a divided group of plaintiffs of family members of victims.

28. "Hora de acusar a los acusadores," *Página/12*, Dec. 7, 2004:8–9. See Chávez 2007 for a clear and concise discussion of recent changes to the council.

29. This enormous and elegant wooden table had been manufactured four years earlier and was said to be worth $40,000.

30. I have adopted the common practice within Argentina of using the word "collectivity" (*colectividad*) in regard to Argentine Jews. This term is generally used to denote the diverse organized Jewish religious, social, and political organizations and their members, while at once recognizing the differences in attitudes and perceptions that exist among these. I have chosen to use the word "community" to refer to the broader set of all self-identifying Argentines of Jewish descent, whether or not these have any participation in organized Jewish life. In Argentina, what I am calling "community" is often referred to as the *calle judía*, or the "Jewish street."

31. Beraja was subsequently imprisoned for his role in the bankruptcy and corruption scandal surrounding the collapse of a local bank, the Banco de Mayo, which resulted in the evaporation of the savings of many members of the Jewish community.

32. The founding of APEMIA developed out of a growing disagreement between Laura Ginsberg and other members of Memoria Activa. After the convulsive political and social events of December 19–20, 2001, when popular protest forced the resignation of President de la Rúa, Argentina went through a difficult process of political reorganization, with the naming of four new presidents in a span of two weeks. During one of these ephemeral administrations, that of Adolfo Rodríguez Saá, one of Memoria Activa's lawyers, Alberto Zuppi, was named minister of justice. Memoria Activa approved this move, hoping that this would lead to concrete advances in the AMIA investigation. However, Ginsberg was strongly opposed to the legal representation of Memoria Activa assuming an active government post, and left Memoria Activa. APEMIA has called for the establishment of an independent investigative commission and the release of all government documents related to the attack.

33. On neoliberalism, see Harvey 2005; Saad-Filho and Johnson 2005. For an overview of neoliberalism in Argentina, see Teubal 2004.

34. At the time of the constitution's adoption, these included the UDHR, the American Convention on Human Rights, the ICESCR, the ICCPR, and the conventions against torture, genocide, racial discrimination, discrimination against women, and the rights of the child. Newer conventions can achieve constitutional status after ratification, by means of a two-thirds vote in Congress. For analysis of the implications of this constitutional status for international conventions, see Grugel and Peruzzotti 2010; Smulovitz 2010.

35. Recuperated businesses have been the focus of a number of works, including Fajn et al. 2003; Fernández Álvarez 2004; García Allegrone et al. 2004; Heller 2004; Landau et al. 2004; lavaca 2004; Magnani 2003; Rebón 2004; Rebón and Saavedra 2006; Ruggeri 2005. For texts in English, see Faulk 2008a, 2008b; Vieta and Ruggeri 2009; and the English translation of lavaca's *Sin Patrón* 2007.

36. Information on the history of the hotel comes from the author's interviews with hotel workers and was corroborated by archival sources, especially coverage from local

mainstream and alternative media including *Clarín*, *ANRed*, *Página/12*, and *lavaca*. Information on the takeover and early days of the cooperative comes primarily from the author's interviews with members and others who closely accompanied the process.

37. Zanón was officially expropriated by the Legislature of the province of Neuquén in August 2009, to be turned over to the workers' cooperative FaSinPat (Fábrica Sin Patrón). After nine years of struggle, and eight of worker-controlled management, the more than 450 workers at Zanón formally gained the right to operate the installation. However, while celebrating these long-sought developments, they continue to insist on the need for the nationalization of the factory. For more information, see www.obreros dezanon.com.ar/html/index1 (accessed Aug. 17, 2009); "Una para festejar: Zanon es de los trabajadores," *Cooperativa lavaca*, www.lavaca.org (accessed Aug. 17, 2009).

38. Cited in a cooperative-produced pamphlet, collected Feb. 2005.

39. For more on privatizations in Argentina, see Vilas 2004; Azpiazu 2002.

40. Quoted in an interview published in *Página/12*, Aug. 21, 2007.

41. From a statement distributed by the Cooperative, April 9, 2012.

42. Andreas Huyssen has likewise proposed that, in addition to considering the victims and oppressors/perpetrators, it is necessary also to look at a third actor: the beneficiary. He argues that in Latin American countries like Chile and Argentina the violation of human rights benefited the local and foreign proponents of neoliberal policies."Se produce una competencia entre distintas memorias," *Página/12*, May 24, 2010.

Chapter 3

1. "We hear the shofar, with its millenarian call that accompanies us and calls us together, so that it can bring down the walls of impunity."

2. Hemos escuchado al shofar. Terminamos como siempre con nuestras voces:
por nuestros 30,000 desaparecidos, víctimas del terrorismo del estado en nuestro país, exigimos JUSTICIA
por los niños, robados de sus hogares durante la última dictadura, que aún hoy siguen buscando su verdadera identidad, exigimos JUSTICIA
por los muertos en el atentado a la Embajada de Israel exigimos JUSTICIA
por nuestros familiares y amigos, víctimas del atroz atentado a la sede de la AMIA en nuestro país, exigimos JUSTICIA
justicia, justicia, perseguirás
צֶדֶק צֶדֶק תִּרְדֹּף [typically spoken in both Spanish and Hebrew]

3. The figure 90,000 is given in *Noticias*, Mar. 22, 1992:74. Other sources estimate the number to be between 80,000 and 150,000.

4. Survey conducted by Ricardo Rouvier & Asociados, between December 18 and 30, 2006.

5. The DAIA's Center for Social Studies (Centro de Estudios Sociales) compiles yearly reports on anti-Semitism in Argentina, available on its website, www.daia.org.ar. It also provides a list and related media coverage of all reported instances of anti-Semitism in Argentina. In addition, see Lvovich 2003.

6. Menem, who converted to Catholicism while pursuing his career in politics,

pushed the revocation of this article of the constitution upon coming into office. This constitution still stipulates in Article 2 that the state upholds the Roman Catholic faith.

7. See Courtis 2000 on the semantics of discrimination in relation to the Argentine Korean community. See also the work by Jeffrey Lesser on the Brazilian Jewish community, including his provocatively titled article, "How the Jews Became Japanese and Other Stories of Nation and Ethnicity," in which he explores how the categories of sameness and difference are deployed in relation to ethnicity within Latin American racial classifications (Lesser 2004).

8. Many others have also noted this widespread aspect of the media coverage. See Elkin 1998:265, and Alejandro Doria in his contribution to the film *18–J*.

9. A full discussion of both Menem and Alfonsín's relationships to the Argentine Jewish collectivity lies beyond the scope of this chapter (see Melamud 2000 for an analysis of this era). The Jewish collectivity tended to judge Alfonsín's politics of cultural pluralism as more sincere. Nonetheless, his foreign policy of aligning Argentina with an emerging coalition of countries from what we now call the Global South estranged many, especially the more conservative elements of the community. Thus, he expressed support for the PLO and the postcolonial Arabic states, in opposition to the United States and Israel. Menem gained initial support from the reluctant Jewish collectivity through his politics of alignment with the United States, including the withdrawal of Argentina's membership in the Movement of Non-Aligned States when he deployed Argentine ships to the Persian Gulf during the first Gulf War (Melamud 2000:43). He also became the first Argentine president to officially visit the State of Israel, something that Alfonsín had promised but not fulfilled. In addition, he promoted some valuable measures, such as lifting questions on religion from codes for aspiring military officers. The legitimacy of the Catholic Church in Argentina, already damaged by the support it had lent the dictatorship, was also weakened by the reforms during his presidency, further opening politics, the arts, and other areas of Argentine life to Jewish Argentines. However, the government's (mis) handling of the AMIA investigation would soon overshadow these earlier achievements.

10. La idea básica de esta obra es un reclamo. No un recordatorio o un homenaje
Un reclamo materializado a través de cada uno de sus elementos
Un círculo de granito oficia de base del conjunto y simboliza la totalidad alrededor de lo que todo gira
Estacas de quebracho de diferentes tamaños y texturas se incrustan en la piedra fundiéndose en un mismo destino se ordenan formando una masa única pero manteniendo su singularidad
El monumento se presenta en actitud expectante hacia el palacio de tribunales y se proyecta al exterior como un vector de búsqueda
La base martillada y rota en un sector señala un reloj detenido a las 9:53
El texto bíblico tallado en el granito "justicia, justicia, perseguirás" (duet xvi) es una apelación a la memoria activa

11. Pierre Nora's massive 1984 work on "lieux de mémoire" is well known for its theoretical contributions on this subject (see Nora 2001). On post-Franco Spain, see Resina 2000. A powerful cinematographic treatment of this issue in relation to the

Armenian genocide is Atom Egoyan's 2002 film, *Ararat*. For Latin America, see Coronil and Skurski 1991; Rappaport 1990; Sánchez G. 2003; Skurski 1996.

12. This is from a speech Goldman made in 2007, in memory of a teacher killed during a protest. The full text of the speech was published in *Página/12* on October 15, 2007.

13. Emphasis added. From the speech by Laura Ginsberg on the third anniversary of the AMIA attack, July 18, 1997. The full text is available at www.memoriaactiva.com. The following is the original of the last two paragraphs of this speech:

Y, porque esa mañana salieron de sus casas como todas las mañanas, merecen justicia. Y porque no olvidaremos exigimos justicia. Y porque la ley de la vida dice que los padres no entierren a sus hijos, reclamamos justicia. Y por todos los que ya no verán crecer a sus hijos pedimos justicia. Y por todos los que no se harán viejos junto a los suyos exigimos justicia. Y porque los amamos gritamos justicia. Y porque nos amaron merecen justicia. Y porque creyeron vivir en un país libre y seguro demandamos justicia. Y porque sus voces reclaman desde el centro mismo de la tierra exigimos justicia. Y porque repudiamos el terrorismo en cualquiera de sus manifestaciones, la violencia, el odio entre los pueblos y la discriminación y porque esclarecer el atentado es una responsabilidad ineludible luchamos por justicia. Y merecen justicia, porque del lugar del universo en donde estén, o desde adentro nuestro, sólo después de hacer justicia nuestros muertos podrán descansar en paz. Los muertos de la AMIA: presentes.

14. All HIJOS citations are taken from www.hijos-capital.org.ar (accessed Feb. 25, 2007).

15. A similar point is made in Peruzzotti 2002: see esp. 89.

16. On the status of workers' rights and the history of the important workers unions throughout the 1960s and 1970s, see James 1988b; Robben 2005. For the 1980s, see Tedesco 1999.

17. Julia Paley makes a similar point for Chile under Pinochet (Paley 2001).

18. Ley Nacional de Empleo 24.103 (1991), Ley 24.465 (1995); Ley 24.557 (1995), and Presidential Decree 2609/93.

19. García Allegrone, Partenio, and Fernández Álvarez also present an argument against seeing the recuperated businesses as a new phenomenon by placing them in the historical context of such takeovers in Argentina (García Allegrone et al. 2004).

20. This quote comes from raw documentary footage filmed by the alternative media cooperative Alavío in 2006. Similar sentiments were frequently expressed in conversations I had with cooperative members throughout 2005 and 2006.

21. See Fassi and Gebhardt 2000 for a detailed study of this law.

22. From a statement released on April 17, 2011.

23. Articles 14 and 14bis of the Argentine constitution detail the rights of workers along these lines.

Chapter 4

1. See Vaisman 2008 for a cogent analysis of processes of social reconstruction among the porteño middle class in the post-neoliberal era.

2. Carlos Menem, sure of a devastating defeat, pulled out of the second round run-off election, leaving Kirchner to assume the presidency without the confirmation of a definitive electoral victory.

3. Kirchner's death from heart failure in October 2010 opened a moment of retrospection on his time in the presidency. In this, one of the most noted achievements attributed to his government was the reform of the Supreme Court. For detailed information on recent prosecutions concerning the Dirty War era, see Centro de Estudios Legales y Sociales Annual Reports, 2002–2011. Though the reopening of trials was initially bogged down by numerous obstructions and delays, by 2011 a number of highly important sentences had been handed down, including the sentencing to life imprisonment of Videla on December 22, 2010. This is his second life sentence; his first, from 1985, was upheld when the Supreme Court ruled unconstitutional the pardon he had received under Menem in 1990. However, many human rights organizations see this new sentence as significant especially because it was reached entirely under the auspices of the common penal code. That is, his trial was not conducted under any sort of special rules or conditions. It was, in short, a symbol and example of the functioning of a normal code of law, applying equally to any and all members of society. This point is made eloquently by Mario Wainfield in "Tardó pero va llegando," *Página/12*, Dec. 26, 2010.

4. All quotations from Kirchner's speech at the Colegio Militar and at ESMA are from "ESMA, colegio militar y otras ceremonias," *Página/12*, Mar. 2004, and "Actos en la ESMA, El Colegio Militar y Plaza de Mayo," *Página/12*, Mar. 24, 2004.

5. Quoted in "Quedaron los clavos para la historia," *Página/12*, Mar. 25, 2004.

6. This citation and the following one are taken from press coverage of this event, which was carried by all the major local newspapers. Full speech available at www.presidencia.gov.ar/index.php?option=com_content&view=article&id=24549&catid=28:discursos-ant (accessed April 8, 2012).

7. See Brodsky 2005, and its accompanying website, www.lamarcaeditora.com/memoriaenconstruccion, for records of this process.

8. See, for example, Frente Popular Darío Santiallán (www.frentedariosantillan.org); Adolfo Pérez Esquivel, *24 de Marzo: Memoria y Resistencia*, Servicio Informativo Alai-amlatina, Mar. 5, 2007, http://alainet.org/active/16157&lang=es (accessed Mar. 5, 2007); *24 de marzo, una fecha en disputa, Doble discurso: para muestra basta una Perla, Indymedia Argentina*, Mar. 27, 2007, www.lafogata.org/07arg/arg3/arg.29.4.htm (accessed April 29, 2007); "Más 'monumentos' kirchneristas para cristalizar los derechos humanos en el pasado," *Boletín quincenal* no. 62, Mar. 26, 2007, www.prensadefrente.org (accessed Mar. 26, 2007).

9. "Febres se mordió la lengua," *Página/12*, Dec. 14, 2007.

10. A full analysis of the way the dictatorship era is remembered and commemorated lies beyond the scope of this book. There is, however, a significant body of scholarship that takes up the theme, as well as, in recent years, considerable diffusion of such events electronically by the groups themselves and by small, independent news organizations. See, for example, the websites of counterimpunity groups like the several

Madres and HIJOS groups, as well as media collectivities like lavaca and Grupo Alavío. For an early analysis, see Jelin 1994. More recently, see Robben 2005; Tandeciarz 2007.

11. From the CEJIL website, www.cejil.org (accessed Sept. 17, 2007).

12. Citations taken from the presentation by Memoria Activa in front of the IACHR, case n 12.204, AMIA-Argentina.

13. The Ecuadorian constitution of 1998 includes the right to "sumak kawsay" or "good living," which includes living in harmony with the environment. In 2011 Bolivia also passed a law that grants nature equal rights to humans and affords a long list of protections to the environment.

14. From the presentation in front of the IACHR of Alejandro Rúa, in representation of the Argentine State, Mar. 4, 2005.

15. See for example, Amitai Etzioni's edited collection *New Communitarian Thinking* (1995).

16. All quotes in this section, unless otherwise attributed, are from interviews I conducted between January 2005 and March 2006.

17. "Cuando la música es una cooperativa," *Página/12*, Dec. 16, 2005.

18. Current manifestations include the Instituto Movilizador de Fondos Cooperativos (IMFC), founded in 1958, and the related Instituto de la Cooperación (IDEL-COOP), created by an earlier version of the IMFC in 1973.

19. On the INAES, see www.inaes.gov.ar; lavaca 2004:22–24. INAES replaced in practice the requirement that cooperatives to pass through older manifestations of such institutions, such as the National Institute of Cooperatives (Instituto Nacional de Cooperativas), which had become increasingly restrictive, expensive, and bureaucratic.

20. Cited in "El strip-tease de los reyes: ¿Cuenta regresiva para Zanón?" *lavaca*, Nov. 20, 2007, www.lavaca.org (accessed Nov. 20, 2007). Godoy made similar statements in conversations we shared during my fieldwork. The high-quality reporting of *lavaca*, an alternative media cooperative, provides an important counterbalance to the increasing consolidation of major media sources into fewer and fewer hands in Argentina (and elsewhere).

21. The major umbrella movements are the Movimiento Nacional de Empresas Recuperadas (National Movement of Recuperated Businesses, or MNER) and a similar though antagonistic movement, the Movimiento Nacional de Fábricas Recuperadas por sus trabajadores (National Movement of Worker Recuperated Factories, or MNFR). Contrary to what their names seem to suggest, it is not the case that the MNFR represents manufacturers and MNER other kinds of businesses; rather, each movement encompasses both. The MNFR is a splinter group of the MNER that formally separated in 2003. Led by lawyer and politician Luis Caro, the MNFR rejects the MNER's motto of occupy, resist, produce (*ocupar, resistir, producir*), arguing that occupation is illegal under current law and therefore illegitimate. Thus it does not support the reentry and occupation of installations. While the MNFR insists on staying within a kind of legality, the MNER rejects this "legality" as itself illegal, focusing instead on the right to work and the primacy of collective well-being. However, many claim that the definitive split between the two groups, which played out most visibly in the struggle for control of the

metalworks factory IMPA, came not over disputes over strategy but when Caro agreed to run for office on the same list as former carapintada Alfredo Rico. For more on these umbrella organizations, see Fernández Álvarez 2004:349–350; lavaca 2004; Magnani 2003; Rebón 2004; Rebón and Saavedra 2006.

22. At the time of this writing, Jorge Julio López remains missing. His disappearance, widely publicized as "disappearance 30,001," has once again brought into the spotlight the continuity of mafia-style hierarchies and relationships among the security forces, particularly in the province of Buenos Aires.

23. "Basta de clausuras," press release from Red de Cultura Boedo, Nov. 24, 2006.

24. An example of this idea can be seen in the work of a group of investigators from the Centro Cultural de la Cooperación who consider the differing manifestations of the idea of participation in post-crisis Argentina. See Landau et al. 2004. For a discussion of similar ideas in Chile, see Dockendorff et al. 2010.

25. The history and nature of electoral democracy in Argentina has been the object of much scholarly attention. See, for example, Auyero 2001; Levitsky 2003; Levitsky and Murillo 2005; Levitsky and Wolfson 2004; Mainwaring and López 2000; and O'Donnell 1999.

26. The Iurcovich family had, in 2005, "sold" the hotel again to a firm registered as Mercoteles. This is problematic and was contested, since, as discussed in Chapter 2, the Iurcovich family had not returned the 4 million peso payment that the Chilean firm Solari had made. However, the purchase by Mercoteles was eventually deemed legal by Commercial Circuit Judge Paula Hualde in 2007. The general director of Mercoteles as of 2003 was Samuel Kaliman, brother-in-law to Iurcovich. This and other evidence have led the Cooperativa BAUEN to assert that the Iurcovich family created a "phantom business" (*una empresa fantasma*) to avoid legal responsibility for their role in running the hotel into insolvency.

27. Eduardo Murúa (MNER), "Desde una quiebra a una esperanza," *Página/12*, Sept. 29, 2003.

Chapter 5

1. "Todo es historia, en versión multitudinaria," *Página/12*, May 26, 2010. See also *La Nación*, www.lanacion.com.ar/1268489-en-un-clima-de-euforia-y-emocion-una-multi tud-presencio-el-cierre-de-los-festejos-por-el-bicentenario (accessed May 26, 2010).

2. "Bicentenario: La ausencia de la comunidad judía argentina y el Estado de Israel en el Paseo del Bicentenario," *Iton Gadol*, May 26, 2010.

3. The current institutional framework for the protection of human rights in the international sphere in many ways grew directly out of a breaking down of the state–citizen relationship. The massive numbers of people left stateless after the political reorganization of Europe following the First World War was a major impetus for the growth of the twentieth-century notion of human rights, initially dedicated to the right to protection of those without a state (Arendt 1951; see also Guy 2000b, esp. chap. 5, for the effects of this on early twentieth-century Argentina). The horrors of Second World War played a major role as well in confirming this need.

4. See, for example, "Trabajo con todos los derechos sociales para terminar con el 'escándalo de la pobreza,'" ANRed, Aug. 21, 2009, www.anred.org/article.php3?id_article=3118 (accessed Aug. 21, 2009), and related articles on the ANRed website.

5. See, for example, www.pagina12.com.ar/diario/elpais/1-167181-2011-04-28.html; and www.pagina12.com.ar/diario/elpais/1-181010-2011-11-11.html (accessed April 28, 2011).

6. Eduardo Jozami, "El momento de la despedida," *Página/12*, Oct. 30, 2010.

7. Ibarra was deposed from office after a fire in a nightclub in the neighborhood of Once, just blocks from the AMIA, killed 194 young people on December 30, 2004. In a hotly contested battle that sharply divided both the city legislature and the family members of victims, Ibarra was eventually impeached for his government's failure to effectively enforce security codes for public buildings. The lack of adequate inspections of buildings led family members of victims to allege that the death of their loved ones was due to corruption within the government and impunity for inspection officials and the business owners who bribed them. In addition, many attributed the high death count to the continued lack of a coordinated emergency rescue system for the city of Buenos Aires, a demand that Memoria Activa has made for years and that figures as one of the key points in the IACHR resolution.

8. See http://lavaca.org/notas/una-para-festejar-zanon-es-de-los-trabajadores (accessed Aug. 17, 2009).

9. The text of the letter that Memoria Activa sent was distributed in a number of ways, including through Memoria Activa's email list and website, and was also published in *Página/12*, Mar. 17, 2011, www.pagina12.com.ar/diario/elpais/subnotas/164341-52571-2011-03-17.html.

10. On March 30, 2012, just days after Memoria Activa and the Argentine state met in the offices of the IACHR for the first time in two years, Judge Lijo ordered that the case against Menem, Galeano, Fino Palacios, Hugo Anzorreguy, Carlos Castañeda, and others implicated in obstructing the investigation into the *pista siria* be brought to trial. The IACHR observer, Rodrigo Escobar Gil, had raised serious concerns about the Argentine state's failure to fulfill the terms of the agreement with Memoria Activa, and the case may move forward to the Inter-American Court of Human Rights.

Bibliography

Abrams, Philip. 1988 [1977]. Notes on the Difficulty of Studying the State. *Journal of Historical Sociology* 1 (1):58–89.

Abregú, Martín. 2000. Human Rights after the Dictatorship: Lessons from Argentina. *NACLA* 34 (1):12–18.

Adelman, Jeremy. 1999. *Republic of Capital: Buenos Aires and the Legal Transformation of the Atlantic World*. Stanford, CA: Stanford University Press.

Aizenberg, Edna. 2000. Las madres de la Calle Pasteur: la lucha por el pluralismo en la Argentina. *Revista Iberoamericana* 66 (191):339–345.

Álvarez, Sonia, Evelina Dagnino, and Arturo Escobar, eds. 1998. *Cultures of Politics, Politics of Cultures: Re-visioning Latin American Social Movements*. Boulder, CO: Westview Press.

Anderson, Benedict. 1991 [1983]. *Imagined Communities*. New York: Verso.

Andrews, George Reid. 1980. *The Afro-Argentines of Buenos Aires, 1800–1900*. Madison: University of Wisconsin Press.

Archetti, Eduardo P. 1997. Multiple Masculinities: The Worlds of Tango and Football in Argentina. Pp. 200–216 in *Sex and Sexuality in Latin America*, edited by Daniel Balderston and Donna J. Guy. New York: New York University Press.

Arditti, Rita. 1999. *Searching for Life: The Grandmothers of the Plaza de Mayo and the Disappeared Children of Argentina*. Berkeley: University of California Press.

Arendt, Hannah. 1951. *The Origins of Totalitarianism*. New York: Harcourt, Brace.

Auyero, Javier. 2001. *Poor People's Politics: Peronist Survival Networks and the Legacy of Evita*. Durham, NC: Duke University Press.

———. 2006. The Political Makings of the 2001 Lootings in Argentina. *Journal for Latin American Studies* 38:241–265.

———. 2007. *Routine Politics and Violence in Argentina: The Grey Zone of State Power*. Cambridge Studies in Contentious Politics. Cambridge: Cambridge University Press.

Azpiazu, Daniel. 2002. *Las privitizaciones en Argentina*. Buenos Aires: CIEPP/Fundación OSDE.

Balaban, Oded, and Amos Megged, eds. 2003. *Impunidad y derechos humanos en América Latina: perspectivas teóricas*. La Plata: Ediciones al Margen; University of Haifa.

Bardenstein, Carol. 1998. Threads of Memory and Discourses of Rootedness: Of Trees, Oranges and the Prickly Pear Cactus in Israel/Palestine. *Edebiyât* 8:1–36.

———. 1999. Trees, Forests, and the Shaping of Palestinian and Israeli Collective Memory. Pp. 148–168 in *Acts of Memory: Cultural Recall in the Present*, edited by Jonathan Crewe, Mieke Bal, and Leo Spitzer. Hanover, NH: Dartmouth College Press.

Barrera, Leticia. 2010. Relocalizing the Judicial Space: Place, Access and Mobilization in Judicial Practice in Post-Crisis Argentina. *Law, Culture and the Humanities*. Published online, Nov. 25, 2010:1–24. http://lch.sagepub.com/content/early/2010/11/12/1743872110379184.abstract.

Battistini, Osvaldo R., ed. 2004. *El trabajo frente al espejo: continuidades y rupturas en los procesos de construcción identitaria de los trabajadores*. Buenos Aires: Prometeo Libros.

Bergman, Marcelo, and Mónica Szurmuk. 2001. Gender, Citizenship, and Social Protest: The New Social Movements in Argentina. Pp. 383–401 in *The Latin American Subaltern Studies Reader*, edited by Ileana Rodríguez. Durham, NC: Duke University Press.

Bickford, Louis. 2000. Human Rights Archives and Research on Historical Memory: Argentina, Chile, Uruguay. *Latin American Research Review* 35 (2):160–182.

Blake, Charles H., and Stephen D. Morris, eds. 2009. *Corruption and Democracy in Latin America*. Pittsburgh: University of Pittsburgh Press.

Bonner, Michelle. 2007. *Sustaining Human Rights: Women and the Argentine Human Rights Organizations*. University Park: Pennsylvania State University Press.

Boyarin, Jonathan. 1992. *Storm from Paradise: The Politics of Jewish Memory*. Minneapolis: University of Minnesota Press.

Brennan, James P. 1994. *The Labor Wars in Córdoba, 1955–1976: Ideology, Work, and Labor Politics in an Argentine Industrial City*. Cambridge, MA: Harvard University Press.

Brodsky, Marcelo. 2005. *Memoria en construcción: el debate sobre la ESMA*. 1st ed. Buenos Aires: La Marca Editora.

Brysk, Alison. 1994. *The Politics of Human Rights in Argentina: Protest, Change, and Democratization*. Stanford, CA: Stanford University Press.

Caballero, Roberto. 2005. *AMIA: la verdad imposible. Por qué el atentado más grande de la historia argentina quedó impune*. Buenos Aires: Editorial Sudamericana.

Caldeira, Teresa P. R. 2000. *City of Walls: Crime, Segregation, and Citizenship in São Paulo*. Berkeley: University of California Press.

———, and James Holston. 1999. Democracy and Violence in Brazil. *Comparative Studies in Society and History* 41 (4):691–729.

Cernadas de Bulnes, Mabel. 2005. Las aporías de la democracia recobrada: la construcción del ciudadano en Argentina. *HAOL* 8:123–134.

Chatterjee, Partha. 2004. *The Politics of the Governed: Reflections on Popular Politics in Most of the World*. New York: Columbia University Press.

Chávez, Rebecca Bill. 2007. The Appointment and Removal Process for Judges in Argentina: The Role of Judicial Councils and Impeachment Juries in Promoting Judicial Independence. *Latin American Politics and Society* 49 (2):33–58.

Cmiel, Kenneth. 2004. The Recent History of Human Rights. *American Historical Review* 109 (1):117–135.

Colectivo Situaciones. 2002. *19 y 20: apuntes para el nuevo protagonismo social.* Buenos Aires: Ediciones de Mano en Mano.

Comaroff, John, and Jean Comaroff. 2001. Millennial Capitalism: First Thoughts on a Second Coming. Pp. 1–56 in *Millennial Capitalism and the Culture of Neoliberalism*, edited by John Comaroff and Jean Comaroff. Durham, NC: Duke University Press.

———. 2004. Criminal Justice, Cultural Justice: The Limits of Liberalism and the Pragmatics of Difference in the New South Africa. *American Ethnologist* 31 (2):189–204.

CONADEP. 1984. *Nunca más: informe de la comisión nacional sobre la desaparición de personas.* Buenos Aires: Eudeba.

Coronil, Fernando. 1995. Transculturation and the Politics of Theory: Countering the Center, Cuban Counterpoint. Pp. ix–lvi in *Cuban Counterpoint: Tobacco and Sugar.* Durham, NC: Duke University Press.

———. 1997. *The Magical State: Nature, Money, and Modernity in Venezuela.* Chicago: University of Chicago Press.

———. 2005. Estado y nación durante el golpe contra Hugo Chávez. *Anuario de estudios americanos* 62 (1):87–112.

———, and Julie Skurski. 1991. Dismembering and Remembering the Nation: The Semantics of Political Violence in Venezuela. *Comparative Studies in Society and History* 33 (2):288–337.

Corradi, Juan, Patricia Weiss Fagen, and Manuel Antonio Garretón. 1992. Fear: A Cultural and Political Construct. Pp. 1–10 in *Fear at the Edge: State Terror and Resistance in Latin America*, edited by Juan Corradi, Patricia Weiss Fagen, and Manuel Antonio Garretón. Berkeley: University of California Press.

Corrigan, Philip, and Derek Sayer. 1985. *The Great Arch: English State Formation as Cultural Revolution.* New York: Basil Blackwell.

Cotarelo, María Celia, and Nicolás Iñigo Carrera. 2004. Looting in Argentina: 1989–90 and December 2001. Paper read at Society for Latin American Studies Annual Conference, April 2–4, 2004, Leiden.

Courtis, Corina. 2000. *Construcciones de alteridad. Discursos cotidianos sobre la inmigración coreana en Buenos Aires.* Buenos Aires: Eudeba.

Couso, Javier, Alexandra Huneeus, and Rachel Sieder, eds. 2010. *Cultures of Legality: Judicialization and Political Activism in Latin America.* Cambridge: Cambridge University Press.

Cucchetti, Humberto. 2007. El proceso electoral en la Argentina 2007. *Nuevo Mundo Mundos Nuevos* 7. http://nuevomundo.revues.org.

de Sardan, J.P. Olivier. 1999. A Moral Economy of Corruption in Africa? *Journal of African Studies* 37 (1):25–52.

Dinerstein, Ana. 2004. Más allá de la crisis. La naturaleza del cambio político en Argentina. *Revista Venezolana de Economia y Ciencias Sociales, Central University of Caracas* 1/2004:241–270.

Dockendorff, Cecilia, José Antonion Román Brugnoli, and María Alejandra Energici Sprovera. 2010. La neoliberalización de la solidaridad en el Chile democrático: una mirada comparativa sobre discursos solidarios en 1991 and 2006. *Latin American Research Review* 45 (1):189–202.

Dussel, Inés. 2005. The Shaping of a Citizenship with Style: A History of Uniforms and Vestimentary Codes in Argentinean Public Schools. Pp. 97–124 in *Materialities of Schooling: Design, Technology, Objects, Routines*, edited by Martin Lawn and Ian Grosvenor. Oxford: Symposium Books.

Eigen, Peter. 2002. Corruption in a Globalized World. *SAIS Review* 22 (1):45–59.

Elkin, Judith. 1998. *The Jews of Latin America.* New York: Holmes and Meier.

Englund, Harri. 2006. *Prisoners of Freedom: Human Rights and the African Poor.* Berkeley: University of California Press.

Escobar, Arturo, and Sonia Álvarez, eds. 1992. *The Making of Social Movements in Latin America: Identity, Strategy, and Democracy.* Boulder, CO: Westview Press.

Escudé, Carlos. 1991. Argentina: The Costs of Contradiction. Pp. 3–38 in *Exporting Democracy: The US and Latin America, Case Studies*, edited by Abraham F. Lowenthal. Baltimore: Johns Hopkins University Press.

Escudero, Lucrecia. 1997. *Malvinas: El gran relato: fuentes y rumores en la informacion de guerra.* Buenos Aires: Gedisa.

Etzioni, Amitai, ed. 1995. *New Communitarian Thinking: Persons, Virtues, Institutions, and Communities.* Fairfax: University of Virginia Press.

Fajn, Gabriel (coord.), et al. 2003. *Fábricas y empresas recuperadas: protesta social, autogestión y rupturas en la subjectividad.* Buenos Aires: Centro Cultural de la Cooperación.

Fals Borda, Orlando. 1992. Social Movements and Political Power in Latin America. Pp. 303–315 in *The Making of Social Movements in Latin America: Identity, Strategy, and Democracy*, edited by Arturo Escobar and Sonia Álvarez. Boulder, CO: Westview Press.

Farer, Tom. 1997. The Rise of the Inter-American Human Rights Regime: No Longer a Unicorn, Not Yet an Ox. *Human Rights Quarterly* 19 (3):510–546.

Farmer, Paul, and Nicole Gastineau. 2009. Rethinking Health and Human Rights: Time for a Paradigm Shift. Pp. 138–166 in *Human Rights: An Anthropological Reader*, edited by M. Goodale. Oxford: Wiley-Blackwell.

Fassi, Santiago, and Marcelo Gebhardt. 2000. *Concurso y quiebra (ley comentada).* Buenos Aires: Editorial Astrea.

Faulk, Karen. 2008a. *If They Touch One of Us, They Touch All of Us:* Cooperativism as a Counterlogic to Neoliberal Capitalism. *Anthropological Quarterly* 81 (3):579–614.

———. 2008b. The Walls of the Labyrinth: Impunity, Corruption, and the Limits of Politics in Contemporary Argentina. Ph.D. dissertation, Anthropology, University of Michigan, Ann Arbor.

Feierstein, Ricardo. 1999. *Historia de los judíos argentinos.* Buenos Aires: Ameghino.

Feitlowitz, Marguerite. 1998. *A Lexicon of Terror: Argentina and the Legacies of Torture.* New York: Oxford University Press.

Feldman, Ilana. 2007. Difficult Distinctions: Refugee Law, Humanitarian Practice, and Political Identification in Gaza. *Cultural Anthropology* 22 (1):129–169.

Feldstein, Federico Pablo, and Carolina Acosta-Alzuru. 2003. Argentinean Jews as Scapegoat: A Textual Analysis of the Bombing of the AMIA. *Journal of Communication Inquiry* 27 (2):152–170.

Ferguson, James, and Akhil Gupta. 2002. Spatializing States: Toward an Ethnography of Neoliberalizing Governmentality. *American Ethnologist* 29 (4):981–1002.

Fernández Álvarez, María Inés. 2004. Sentidos asociados al trabajo y procesos de construcción identitaria en torno a las ocupaciones y recuperaciones de fábricas de la Ciudad de Buenos Aires: un análisis a partir de un caso en particular. Pp. 345–365 in *El trabajo frente al espejo: continuidades y rupturas en los procesos de construcción identitaria de los trabajadores,* edited by Osvaldo R. Battistini. Buenos Aires: Prometeo Libros.

Fisher, Jo. 1989. *Mothers of the Disappeared.* Boston: South End Press.

Forment, Carlos. n.d. Argentina's Recuperated Factory Movement and Citizenship: An Arendtian Perspective. Unpublished manuscript.

García Allegrone, Verónica, Florencia Partenio, and María Inés Fernández Álvarez. 2004. Los procesos de recuperación de fábricas: una mirada retrospectiva. Pp. 329–343 in *El trabajo frente al espejo: continuidades y rupturas en los procesos de construcción identitaria de los trabajadores,* edited by Osvaldo R. Battistini. Buenos Aires: Prometeo Libros.

García Canclini, Néstor. 2001. *Consumidores y ciudadanos: conflictos multiculturales de la globalización.* Mexico, D.F.: Grijalbo.

Gargarella, Roberto. 2004. In Search of Democratic Justice—What Courts Should Not Do: Argentina, 1983–2002. Pp. 181–197 in *Democratization and the Judiciary: The Accountability Function of Courts in New Democracies,* edited by Siri Gloppen, Roberto Gargarella, and Elin Skaar. London: Frank Cass.

Gilbert, Abel, and Miguel Vitagliano. 1998. *El terror y la gloria: la vida, el fútbol, y la política en la Argentina del Mundial 78.* Buenos Aires: Norma.

Gill, Lesley. 2004. *The School of the Americas: Military Training and Political Violence in the Americas.* Durham, NC: Duke University Press.

Gohn, Maria da Glória Marcondes. 1995. *História dos movimentos e lutas sociais: a construçao da cidadania dos brasileiros.* São Paulo, SP: Ediçoes Loyola.

Goldsmith, Arthur A. 1999. Slapping the Grasping Hand: Correlates of Political Corruption in Emerging Markets. *American Journal of Economics and Sociology* 58 (4):865–883.

Goldstein, Daniel M. 2003. "In our own hands": Lynching, Justice, and the Law in Bolivia. *American Ethnologist* 30 (1):22–43.

———. 2004. *The Spectacular City: Violence and Performance in Urban Bolivia.* Durham, NC: Duke University Press.

———. 2007. Human Rights as Culprit, Human Rights as Victim: Rights and Security in the State of Exception. Pp. 49–77 in *The Practice of Human Rights: Tracking Law between the Global and the Local,* edited by Mark Goodale and Sally Engle Merry. Cambridge: Cambridge University Press.

Goobar, Walter. 1996. *El tercer atentado: Argentina en la mira del terrorismo internacional.* Buenos Aires: Editorial Sudamericana.

Goodale, Mark. 2007a. Introduction: Locating Rights, Envisioning Law between the Global and the Local. Pp. 1–38 in *The Practice of Human Rights: Tracking Law between the Global and the Local,* edited by Mark Goodale and Sally Engle Merry. Cambridge: Cambridge University Press.

———. 2007b. The Power of Right(s): Tracking Empires of Law and New Modes of Social Resistance in Bolivia (and Elsewhere). Pp. 130–162 in *The Practice of Human Rights: Tracking Law between the Global and the Local,* edited by Mark Goodale and Sally Engle Merry. Cambridge: Cambridge University Press.

———. 2009. *Surrendering the Utopia: An Anthropology of Human Rights.* Stanford, CA: Stanford University Press.

Gordillo, Gastón, and Silvia Hirsch. 2003. Indigenous Struggles and Contested Identities in Argentina: Histories of Invisibilization and Reemergence. *Journal of Latin American Anthropology* 8 (3):4–30.

Graziano, Frank. 1992. *Divine Violence: Spectacle, Psychosexuality, and Radical Christianity in the Argentine "Dirty War."* Boulder, CO: Westview Press.

Greenhouse, Carol, ed. 2010. *Ethnographies of Neoliberalism.* Philadelphia: University of Pennsylvania Press.

Grimson, Alejandro. 2006. Unidad y diversidad en la Argentina. *TodaVía* 15, edición electrónica. www.revistatodavia.com.ar/todavia26/15.grimsonnotaFronteras.html.

Grossman, Claudio. 2005. *Informe del decano Claudio Grossman Observador Internacional de la Comisión Interamericana de Derechos Humanos en el juicio de la AMIA.* IACHR, February 22.

Grugel, Jean, and Enrique Peruzzotti. 2010. Grounding Global Norms in Domestic Politics: Advocacy Coalitions and the Convention on the Rights of the Child in Argentina. *Journal for Latin American Studies* 42:29–57.

Guha, Ranajit. 1985. Nationalism Reduced to Official Nationalism. *ASAA Review* 9 (1):103–108.

Gupta, Akhil. 1995. Blurred Boundaries: The Discourse of Corruption, the Culture of Politics, and the Imagined State. *American Ethnologist* 22 (2):375–402.

Gurevich, Beatriz. 2005a. After the AMIA Bombing: A Critical Analysis of Two Parallel Discourses. Pp. 86–111 in *The Jewish Diaspora in Latin America and the Caribbean: Fragments of Memory*, edited by Kristin Ruggiero. Brighton, East Sussex: Sussex Academic Press.

———. 2005b. *Passion, Politics, and Identity: Jewish Women in the Wake of the AMIA Bombing in Argentina*. Buenos Aires: Universidad del CEMA.

Guterman, Sofia Kaplinsky. 1999. *La gran mentira 1994–1999*. Buenos Aires: Ediciones La Luz.

———. 2004. *Detrás del vidrio*. Buenos Aires: Gobierno de la Ciudad de Buenos Aires.

Gutman, Daniel. 2003. *Tacuara, historia de la primera guerrilla urbana Argentina*. Buenos Aires: Vergara.

Guy, Donna. 1991. *Sex and Danger in Buenos Aires: Prostitution, Family, and Nation in Argentina*. Lincoln: University of Nebraska Press.

———. 2000a. "White Slavery," Citizenship, and Nationality in Argentina. Pp. 72–85 in *White Slavery and Mothers Alive and Dead: The Troubled Meeting of Sex, Gender, Public Health, and Progress in Latin America*. Lincoln: University of Nebraska Press.

———. 2000b. *White Slavery and Mothers Alive and Dead: The Troubled Meeting of Sex, Gender, Public Health, and Progress in Latin America*. Lincoln: University of Nebraska Press.

Guzman Bouvard, Marguerite. 1994. *Revolutionizing Motherhood: The Mothers of the Plaza de Mayo*. Wilmington, DE: Scholarly Resources.

Halbswach, Maurice. 1992 [1942]. *On Collective Memory*. Translated by Lewis A. Coser. Chicago: University of Chicago Press.

Hale, Charles. 2002. Does Multiculturalism Menace? Governance, Cultural Rights and the Politics of Identity in Guatemala. *Journal of Latin American Studies* 34 (3):485–525.

Haller, Dieter, and Cris Shore. 2005. Introduction—Sharp Practice: Anthropology and the Study of Corruption. Pp. 1–26 in *Corruption: Anthropological Perspectives*, edited by Dieter Haller and Cris Shore. London: Pluto Press.

Halperín, Jorge. 2008. El regreso de los gorilas: el sociólogo Lucas Rubinich analiza las ideas que son funcionales a la sociedad desigual. *Página/12*, Feb. 17.

Harvey, David. 2005. *A Brief History of Neoliberalism*. Oxford: Oxford University Press.

Hasty, Jennifer. 2005. The Pleasures of Corruption: Desire and Discipline in Ghanaian Political Culture. *Cultural Anthropology* 20 (2):271–301.

Hayner, Priscilla. 1995. Fifteen Truth Commissions—1974–1994: A Comparative Study. Pp. 323–382 in *Transitional Justice: How Emerging Democracies Reckon with Former Regimes. Volume 2, Country Studies*. Edited by Neil J. Kritz. Washington, DC: United States Institute of Peace.

Heller, Pablo. 2004. *Fábricas ocupadas*. Buenos Aires: Ediciones Rumbos.

Hinton, Alex Laban, and Kevin Lewis O'Neill, eds. 2009. *Genocide: Truth, Memory, and Representation*. Durham, NC: Duke University Press.

Hinton, Mercedes S. 2006. *The State on the Streets: Police and Politics in Argentina and Brazil*. Boulder, CO: Lynne Rienner.

Huneeus, Alexandra. 2010. Rejecting the Inter-American Court: Judicialization, National Courts, and Regional Human Rights. Pp. 112–138 in *Cultures of Legality: Judicialization and Political Activism in Latin America*, edited by Javier Couso, Alexandra Huneeus, and Rachel Sieder. Cambridge: Cambridge University Press.

Hunt, Lynn. 2007. *Inventing Human Rights*. New York: W.W. Norton.

Informe Rattenbach. Comisión Decreto 200/12. www.casarosada.gov.ar/component/content/article/108-gobierno-informa/25773-informe-rattenbach.

Ishay, Micheline R. 2008 [2004]. *The History of Human Rights: From Ancient Times to the Globalization Era*. 2nd ed. Berkeley: University of California Press.

Izaguirre, Ines. 1998. Recapturing the Memory of Politics. *NACLA*, May–June: 28–34.

James, Daniel. 1988a. October 17th and 18th 1945: Mass Protest, Peronism, and the Argentine Working Class. *Journal of Social History* 21:441–61.

———. 1988b. *Resistance and Integration: Peronism and the Argentine Working Class, 1946–1976*. New York: Cambridge University Press.

———. 2000. *Doña María's Story: Life History, Memory, and Political Identity*. Durham, NC: Duke University Press.

Jelin, Elizabeth. 1994. The Politics of Memory: The Human Rights Movement and the Construction of Democracy in Argentina. *Latin American Perspectives* 21 (2):38–58.

———. 1995. La política de la memoria: el movimiento de derechos humanos y la construcción democrática en la Argentina. Pp. 103–146 in *Juicio, castigo y memorias: derechos humanos y justicia en la política argentina*, edited by Adam Przeworski. Buenos Aires: Ediciones Nueva Visión.

———. 1996. Citizenship Revisited: Solidarity, Responsibility, and Rights. In *Constructing Democracy: Human Rights, Citizenship, and Democracy in Latin America*, edited by Elizabeth Jelin and Eric Hershberg. Boulder, CO: Westview Press.

———. 1998. The Minefields of Memory. *NACLA* 32 (3):23–29.

Juris, Jeffrey. 2008. Performing Politics: Image, Embodiment, and Affective Solidarity during Anti-Corporate Globalization Protests. *Ethnography* 9 (1):61–97.

Kalmanowiecki, Laura. 2000. Police, Politics, and Repression in Modern Argentina. Pp. 195–218 in *Reconstructing Criminality in Latin America*, edited by Carlos A. Aguirre and Robert Buffington. Wilmington, DE: Scholarly Resources.

Kiernan, Sergio. 1999. *A Glimmer of Hope: The American Jewish Committee Annual Report on the AMIA Bombing*. New York: American Jewish Committee.

―――. 2000. *Unfinished Business: The AMIA Bombing, Six Years Later*. New York: American Jewish Committee.

―――. 2001. *Seeking the Truth: The AMIA Bombing Goes to Trial*. New York: American Jewish Committee.

Kordon, Diana, et al. 1995. *La impunidad: una perspectiva psicosocial y clínica*. Buenos Aires: Sudamericana.

Kornbluh, Peter. 2003. *The Pinochet File: A Declassified Dossier on Atrocity and Accountability*. New York: New Press.

Lambek, Michael, and Paul Antze. 1996. Introduction: Forecasting Memory. Pp. xi–xxxviii in *Tense Past: Cultural Essays in Trauma and Memory*, edited by Paul Antze and Michael Lambek. New York: Routledge.

Lanata, Jorge, and Joe Goldman. 1994. *Cortinas de humo: una investigación independiente sobre los atentados contra la embajada de Israel y la AMIA*. Buenos Aires: Planeta.

Landau, Matías (coord.), Alejandro Capriati, Nicolás Dallorso, Melina Di Falco, Lucas Gastiarena, Flavia Llanpart, Agustina Pérez Rial, Ivana Socoloff. 2004. *Los discursos de la participación: una mirada hacia la construcción de la figura del ciudadano en la prensa escrita de la Ciudad de Buenos Aires*. Buenos Aires: Centro Cultural de al Cooperación.

lavaca, Cooperativa de trabajo. 2004. *Sin Patrón: fábricas y empresas recuperadas por sus trabajadores. Una historia, una guía*. 2007 edition in English, *Sin Patrón: Stories from Argentina's Worker-Run Factories*. Buenos Aires: Cooperativa de trabajo lavaca.

Lazar, Sian. 2005. Citizens Despite the State: Everyday Corruption and Local Politics in El Alto, Bolivia. Pp. 212–228 in *Corruption: Anthropological Perspectives*, edited by Dieter Haller and Cris Shore. London: Pluto Press.

―――. 2008. *El Alto, Rebel City: Self and Citizenship in Andean Bolivia*. Durham, NC: Duke University Press.

Lesser, Jeffrey. 2004. How the Jews Became Japanese and Other Stories of Nation and Ethnicity. *Jewish History* 18:7–17.

Levinas, Gabriel. 1998. *La ley bajo los escombros*. Buenos Aires: Editorial Sudamericana.

Levitsky, Steven. 2003. *Transforming Labor-Based Parties in Latin America: Argentine Peronism in Comparative Perspective*. Cambridge: Cambridge University Press.

―――, and María Victoria Murillo, eds. 2005. *Argentine Democracy: the Politics of Institutional Weakness*. University Park: Pennsylvania State University Press.

Levitsky, Steven, and Leandro Wolfson. 2004. Del sindicalismo al clientelismo: la transformación de los vínculos partido-sindicatos en el peronismo, 1983–1999. *Desarrollo Económico* 44 (173):3–32.

Llonto, Pablo. 2005. *La vergüenza de todos: el dedo en la llaga del Mundial 78.* Buenos Aires: Ediciones Madres de Plaza de Mayo.

Low, Setha M. 2003. *Behind the Gates: Life, Security, and the Pursuit of Happiness in Fortress America.* New York: Routledge.

Lozada, Salvador María. 1999. *Los derechos humanos y la impunidad en la Argentina (1974–1999): de López Rega a Alfonsín y Menem.* Buenos Aires: Grupo Editor Latinoamericano Nuevohacer.

Lvovich, Daniel. 2003. *Nacionalismo y antisemitismo en la Argentina.* Buenos Aires: Javier Vergara, Grupo Zeta.

Magnani, Esteban. 2003. *El cambio silencioso: empresas y fábricas recuperadas por sus trabajadores en la Argentina.* Buenos Aires: Prometeo Libros.

Mainwaring, Scott, and Ernesto López, eds. 2000. *Democracia: discusiones y nuevas aproximaciones.* Quilmes, Argentina: Universidad Nacional de Quilmes.

Malkki, Liisa. 1992. National Geographic: The Rooting of Peoples and the Territorialization of National Identity among Scholars and Refugees. *Cultural Anthropology* 7 (1):24–43.

Maris Ageitos, Stella. 2002. *Historia de la impunidad: de los actos de Videla a los indultos de Menem.* Buenos Aires: Adriana Hidalgo.

Marquardt, Kairos. In press. Participatory Security: Citizen Security, Participation, and the Inequities of Citizenship in Urban Peru. *Bulletin of Latin American Research* 31 (2).

Marshall, Thomas Humphrey. 1950. *Citizenship and Social Class.* Cambridge: Cambridge University Press.

Marx, Karl. 1977 [1843]. On the Jewish Question. Pp. 38–62 in *Karl Marx: Selected Writings,* edited by David McLellan. Oxford: Oxford University Press.

Mason, Tony. 1995. *Passion of the People? Football in South America.* Critical Studies in Latin American and Iberian Culture. London: Verso.

Mato, Daniel, ed. 2004. *Políticas de ciudadanía y sociedad civil en tiempos de globalización.* Caracas: Facultad de Ciencias Económicas y Sociales, Universidad Central de Venezuela.

Melamud, Diego. 2000. *Los judíos y el menemismo: un reflejo de la sociedad argentina.* Buenos Aires: Editorial Sudamericana.

Merry, Sally Engle. 1997. Legal Pluralism and Transnational Culture: The Ka Hoʻokolokolonui Kanaka Maoli Tribunal, Hawaiʻi, 1993. Pp. 28–48 in *Human Rights, Culture and Context: Anthropological Perspectives,* edited by Richard A. Wilson. London: Pluto Press.

———. 2005. Anthropology and Activism: Researching Human Rights across Porous Boundaries. *Political and Legal Anthropology Review* 28 (2):240–257.

———. 2006. Transnational Human Rights and Local Activism: Mapping the Middle. *American Anthropologist* 108 (1):38–51.

Merton, R. K. 1968. *Social Theory and Social Structure*. New York: Free Press.

Mignolo, Walter. 2005. *The Idea of Latin America*. Blackwell Manifestos. Malden, MA: Blackwell.

Miller, Jonathan M. 2000. Evaluating the Argentine Supreme Court under Presidents Alfonsin and Menem (1983–1999). *Southwestern Journal of Law and Trade in the Americas* 7:369–433.

Mirelman, Victor A. 1975. The Semana Trágica of 1919 and the Jews of Argentina. *Jewish Social Studies* 37:61–73.

Mittlebach, Federico. 1986 [1984]. *Punto 30: informe sobre desaparecidos*. Buenos Aires: Ediciones de la Urraca.

Moro, Carlos Emilio. 2006. *Ley 26.086. Concursos y quiebras. Modificación de la ley 24.522*. Buenos Aires: Ad-Hoc.

Moya, Jose C. 2004. The Positive Side of Stereotypes: Jewish Anarchists in Early-Twentieth-Century Buenos Aires. *Jewish History* 18:19–48.

Muir, Sarah. 2011. Producing the Future in Post-Crisis Buenos Aires: Popular Knowledge and the Argentine Middle Class. Ph.D. dissertation, Anthropology, University of Chicago.

Munck, Ronaldo. 1998. Mutual Benefit Societies in Argentina: Workers, Nationality, Social Security and Trade Unionism. *Journal of Latin American Studies* 30 (3):573–590.

Navarro, Marysa. 1989. The Personal Is Political: Las Madres de Plaza de Mayo. Pp. 241–259 in *Power and Popular Protest: Latin American Social Movements*, edited by Susan Eckstein. Berkeley: University of California.

Nino, Carlos S. 1996. *Radical Evil on Trial*. New Haven, CT: Yale University Press.

Nora, Pierre. 2001 [1984]. *Rethinking France: Les Lieux de mémoire*. Translated by Mary Trouille. Chicago: University of Chicago Press.

O'Donnell, Guillermo. 1997 [1983]. ¿Y a mí, qué mierda me importa? Notas sobre sociabilidad y política en la Argentina y Brasil. Pp. 165–193 in *Contrapuntos: ensayos escogidos sobre autoritarismo y democratización*, edited by Guillermo O'Donnell. Buenos Aires: Paidós.

———. 1999. *Counterpoints: Selected Essays on Authoritarianism and Democratization*. Notre Dame, IN: Notre Dame University Press.

Ong, Aihwa. 1996. Cultural Citizenship as Subject-Making: Immigrants Negotiate Racial and Cultural Boundaries in the United States. *Current Anthropology* 37 (5):737–762.

———. 1999. *Flexible Citizenship: The Cultural Logics of Transnationality*. Durham, NC: Duke University Press.

———. 2003. *Buddha Is Hiding: Refugees, Citizenship, and the New America*. Berkeley: University of California Press.

Oquendo, Ángel. 2008. Upping the Ante: Collective Litigation in Latin America. *Columbia Journal of Transnational Law* 47:248–291.

Ortiz, Fernando. 1995 [1947]. *Cuban Counterpoint: Tobacco and Sugar.* Translated by Harriet de Onís. Durham, NC: Duke University Press.

Paley, Julia. 2001. *Marketing Democracy: Power and Social Movements in Post-Dictatorship Chile.* Berkeley: University of California Press.

Pateman, Carole. 1983. Feminist Critiques of the Public/Private Dichotomy. Pp. 118–140 in *Public and Private in Social Life,* edited by Stanley Benn and G. F. Gaus. London: St. Martin's Press.

Perelli, Carina. 1994. Memoria de sangre: Fear, Hope, and Disenchantment in Argentina. Pp. 39–66 in *Remapping Memory: The Politics of Time-Space,* edited by Jonathan Boyarin. Minneapolis: University of Minnesota Press.

Perelman, Mariano D. 2007a. ¿Rebusque o trabajo? Un análisis a partir de las transformaciones del cirujeo en la Ciudad de Buenos Aires. Pp. 245–268 in *Recicloscopio: miradas dobre recuperadores urbanos de residuos de América Latina,* edited by Pablo J. Schamber and Francisco M. Suárez. Buenos Aires: Prometeo Libros.

———. 2007b. Theorizing Unemployment: Toward an Argentina Anthropology of Work. *Anthropology of Work Review* 28 (1):8–13.

———. 2011. La construcción de la idea del trabajo digno en cirujas de la ciudad de Buenos Aires. *Intersecciones en Antropología* 12:155–168.

Pérez Aguirre, Luis. 1992. The Consequences of Impunity in Society. Pp. 107–120 in *Justice, Not Impunity.* Geneva: International Commission of Jurists.

Peruzzotti, Enrique. 2002. Towards a New Politics: Citizenship and Rights in Contemporary Argentina. *Citizenship Studies* 6(1):77-93.

Plotkin, Mariano Ben. 1995. Rituales políticos, imágenes y carisma: la celebración del 17 de octubre y el imaginario peronista 1945–1951. Pp. 171–217 in *El 17 de octubre de 1945,* edited by Juan Carlos Torre. Buenos Aires: Espasa Calpe Argentina S.A./Ariel.

———. 2003. *Mañana es San Perón: A Cultural History of Peron's Argentina.* Translated by Keith Zahniser. Wilmington, DE: Scholarly Resources. Original edition, 1993.

Poritzker, Karina, and Marcos Salgado. 2005. *El veredicto: un documento revelador. Razones públicas y secretas de la impunidad en el atentado a la AMIA.* Buenos Aries: Sumate.

Postero, Nancy. 2007. *Now We Are Citizens.* Stanford, CA: Stanford University Press.

———. 2010. The Struggle to Create a Radical Democracy in Bolivia. *Latin American Research Review* 45 (Special Issue: Living in Actually Existing Democracies):59–78.

Rabinow, Paul. 2005. Midst Anthropology's Problems. Pp. 40–54 in *Global Assemblages: Technology, Politics, and Ethics as Anthropological Problems,* edited by Aihwa Ong and Stephen J. Collier. Oxford: Blackwell.

Rappaport, Joanne. 1990. *The Politics of Memory: Native Historical Interpretation in the Colombian Andes.* Cambridge: Cambridge University Press.

Rebón, Julián. 2004. *Desobedeciendo al desempleo: la experiencia de las empresas recuperadas*. Buenos Aires: Ediciones P.ica.so/La Rosa Blindada.

———, and Ignacio Saavedra. 2006. *Empresas recuperadas: la autogestión de los trabajadores*. Edited by José Nun. Claves para Todos. Buenos Aires: Capital Intelectual.

Reed, Darryl, and J. J. McMurtry, eds. 2009. *Co-operatives in a Global Economy: The Challenges of Co-operation across Borders*. Newcastle upon Tyne: Cambridge Scholars Publishing.

Resina, Joan Ramon, ed. 2000. *Disremembering the Dictatorship: The Politics of Memory in the Spanish Transition to Democracy*. Atlanta: Rodopi.

Riles, Annelise. 2006. Anthropology, Human Rights, and Legal Knowledge: Culture in an Iron Cage. *American Anthropologist* 108 (1):52–65.

Robben, Antonius C. G. M. 2000. State Terror in the Netherworld: Disappearance and Reburial in Argentina. Pp. 91–113 in *Death Squad: The Anthropology of State Terror*, edited by Jeffrey A. Sluka. Philadelphia: University of Pennsylvania Press.

———. 2005. *Political Violence and Trauma in Argentina*. Philadelphia: University of Pennsylvania Press.

Rodríguez, Ileana. 2009. *Liberalism at Its Limits: Crime and Terror in the Latin American Cultural Text*. Pittsburgh: University of Pittsburgh Press.

Rodríguez, Juan Carlos. 2010. "El cine militante es el cine abierto a la demanda de los compañeros": una conversación con Fabián Pierucci del Grupo Alavío y Ágora TV. *A Contracorriente* 7 (2):294–314.

Roht-Arriaza, Naomi, ed. 1995. *Impunity and Human Rights in International Law and Practice*. New York: Oxford University Press.

———. 1999. The Need for Moral Reconstruction in the Wake of Past Human Rights Violations: An Interview with José Zalaquett. Pp. 195–213 in *Human Rights in Political Transitions: Gettysburg to Bosnia*, edited by Carla Hesse and Robert Post. New York: Zone Books.

Romero, Luis Alberto. 2002 [1994]. *A History of Argentina in the Twentieth Century*. Translated by James P. Brennan. University Park: Pennsylvania State University Press.

Roniger, Luis. 2003. El discurso de los derechos humanos: problemas interpretativos en su inserción local. Pp. 115–130 in *Impunidad y derechos humanos en América Latina: perspectivas teóricas*, edited by Oded Balaban and Amos Megged. La Plata, Buenos Aires: Ediciones al Margen.

Rosaldo, Renato. 1994. Cultural Citizenship in San Jose, California. *PoLAR* 17 (2):57–64.

Ruggeri, Andrés. 2005. *Las empresas recuperadas en la Argentina: informe del segundo relevamiento del programa*. Buenos Aires: Facultad de Filosofía y Letras. SEUBE. Universidad de Buenos Aires.

Saad-Filho, Alfredo, and Deborah Johnson, eds. 2005. *Neoliberalism—A Critical Reader*. London: Pluto Press.

Sábato, Hilda. 1992. Citizenship, Political Participation and the Formation of the Public Sphere in Buenos Aires 1850s–1880s. *Past and Present* 136:139–163.

———. 2004 [1998]. *La política en las calles: entre el voto y la movilización, Buenos Aires, 1862–1880.* Bernal, Buenos Aires: Universidad Nacional de Quilmes.

Salinas, Juan. 1997. *AMIA: el atentado.* Buenos Aires: Planeta.

Sánchez G., Gonzalo. 2003. *Guerras, memorias e historia.* Bogotá: Instituto Colombiano de Antropología e Historia.

Sarlo, Beatriz. 1988. El campo intelectual: un espacio doblemente fracturado. Pp. 96–107 in *Represión y reconstrucción de una cultura: el caso argentino,* edited by Saúl Sosnowski. Buenos Aires: EUDEBA.

———. 1994. *Escenas de la vida posmoderna.* Buenos Aires: Compañía Editora Espasa Calpe.

Schirmer, Jennifer. 1994. The Claiming of Space and the Body Politic within National-Security States: The Plaza de Mayo Madres and the Greenham Common Women. Pp. 185–200 in *Remapping Memory: The Politics of TimeSpace,* edited by Jonathan Boyarin. Minneapolis: University of Minnesota Press.

SERPAJ, Tribunal Permanente de los Pueblos. 1992. *La impunidad juzgada: el caso argentino.* Buenos Aires: Fundación Servicio Paz y Justicia.

Shumway, Nicolas. 1991. *The Invention of Argentina.* Berkeley: University of California Press.

Sikkink, Kathryn. 1996. The Emergence, Evolution, and Effectiveness of the Latin American Human Rights Network. Pp. 59–84 in *Constructing Democracy: Human Rights, Citizenship, and Society in Latin America,* edited by Elizabeth Jelin and Eric Hershberg. Boulder, CO: Westview Press.

———. 2008. From Pariah State to Global Protagonist: Argentina and the Struggle for International Human Rights. *Latin American Politics and Society* 50 (1):1–29.

Skurski, Julie. 1996. The Ambiguities of Authenticity in Latin America: *Doña Bárbara* and the Construction of National Identity. Pp. 371–402 in *Becoming National,* edited by Geoff Eley and Ronald Grigor Suny. New York: Oxford University Press.

Sluka, Jeffrey A. 2000. Introduction: State Terror and Anthropology. Pp. 1–45 in *Death Squad: The Anthropology of State Terror,* edited by Jeffrey A. Sluka. Philadelphia: University of Pennsylvania Press.

Smith, Daniel Jordan. 2008. *A Culture of Corruption: Everyday Deception and Popular Discontent in Nigeria.* Princeton, NJ: Princeton University Press.

Smulovitz, Catalina. 2010. Judicialization in Argentina: Legal Culture of Opportunities and Support Structures? Pp. 234–253 in *Cultures of Legality: Judicialization and Political Activism in Latin America,* edited by Javier Couso, Alexandra Huneeus, and Rachel Sieder. Cambridge: Cambridge University Press.

Soriano, Osvaldo. 1987 [1974]. *No habrá más penas ni olvido.* Barcelona: Ediciones B.

Speed, Shannon, and Jane Collier. 2000. Limiting Indigenous Autonomy in Chiapas, Mexico: The State Government's Use of Human Rights. *Human Rights Quarterly* 22 (4):877–905.

Stewart, Kathleen. 2007. *Ordinary Affects.* Durham, NC: Duke University Press.

Striffler, Steve. 2002. *In the Shadows of State and Capital: The United Fruit Company, Popular Struggle, and Agrarian Restructuring in Ecuador, 1900–1995.* Durham, NC: Duke University Press.

Sutton, Barbara. 2007. *Poner el cuerpo*: Women's Embodiment and Political Resistance in Argentina. *Latin American Politics and Society* 49 (3):129–162.

———. 2010. *Bodies in Crisis: Culture, Violence, and Women's Resistance in Neoliberal Argentina.* New Brunswick, NJ: Rutgers University Press.

Svampa, Maristella. 2001. *Los que ganaron. La vida en los countries y barrios privados.* Buenos Aires: Biblos.

———. 2002. *19 y 20. Apuntes sobre el nuevo protagonismo social.* Buenos Aires: CEDES.

———. 2005a. Ciudadanía, estado y globalización: una mirada desde la Argentina contemporánea. Pp. 263–290 in *Debates de Mayo: nación, cultura y política*, edited by José Nun. Buenos Aires: Gedisa Editorial.

———. 2005b. *La sociedad excluyente: Argentina bajo el signo del neoliberalismo.* Buenos Aires: Taurus.

Sveaass, Nora. 1994a. The Organized Destruction of Meaning. Pp. 45–63 in *Pain and Survival: Human Rights Violations and Mental Health*, edited by Nils Johan Lavik et al. Oslo: Scandinavian University Press.

———. 1994b. The Psychological Effects of Impunity. Pp. 211–221 in *Pain and Survival: Human Rights Violations and Mental Health*, edited by Nils Johan Lavik et al. Oslo: Scandinavian University Press.

Tandeciarz, Silvia R. 2007. Citizens of Memory: Refiguring the Past in Post-Dictatorship Argentina. *Publications of the Modern Language Association of America* 122 (1):151–169.

Tate, Winifred. 2007. *Counting the Dead: The Culture and Politics of Human Rights Activism in Colombia.* California Series in Public Anthropology. Berkeley: University of California Press.

Taussig, Michael. 1999. *Defacement: Public Secrecy and the Labor of the Negative.* Stanford, CA: Stanford University Press.

———. 2003. *Law in a Lawless Land: Diary of a Limpieza in Colombia.* New York: New Press.

Taylor, Charles. 1992. *Multiculturalism and the Politics of Recognition: An Essay.* Princeton, NJ: Princeton University Press.

Taylor, Diana. 1998. Making a Spectacle: The Mothers of the Plaza de Mayo. Pp. 74–85 in *Radical Street Performance: An International Anthology*, edited by Jan Cohen-Cruz. London: Routledge.

Tedesco, Laura. 1999. *Democracy in Argentina: Hope and Disillusion.* London: Frank Cass.

Teubal, Miguel. 2004. Rise and Collapse of Neoliberalism in Argentina. *Journal of Developing Societies* 20 (3–4):173–188.

Thwaites Rey, Mabel. 2004. *La autonomía como búsqueda, el estado como contradicción.* Buenos Aires: Prometeo Libros.

Tilly, Charles. 1994. Afterword: Political Memories in Space and Time. Pp. 241–256 in *Remapping Memory: The Politics of TimeSpace*, edited by Jonathan Boyarin. Minneapolis: University of Minnesota Press.

Torre, Susana. 1996. Claiming the Public Space: The Mothers of the Plaza de Mayo. Pp. 241–250 in *The Sex of Architecture*, edited by Diana Agrest, Patricia Conway, and Leslie Kanes Weisman. New York: Harry N. Abrams.

Trouillot, Michel-Rolph. 2000. Abortive Rituals: Historical Apologies in the Global Era. *Interventions* 2 (2):171–186.

Tulchin, Joseph S., and Ralph H. Espach, eds. 2000. *Combating Corruption in Latin America.* Washington, DC: Woodrow Wilson Center Press.

Vaisman, Noa. 2008. Talk, Dreamwork, and Specters: (Re)Constructing Patterns of Self, Truth, and Society in Present-Day Buenos Aires. Ph.D. dissertation, Anthropology, Cornell University, Ithaca, NY.

Verbitsky, Horacio. 1995. *El vuelo.* Buenos Aries: Planeta–Espejo de la Argentina.

Vezzetti, Hugo. 2002. *Pasado y presente. Guerra, dictadura y sociedad en la Argentina.* Buenos Aires: Siglo XXI.

Vieta, Marcelo, and Andrés Ruggeri. 2009. Worker-Recovered Enterprises as Workers Cooperatives: The Conjunctures, Challenges, and Innovations of Self-Management in Argentina and Latin America. Pp. 178–225 in *Co-operatives in a Global Economy: The Challenges of Co-operation across Borders*, edited by Darryl Reed and J. J. McMurtry. Newcastle upon Tyne: Cambridge Scholars Publishing.

Vilas, Carlos M. 2004. Water Privatization in Buenos Aires. *NACLA* 38 (1):34–40.

Villalba Welsh, Alfredo. 1984. *Tiempos de ira, tiempos de esperanza: 50 años de vida política a través de la Liga Argentina por los Derechos del Hombre.* Buenos Aires: Rafael Cedeño Editor.

Waisbord, Silvio. 2000. *Watchdog Journalism in South America: News, Accountability, and Democracy.* New York: Columbia University Press.

Yashar, Deborah J. 2005. *Contesting Citizenship in Latin America.* Cambridge: Cambridge University Press.

Yerushalmi, Yosef Hayim. 1982. *Zakhor: Jewish History and Jewish Memory.* Seattle: University of Washington Press.

Zaretsky, Natasha. 2008. Singing for Social Change: Nostalgic Memory and the Struggle for Belonging in a Buenos Aires Yiddish Chorus. Pp. 231–265 in *Rethinking*

Jewish-Latin Americans, edited by Jeffrey Lesser and Raanan Rein. Albuquerque: University of New Mexico Press.

Zemon-Davis, Natalie, and Randolph Starn. 1989. Introduction: Memory and Counter-Memory. *Representations* 26:1–6.

Index

Stanford Studies in Human Rights brings together established and emerging voices from the interdisciplinary field of human rights studies. The series publishes work from a range of perspectives, including ethnographic studies of human rights in practice, critical reflections on the idea of human rights, new proposals for a more effective international human rights system, and historical accounts of the rise of human rights as a globalized moral discourse.

Values in Translation: Human Rights and the Culture of the World Bank
Galit A. Sarfaty
2012

Disquieting Gifts: Humanitarianism in New Delhi
Erica Bornstein
2012

Stones of Hope: How African Activists Reclaim Human Rights to Challenge Global Poverty
Edited by Lucie E. White and Jeremy Perelman
2011

Judging War, Judging History: Behind Truth and Reconciliation
Pierre Hazan
2010

Localizing Transitional Justice: Interventions and Priorities after Mass Violence
Edited by Rosalind Shaw and Lars Waldorf, with Pierre Hazan
2010

Surrendering to Utopia: An Anthropology of Human Rights
Mark Goodale
2009

Human Rights for the 21st Century: Sovereignty, Civil Society, Culture
Helen M. Stacy
2009

Human Rights Matters: Local Politics and National Human Rights Institutions
Julie A. Mertus
2009